To: I. SANTANA

Drafted To Serve

POPE JOHN PAUL II
A SAINT

Keep on,

Making Miracles Happen!

JD 10-14-14

A True Story as told by JD

1st Run Proof

Published by Great American Press
4155 East Jewell Ave. Suite 610 Denver, CO 80222 USA

Copyright © 2011 by Joseph Daniluk

All rights reserved. No part of this book may be
reproduced, scanned, or distributed in any printed or
electronic form without prior written permission.
Please do not participate in or encourage piracy of
copyrighted materials in violation of the author's rights.
Purchase only authorized editions.

Library of Congress Cataloging-in-Publication Data

Daniluk, Joseph

Drafted To Serve Pope John Paul II A Saint Making Miracles Happen
A True Story As Told By JD

ISBN 978-0-9903416-3-5

This is a true story, told as the events took place at the
time. Names of characters are actual for those living
who granted the author permission to include their real
names, and for public figures, as well as those public
figures who are no longer living. All other character
identities, representing persons encountered or involved
at the time, are pseudonyms invented by the author.
Any references, quotes, and/or descriptions regarding
the foregoing are as recollected by the author.

Documents included are copies of the originals and redacted as necessary.

Photos included were taken by the author at the time as noted in the accompanying text.

The cover photo was taken by photographer, Paul Gana.

DEDICATION

To our Heavenly Father

And

To Pope John Paul II

And

To the love of my life, my dearly beloved wife, editor,
and Soul Mate:

CONTENTS

Contents
Con't.

ACKNOWLEDGEMENTS

I wish to thank and express my deep appreciation for the friendship, involvement, and participation in the events of this story, and the creation of this book to each of the following:

- My Sons:
  Stephen, Web Designer and Programmer
      and
  Christopher, Cover Designer

- TP My dear friend and partner in this story
- Tommy Amato
- William Fox
- General James Hall, USAF, Ret,
- Chuckles

And

- To the Artistry of Paul Gana, Photographer, for the Cover Photo

And

- To all my family and friends who have put up with me and supported me during the process of writing and publishing this story, my heartfelt thanks.

INTRODUCTION

Believe in miracles they really happen

God intervenes and works within us each day to guide us and fulfill His ultimate plan. Unseen through our eyes, God remains ever-present. The experiences and events shared in this book offer a first-hand account of how close God really is and how he can manifest His presence in our daily lives.

While on this earth, Pope John Paul II taught, by example and through prayer, that with God all things are possible. While in Colorado in 1993, it was reported, that each evening he adjourned to a garden to pray*. Looking back, I believe he prayed to God for help in caring for his flock. Finally, I have come to accept the possibility that my partner and I became part of God's answer to the Pope's prayers.

I also believe my thoughts and prayers to Pope John Paul II and to God, for help and guidance as we answered the *call* to assist, were answered in a most astonishing way. The only term to adequately describe what took place is the word miracle. But, I'll tell you what happened and let you decide for yourself.

Pope John Paul II

This Pope was a man of strength and vision. He cared for his flock, and strengthened the bonds between the church and its young people throughout the world. He initiated World Youth Day, which is now in its 28th year.

In 1984 at the close of the Holy Year of Redemption, over 300,000 young people from around the world responded to the Pope's invitation for an International Jubilee of Youth on Palm Sunday in St. Peter's Square. That Sunday, he looked out to the crowds that had arrived and said, "What a fantastic spectacle is presented on this stage by your gathering here today! Who claimed today's youth has lost their sense of values? Is it really true they cannot be counted on?"

The First World Youth Day

The following year, Our Holy Father welcomed thousands of young people to join him again. Later, on December 20, 1985, he announced the institution of World Youth Day (WYD). The first official WYD was held in 1986. During subsequent years, World Youth Day traveled from country to country and continues to this day.

1986- Rome, Italy	Always be prepared to make a defense to anyone who calls you to account for the hope that is in you. - 1Pt 3:15
1987- Buenos Aires, Argentina	We ourselves have known and put our faith in God's love towards ourselves. - 1Jn 4:16
1989- Santiago de Compostela, Spain	I am the way, the truth, and the life - Jn 14:6
1991- Czestochowa, Poland	You have received a spirit of sonship.- Romans 8:15
1993- Denver, Colorado, USA	**I came that they might have life, and have it to the full. Jn 10:10**

I was fortunate to be part of World Youth Day VIII in August of 1993, when the event was held in Denver. The Pope's theme for this particular event was taken from the Gospel of John 10:10.

"I came that they might have life, and have it to the full."

Little did I realize the impact of those words, until I lived through the extraordinary events that took place in 1993, and which I continue to appreciate.

The Story

I was jobless and with a family to care for when Denver was announced as the destination for World Youth Day. My entrepreneurial nature recognized opportunity knocking - to take advantage of what would be a massive public event. And with it my journey began. And 18 months later it ends as the Pope's jet departs Denver. Or so I thought, as I find myself laying word after word onto the screen to share the story with you and the rest of the world.

Part I is an adventure story in and of itself. Beginning with the back story it provides you with an understanding of the characters involved by exposing the events and their activities leading up to the Pope's arrival. Taking what had been submitted to the Vatican, I expanded the factual narration (film at 11 summary approach) into a descriptive story, including many of the individuals participating and the who, what, where, and how everything came about, without embellishment, and with a good dose of language sanitizer. Most of the names of the characters involved and still living have been changed.

Part II provides you with a ringside seat to the astounding events that take place, when the *Call* (from God) comes. For us to help take care of the Pope's flock of 20,000 kids marching to meet their beloved Pope. Illustrating the beauty, the love, and mystery of how God intervenes and works with and among us each day to fulfill His ultimate plan. The story portrays what I believe is an incredible relationship between God and his humble servant, Pope John Paul II. Written originally as a factual description of events, and submitted to the Vatican in support of the efforts to canonize Pope John Paul II, I suddenly realized during the process, (and maybe touched by the hand of God Himself) the time had come to expand and share this story with the world.

My intent is to tell you my story, about my journey, and about how my involvement in Pope John Paul II's WYD-8 impacted my life, and the lives of those participating around me.

Some may see certain events in this story as miracles; others will not. You decide. And possibly you will find the answer that still eludes my partner and me. Of all the people on the planet, what, in all the heavens, prompted the Good Lord to draft two crazy characters, like us, into the service of Pope John Paul II?

Believe in Miracles – Ask for them - And they'll Happen!

*As Pictured on the Cover

~ *v* ~

PREFACE

Drafted To Serve: Pope John Paul II - A Saint - Making Miracles Happen is a true story. Chronicling the actual actions and experiences of my partner and I as they took place in 1992 and 1993. It is about the Spirit of God, and His relationship with Pope John Paul II, and His love for that individual, as God journeyed with him on his travels to spread the word of God's love of all.

At the time, my partner, TP, and I made a pact and agreed to tell no one our incredible story. Given what we experienced, we decided to keep silent. The events were unexplainable to the logical mind. And, if we shared them, we might be considered out of our minds, or intent on exploiting the Pope and the Church. The possible negative fallout could affect not only us personally. It could damage our families and create a whirlwind of negative publicity that could tarnish them and our standing in the community for years. Sharing this story was risky business. TP knew it and I knew it. So, we made the pact to tell no one but the Church of our experiences.

During 2011 and early 2012, several news stories reported that the Vatican was having difficulty finding sufficient miracles attributable to Pope John Paul II to meet the requirements to bestow sainthood. In time, I became motivated to help the Church by providing a written account of the miracles I had witnessed, and attribute to Pope John Paul II's intercession, in answer to my prayers. The resulting document, an earlier draft of Part 2 of this story, was sent to the Vatican in February 2013. In May 2013, in an effort to expand and more completely clarify the unique nature of the events, and the characters involved, a second and expanded Part 2 document was sent to the Vatican, which included a draft of the first three chapters of Part 1 along with my sworn affidavit to the truth of the content.

About six weeks later on June 30, 2013 Pope Francis announced that Pope John Paul II would be canonized officially on April 27, 2014. Coincidence? After the announcement, I felt compelled to complete the story in Part 1 and share the entire story with the world.

When I look back on the events of 1993, I have to ask myself, *how in the world did I end up involved?* I believe the Good Lord knew if He had burned an engraved invitation on a stone tablet, and FedEx'd it to me, requesting me to spend just one day helping John Paul reach out and connect with his flock, I would have, as graciously as possible, declined due to my busy schedule.

Instead of an engraved invitation, for over a year God helped me muddle through a series of activities and experiences leading me to exactly where He needed me to be. Ready, willing, and able to assist Pope John Paul II tend to his flock for a day, with no clue, at the time, He was involved or what He had in mind for me.

Join me, as the story unfolds, and the Pope makes miracles happen. I will provide an account of how we created the lemonade stand, how it became the *lemonaid* stand to help thousands of Pilgrims complete their journey to see their beloved Pope

And, *more importantly*;

How a prayer to Saint John Paul II,
Might just cause a miracle to happen in your life!

I hope you enjoy this story and share this adventure with others.

May God bless you and yours!

Joseph Daniluk

Drafted To Serve

POPE JOHN PAUL II
A SAINT

Making Miracles Happen

PART I

THE POPE IS COMING!

JANUARY 22, 1992

DENVER COLORADO

CHAPTER 1

The Back Story

Fifteen years after World Youth Day 8 (1993)
we are called to tell our story...

After months of extreme consternation, trying to formulate a method to integrate into this story two key factors: the 20 year time lapse between the events in the story being told, and the last miracle, which took place years after the Pope left Denver in 1993. I finally asked myself the key question: if Angels were involved, what took place, and how did the last miracle come about?

Finally, late one sunny summer afternoon in 2012, as I contemplated this dilemma, I suddenly found myself observing a meeting taking place in the heavens within the confines of my mind. As I watched the events unfold, I suddenly realized it was the answer I was seeking.

It provided a plausible explanation as to how, with the passage of time, changing circumstances, and what was once a good and solid decision, i.e. to keep this story a secret, the heavens moved to undo the decision. It may have been nothing more than an overactive imagination, but it was so cool I decided to include it as a precursor to the story for the enjoyment of my readers.

I immediately began to write what I saw in my mind.

The Secret Pact Remained Intact!

And Looking Back

I can just Imagine…

How it was Cracked!

* * *

1

Heavenly Memorandum

From: *St. Peter*

To Angels: *Gabriel, Judith, and Jeremiah.*

Subject: *Status Update Meeting*
             Re - John Paul II's canonization

Location: *Meeting room three at the intersection of*
             Joy and Happiness.

Time: *ASAP*

Attendance Required

 # Saint Peter's
Heavenly Meeting

"**A**ngels! Gabriel, Jeremiah, wait up! I take it you received the memo? Mind if I tag along with you?" Angel Judith asked.

Gabriel responded, "Of course. Come along, my dear, we'll arrive together."

As the three angels joined St. Peter at the heavenly table and exchanged greetings, St. Peter said, "Thank you for coming.

Recently, John Paul II stopped by the Pearly Gates and mentioned he hadn't received any word about his canonization which the Good Lord ordered. Since you three were selected to take care of this project, I thought we ought to get together to see where we're at presently, as well as your current plans to get this project completed. So Angel Judith, why don't we start with you? Please fill me in."

Judith responded, "Well, St. Peter, since John Paul II's arrival here in 2005, the Church has been making every effort to canonize him. Sadly it's been unsuccessful, due to the failure to find the required miracles. These, as you know, must be directly attributed to John Paul's intercession with God on behalf of the individual praying for his intervention. Gabriel has been working on the two miracles reported so far. Gabriel?"

Gabriel answered, "Thank you, Judith. So far, John Paul has only two miracles reported. The first was the nun cured of Parkinson disease. The other was the Costa Rican woman, cured of an inoperable brain aneurysm, after she claimed she heard a voice telling her to get up, and then she saw a magazine with a photo of John Paul gesturing for her to get up. She did and was cured. The Church still doesn't know about the miracles that occurred during John Paul's celebration of World Youth Day 8, which affected and benefitted so many."

Jeremiah interjected, "Miracles are just not being reported to the Church these days. You know how it is, St. Peter. So many miracles are credited to luck or good fortune, and nearly all the rest are lost to fear, the fear of ridicule or notoriety when telling others about their miracle."

After a moment, St. Peter responded, "OK, let's focus on the WYD-8 miracles. Why haven't they been reported? I thought we selected Joe and TP for that project because of their storytelling abilities. Why haven't they reported the miracles they witnessed?"

Jeremiah answered, "Those two characters were so overwhelmed by the miracles they witnessed that they swore themselves to secrecy, a secret pact forevermore. They feared their lack of credibility would result in people questioning their motives for reporting the miracles. It seems the miracles remain incredulous in their own minds. When it happened they believed public revelation would result in such disbelief that they would be scorned and ridiculed. So they have remained silent. My concern is that they'll take the miracles to their graves. Gabriel, tell St. Peter about 1998."

"Well, in '98, Joe had his brother RJ arrange a meeting for him with Denver Archbishop Chaput. During the meeting, despite his best efforts, Joe failed miserably to describe the most significant miracle to the archbishop. Actually watching him stammer and stutter as he tried to tell the story was kinda humorous as he just couldn't figure out how to compress the story

• • •

into the allotted time the archbishop gave him. He couldn't convey the facts, the credibility, or the substance necessary to capture the archbishop's attention, his imagination, or his interest in examining the bare facts of the events. So the meeting ended up being more of a courtesy to his brother. But the archbishop graciously thanked him for his efforts, and then told him explicitly to submit the story to him in writing, and he would send it to Rome. Joe and TP still haven't done it. And the archbishop was right. These miracles are going to have to be written first and then reported to Rome."

"Anything else to report, my Angels?" St. Peter inquired. Silently, shaking their heads negatively, the Angels waited for St. Peter to continue.

After thoughtful consideration, St. Peter said, "We need to get this project moving. Have you formulated a plan on how to proceed?"

Judith replied, "Yes, we have. We're all in agreement. We think that a…"

"Don't even say it." St. Peter interrupted instantly and sternly. "You know that hasn't been done in a very long time. It's just not used these days. That would require the special approval of the Good Lord Himself. Are you certain that's the correct course of action, and is it really necessary?" Looking intently from one angel to the next awaiting an answer.

Gabriel responded, "We truly believe that this is the only way we're going to get those two characters off the dime and moving forward again."

Shaking his head, St. Peter replied, "OK, I'll take your plan upstairs for approval. Under the circumstances, I don't have much hope for a positive reply. Let me be clear, I'm only requesting one. Jeremiah, you've never done one have you?" he asked, looking at Jeremiah who started shaking his head negatively. St. Peter continued, "All right, if we get approval to proceed, Jeremiah you handle it. Make it short and sweet. I'll get back to you later and let you three know the final decision. I thank each of you for the update. Now let's see if we can get this project completed soon. Mccting adjourned."

Spring 2008
The Call Comes

...there was so much light
I could see the blood flowing through my hands...

Early one morning, about three years after Pope John Paul II's death in 2005, the phone on my nightstand rang, and rang. Reaching for it, as I tried desperately to get the machinery in my brain to function, I finally grumbled into the device in my hand, "*Who is* this and *what* do you *want*!? Has someone died?"

The voice of my friend TP vibrated through the receiver exclaiming, "JD I gotta see you. Can I come over to your house, right now?" I could hear the desperation in his voice. "I need to meet with you. Like now!"

Squinting at the clock on my night stand, I retorted, "TP, it's just past 4am. Can't we do this later, like, maybe after the sun comes up, or something?"

"JD," he said desperately, "I need to see you now! Can I come over?"

TP lived out in the sticks, at least a good half hour away, enough time to get up, have a cup of coffee, and be fully awake for his arrival. "Fine, come on over," I answered.

The shower had brought me back to life. I stood in front of the mirror, combing my *still black* hair, looking at the reflection thinking I was in pretty good shape at 61, about 5'9", and holding steady, at a stocky 200 pounds with a decent smile, thinking I may just have a few more miles left in me.

Fortunately, TP's call had not roused anyone else, and the house remained quiet, as I sat down to wait for his arrival. The coffee was hot and tasted good. *What on earth, did he want - especially at this hour of the morning...?*

Then I heard the noisy diesel engine in TP's old pickup pulling into the driveway. Bursting into the house and bounding up the stairs two at a time, he put the brakes on, stopping just before knocking me over. His partially un-tucked shirt, buttoned in the wrong holes, and what little hair he had left, not having seen a comb yet, looked somewhat comical as I handed him a steaming cup of coffee and moved into the living room. Clearly, something was up. After three minutes of babbling, he got up and started pacing around as he continued to talk. The words tumbled out of his mouth, almost incoherently. Small talk. Nonsensical words. More pacing. *What's going on with him?*

I finally interrupted him. "TP, why did you drive over here at 4:30 in the morning to talk to me?"

He stopped pacing, sat down on the fireplace hearth, and as he looked up at me, I could see the color draining out of his face as he said, "JD, you ain't gonna' believe this . . . but I gotta tell you what happened!

"Last night, in my trailer out at the ranch, there was no moon, it was a dark night, and it was pitch black when me and the dogs turned in. I was sound asleep when the dogs started barking and woke me up. I could hear them moving around in the trailer as they continued barking ferociously.

"Suddenly, there was this bright white light coming through all the windows creating bright beams across the trailer's darkness. It was like my trailer had been moved inside a football stadium and somebody turned on all the lights. The dogs kept barking at the door. I felt around on the floor for my pants, keeping an eye on the door and the dogs. But before I found them . . ."

He paused, looking down and shaking his head. Then, after a moment, he looked up at me, his eyes widening as he spoke.

"The light that was outside was suddenly inside, completely filling the trailer with this intense light, and the dogs immediately stopped barking. The light blinded me. I couldn't see anything. I put my hands over my eyes.

"As I tried to open them, there was so much light I could see the blood flowing through my hands.

"Suddenly, my eyes became accustomed to the brilliance in the room. I took my hands away. I could see perfectly. Both dogs were lying on the floor, wagging their tails happily, looking up at the kitchen counter. Then I saw this white gown near them. As I started slowly looking upward, following the shape of the gown, I saw this huge figure of a man, filling the trailer from floor to the ceiling, his head almost touching the ceiling."

Again, he paused, as if to rerun the images in his mind.

"I mean, I'm a 6 foot two ex-Marine, and this guy seemed like he was twice my size, standing in front of me in a white gown. While I was thinking about how enormous he was, he just opened his mouth, and started to speak with this unbelievable voice. It sounded almost musical, like it was in perfect pitch and cadence, and perfect volume. The sound, it was beautiful as he spoke, saying...

I have come to tell you,
the time has come,
for you and Joseph to tell the story.

You must make the joy of the miracles of God,
known to all who wish to hear.

then he smiled. And then, just like that, (snapping his fingers) he was gone. He just vanished! The trailer, it turned immediately pitch black. JD, I'm not making this up. I jumped up off the bed and got the light on, and there were the two dogs lying in front of the door with their tails wagging, and their tongues hanging out, happy as could be.

"I've been a basket case since it happened. I hate to admit it, but - I soiled my underwear and had to change the bed sheets. Then I called you and came right over! This whole thing has really freaked me out! I had to talk to you!"

* * *
9

In all the years I've known TP, I had never seen him this rattled. I really hadn't seen anyone in this condition since 'Nam, and I was truly speechless. He seemed like he was shell-shocked. More importantly, resonating through my entire being was one word the Angel had said: "*Joseph.*" No one, except my late grandmother ever calls me Joseph. I was a child the last time I heard that. TP had never called me, or referred to me with others as, *Joseph.* Hearing it now really bothered me.

Feeling I had to choose my words carefully, I stalled for a little time and lit a cigarette. I needed to figure out what to say. I handed the smoke to TP, as he nodded and took it. Repeating the ritual, I lit one for myself, all the while searching for the correct response, for that matter, any response.

Humor, that's the answer, I concluded. I exhaled a drag on my cigarette and finally said, "TP, how much wine did you have to drink last night?"

He turned his head to look at me directly and said, with a chuckle, "Apparently not enough! I should've downed the whole bottle!"

Lightheartedly and gently, I said, "Well, what exactly do you think happened?"

"JD, I honestly don't know. All I really know is what I told you. I mean, when the light came... Then there's this huge being, standing in the middle of my trailer, looking at me! I really don't know what to make of it. . .

"I have to believe it was an angel or some kind of messenger - from God, I guess." Pausing to sip on his coffee and take a drag on his smoke, he continued.

"I almost can't believe I just said that, because, until I met up with you I've never given much thought about God, angels or anything religious. So I don't know. I've never experienced anything like this - in my entire life. My kids decided to be agnostics, and my ex-wife, if she had a religion, I never knew what it was and never inquired. So, what do you think happened, JD?"

I really wasn't certain of how to respond. It was obvious something had happened to TP, but what?

This certainly wasn't the TP I knew and learned to love, or part of TP's character and general approach to life. TP had always been a matter of fact kind of guy. He was capable of selling ice cubes to Eskimos. However, his pitch was always well thought out, carefully planned, and dependent upon the listener's reaction and response. But he blew through the details of his event so quickly, I had no time or opportunity to react.

I've read about angels, I've heard about angels, I've even talked about angels. But, I have never spoken to someone who had actually seen one. I just continued to sit there, in silence, looking at TP, dumbfounded and perplexed, trying to comprehend what had just been said.

TP finally broke the silence, and asked, "Got any more coffee?"

"Yah, help yourself," I replied.

TP rose and went into the kitchen. His absence allowed the analytical side of my brain to function. My conclusion seemed solid. An angel appeared; TP must have been, no – was visited - by an angel. If that's a fact, then we need to respond and follow the angel's instructions.

TP returned to his seat and as he lit up a fresh smoke, I said, "Well, TP, I truly believe you just saw your first angel. Something I've never experienced. I think it's really awesome.

"More importantly, for you to rush over here at 4am, to share the message for us to tell our story, has had a definite impact on me.

"We need to follow the Angel's instructions. We need to get together and do it. We have to quit putting this off! We need to write the story, regardless of the consequences."

"I agree, let's do it." TP exclaimed.

After this conversation with TP, the time, it continued to slip away.

Two Years Later!
2010

For months there had been a nagging thought in my mind. "Joseph." I kept hearing that word repeatedly. I had to get together with TP and discuss our story, even though we had made a pact to never tell. Anyone. Not even a friend. No one. And for fifteen years the pact worked out just fine. Then out of nowhere, TP's Angel shows up, breaks the pact, and I end up haunted.

Late March 2010, I answered the phone one morning and TP says, "How ya doin' bud? It's been awhile!"

"You know, I was just thinking about you and have been for some time recently. What prompts your call, my friend?"

"We have to tell the story!" he blurted out.

Given the months since we last spoke, his call was a surprise. I finally replied, "I cannot believe we are having this conversation. I've been thinking about this for months, and I agree."

TP quickly interjected, "Let's get together tomorrow and at least go take pictures of the locations - the store, the office, and the 'police command center' at the lemonade stand."

The conversation continued, interlaced with tidbits of memories. Until TP added, "We need to get the archbishop to put us in front of some cameras and just tell him the story and get it finally over with."

"TP, you forget. After the Pope left, back in '98, I met with the archbishop. I pitched the deal exactly that way. His response, if you remember, was for us to reduce it to writing so it could be handled properly through channels. And neither one of us wanted to do that. Remember?"

"Well, we need to try again!" He replied.

"No way, TP. I'm not going to go through that again, even if I could. The time has come for you and me to sit down and write the story. Really write it. I'm still very concerned about the publicity and wish we could remain anonymous, if possible.

"But, it's . . . I swear, your angel, my angels, everybody's angels are on my case to get this done. I feel they are providing me with a guide on how to proceed. I'm going to proceed. Trust me! Work with me and help me to get it done. You do remember your angel?"

"Of course I remember the angel, but what about all the crap and notoriety?" He replied, while I felt his frustration coming through the phone.

"C'mon TP, listen to me," I said. "Let's just write about what happened at the lemonade stand and send it to the Vatican. Maybe it'll just get lost in the bureaucracy. We'll only identify ourselves to the Vatican in sworn affidavits, confirming that everything stated is the truth, the whole truth, and nothing but the truth and be done with it!"

Sharing this story was risky business. It could turn our lives upside down. TP knew it and I knew it.

I continued, "TP I have no doubt - I totally believe the Good Lord will guide us and protect us as we proceed to complete this mission. It can't be any worse than riding the rivers in Vietnam, can it? We need to tell the story, to share the awe and wonder of being witness to, and players in, the miracles, and such an astounding series of events. To share the reality of what we saw and experienced, of God's Love for one man completing his heavenly mission on earth.

"You and I both know it was such a fantastic display of God's Love for everyone involved. We have to share this story. Let's do it!"

"How about next Sunday?" he inquired.

I confirmed the meet.

Revisiting the Past

The morning of April 4, 2010, Easter Sunday, TP calls and tells me he's on his way. I pick up my laptop and write an introduction. We saddle up and ride out to fulfill the mission. This day, our plan was to go and revisit the sites where the events took place – just to jog our memories.

Man, did we ever misjudge the amount and degree of change which had taken place. It took a while to remember, and find the old office building where we originally met, where our story began. Gone were all the trees by the front doors and surrounding the north and east side of the building. The parking lot had been expanded, but the outside structure of the building had not changed. As we pulled up to the front door, the memories started rushing in.

Walking up the front steps where we had spent so much time together talking, we found locks on the front door, which did not exist when we were tenants. After sitting on the steps for a while, ruminating, as we had done so many times in the past, we walked around the building and took some pictures.

We then headed out to visit the site where the amazing events took place. Assuming we could drive right to the spot, we quickly discovered most of the area had radically changed. Where there had once been trees and wild grasses growing, we found a concrete jungle. Condominiums and apartment complexes, built along Cherry Creek where the events had taken place, encroached in every direction.

 ## Recollecting
The Lemonade Stand

After what seemed like hours, we found "the spot." Well, sort of. A new bridge had been constructed for pedestrians to cross the creek right at the site of the lemonade stand where we had participated in Pope John Paul II's World Youth Day VIIIr.

Our city, the beautiful city the Pope had selected as his venue to reach out to young people from around the world. Just to meet and pray with him, which they did by the hundreds of thousands. Hearing his call, they came, to be with him. Attendance was estimated afterwards in excess of 500,000. Of which 20,000 - 30,000 marched past us, met us, interacted with us, and consumed our lemonade at this very site. WOW! We're back at the site of God's miracles! What a breathtaking rush! To sit there, watching the ghosts of the marchers trekking on by, waving, singing, and happy as could be. As the rerun in my mind continued, all the accoutrements, and trappings of the lemonade stand appeared next to the bike path. Memories of individuals' happy and smiling faces formed, images of so many, who stopped for refreshments and rest. Incredibly, at the forefront of my memories was the joy! The joy and happiness that everyone at the lemonade stand expressed, demonstrated, and shared with all who were present.

Finally, the effects of old age began signaling that it was time to go. We decided that one day soon we would have to stop at a burger barn somewhere nearby, bring a couple of folding chairs, and have lunch once again at the lemonade, no the *lemonaid* stand. To just reminisce, relive, and remember an unbelievable adventure.

To conclude our outing we headed to the store.

The store where miracles happen! We drove around back and stopped. I got out of the car and took pictures of the truck dock where I stood 17 years ago, where the final events of the day blew us away, as the Holy Spirit of the heavens was revealed, in our reality, in real time, right before our eyes. Silencing us for hours afterwards as we tried to comprehend what we had witnessed.

It was so eerie. TP and I sat on the edge of the concrete barrier, underneath the tree, again, behind the streetlight, contemplating in silence as we had done so very long ago.

Our outing had consumed five or six hours, so we headed home, worn out, and re-committed to writing the story.

But, once again, *scheduling issues* prevented us from getting together, and we continued to procrastinate.

A Year Later 2011

Repeated efforts to get with TP to write this story failed. I started to put an outline together and wrote a couple of snippets, but everyday life, once again, pulled me away. My business schedule again took precedence. Finally, WWD (the World's Worst *economic* Depression) which started in 2008 caught up to my business in 2012. As my business volume diminished, I found myself with more and more surplus time. So once again, 'the story, the book' pulled me in and I started writing. And this time, I am and remain committed and dedicated to completing my mission even at the expense of my business.

Having never written anything of depth or breadth, this project has proven to be a real challenge for me. Time and again, I wanted to throw in the towel and give it up. But, as the words slowly took shape, I realized just how amazing this story about God and John Paul II really was. I began to understand John Paul's commitment to his mission of sharing his knowledge of God's love for all mankind with the world. And the best part was recognizing God's love for John Paul, and finally, realizing that I got to see the manifestation of this relationship, and could now, nearly, comprehend how He interacted with his beloved John Paul and share what I saw with everyone.

As the star and leading character in this story, God, needs no introduction, and I am certainly not competent to describe Him. You're on your own here. But, the other star of the story, Pope John Paul II, I can help you out, with an introduction, as it correlates to the story.

At the time of these events in 1993, the only thing I knew about the Pope was his name. Since then, having had years to think about and contemplate the events, overcoming the trepidation that accompanies involvement in such events, and having carried out only a cursory investigation of this person, this individual, this man called Pope John Paul II, have I been able to realize what took place, and the enormity of what I witnessed. The impact on me was, and remains, so intense language to describe any one of the events escapes me; I become tongue tied when I try. Leaving me with only this venue, this book - to try and convey, and share this experience with you and everyone else.

Now recognizing I have a role, albeit a very, very minor one, in helping John Paul wrap up his earthly undertakings, makes the burden of writing this story so much lighter as each word appears.   I am enjoying the research, the reminiscing, and reflections on the events at the time, while appreciating the new perspective the passage of time has had on the events.

In retrospect, what impresses me the most about Pope John Paul II was his leadership, dedication, and commitment to his missions - one to the church itself and the other to his congregation. Once he recognized his mission to lead and guide a changing church — to enact, correct and nurture the reforms of Vatican II, he developed a plan to achieve and ultimately executed it.

His true love though, seemed to be his other mission, his congregation. Creatively conceiving the concept of world youth day event rallies, as his means and method to share his love, and his message, with everyone, everywhere. He focused on the young, soon to be adults, whom he cherished. Never allowing the bureaucracy of the Church or the Vatican itself to interfere with his commitment to his missions, he always persevered.

Pope John Paul II envisioned and expressed in his first encyclical, *Redemptor Hominis,* his mission for his congregation, and for a troubled world, which was to herald the message 'joy is found in faith, in the belief, in our Creator.' How incredibly powerful those words are – the statement is! The extreme depth of meaning is awesome.

Stop reading here for a moment and contemplate the magnificence of John Paul imagining, creating, and then bringing to life, an idea to fulfill his mission, formulating a plan of action (create World Youth Day events) and then executing it.   He touched the lives of millions pursuing his mission since announcing the institution of World Youth Day on December 20, 1985, and holding the first official WYD in 1986.

I witnessed and shared with a half a million followers the joy and wonder he brought to Denver in WYD-8 in '93. It truly was something to see and experience. And, *more importantly*, I learned how a prayer to Blessed (soon to be Saint) John Paul II, might just cause a miracle to happen in your life!

Despite our best efforts over the years, TP and I were unable to mutually agree on when to get together to begin writing. In mid-2012, I decided I would have to tell the story myself.

CHAPTER 2

And The Story Begins
January 1992

... 30,000 people are expected to show up ...
And that's how the idea ... was born.

Plodding down the hall, I was trying to shake off the grogginess that accompanies a restless night. The welcome smell of fresh coffee brewing in the kitchen filled the air. Turning the corner into the kitchen, now squinting as the morning sun burst into the room, I opened the cabinet to reach for a cup and said to my beautiful wife, Audrey, whose golden blonde locks sparkled in the sunlight, "Good morning my love."

"Good morning, I have to leave for work - kids! We're leaving - get in the car! Will you be home on time tonight?" She replied, as she softly brushed my cheek with a kiss.

I smiled as the kids rushed by, waving to them, and responded, "Yes, I'll be home for dinner."

She smiled back and then looked down and said, "Snugger, you have to find work, please. We're running low on money."

I looked at her, suddenly feeling glum about my current set of circumstances and said, "I know, I'll have to give it some thought and try to figure something out. I still have to get hold of the GAO and see how we're proceeding with the investigation. I'll look through the paper and see if there're any want ads worthy of a response and send out some resumes."

With a loving smile she replied, "Good luck, see you later, bye!" Turning, she descended the stairs and I heard the sound of the closing door echoing through the now-empty house.

Having filled my coffee cup I sat down at the table thinking. Just 18 months ago I was the number two in command of a major government agency in Denver managing 300+ employees and now unable to find a new gig. I grabbed the newspaper.

As it unfolded onto the table, the front page jumped out at me screaming **POPE** in the largest font I'd ever seen in a newspaper. The four characters took up the entire front page. *Oh my God,* I thought, *did the pope die?*

It was then I noticed a few words in a tiny font in the lower right corner: "is coming – see page 2."

Still amazed at the sheer size of the characters on the page, I was thinking it must've taken an extra truck load of black ink to make these four giant characters fill the page. Turning to page 2, it became apparent that this was going to be a really big deal. Pope John Paul II had decided to hold a rally called "World Youth Day" in Denver, Colorado, in mid-August next year. And 20,000 maybe 30,000 people are expected to show up for 10 days to see and hear him speak.

As I reread the article my mind started to race thinking about the opportunities this kind of event could bring. Out of work, out of dough, a family of four to feed, and having reached middle age, necessity seemed to drive me to try to find an opportunity to make some money somehow during this event. There had to be some kind of concession, some kind of service or product to sell to 30,000 fans of the pope coming to Denver from around the world. More importantly, we had time. Today being January 23, 1992, I had about 18 months to put something together. *Hmmm* I thought, *better make a mental note - could be something really worthwhile.*

During the next few months there were sporadic news stories about the pope's visit, continually reminding me to figure out how to take advantage of this opportunity. I relentlessly tried to find work. However, periodic interruptions due to my participation in a Government Accounting Office (GAO) investigation made the search even more difficult. The lack of success with my job hunting efforts caused more and more of my thoughts to go back to the possible opportunities the pope's visit could present.

Finally, one day I picked up the phone and called an old partner of mine, Bill Fox, my executive vice president for five years, when I owned a bank during the mid-70's. The ringing stopped, and upon hearing his voice I said, "Bill, you old water buffalo, how the hell are you? It's JD."

"Fine, just fine JD, how about you?"

After reminiscing about old times and adventures it was time to pop the question. "Bill, have you read about the pope's visit?"

"Yes."

"Well I think it's an incredible opportunity. Do you want to get together again and make some money?"

"Hell yes, what yah got in mind?"

"Let's meet for coffee tomorrow morning at 10am, at Denny's restaurant on Parker Road."

"Done, see you tomorrow, bye."

It was a bright and sunny morning. The aroma of bacon, the clanking of dishes and the murmur of numerous conversations blending together filled the restaurant. At precisely 9:55 Bill pulled into a parking space in front of the window beside me. My good friend, standing about 5'7" tall with a stocky build, having once been a golden gloves boxer, and still sporting his military style navy crew cut, proceeded through the doors, and after exchanging pleasantries for a bit, it was time to get down to business.

"Bill, I've been thinking about this for the past three months, and I feel in my bones, there is a huge opportunity here. I just haven't figured it out yet. Now they're reporting crowds in excess of 50,000 people are expected to come for the papal visit, for 10 days. Denver doesn't have 50,000 extra hotel rooms, enough restaurants to feed so many people three times a day, nor the transportation to move such a volume of people around to various events. The overall logistics are a mind bender.

This event is going to be huge! Now, the question begging for an answer is, how can we make a few bucks on the deal? I've thought about the food and beverage concepts, and ruled them out because there are too many costly variables. Labor, particularly part time labor for 10 days is the biggest problem, so I really don't wanna get involved in a food related project. Lodging is out of the question, because the timetable is too short, leaving us with only transportation or some kind of tourist souvenir concessions for further consideration. As for tourist concessions, thinking back to when I had the franchise to sell Denver Gold and Broncos football teams' paraphernalia, between inventory management control, and employee thefts, it seems too risky a crapshoot, leaving us with only the transportation category!" Bill nodded in agreement as I sipped on my coffee for a moment.

Continuing, I said, "There still hasn't been an agenda published, but it's safe to assume the pope is going to speak periodically at least once a day, maybe more often, and our visitors will want to hear him, wherever he speaks. How do you move 50,000 people around every day? I don't think Denver has enough government buses, and for sure there ain't enough taxis in town to handle this kind of logistics nightmare. Anyway, those are my thoughts so far. What do you think?"

Setting his coffee cup down Bill leaned back and said, "Seems like you've spent a great deal of time and thought on this proposition. Your conclusions are dead on. But, let's go back in time, and if you remember back in Cheyenne, we spent an entire night discussing marketing strategies and came to a conclusion. The only things that will motivate people to part with their money is 'Need, Greed, or Want'. Keeping that in mind, we should re-examine this whole thing. Let's call these 50,000 people 'The

Kids,' as this event is being billed as 'World Youth Day.'"
Catching the waitress with a fresh pot of coffee in her fist, Bill got
her to refill our cups as she was passing by.

Pausing while he stirred about a half-dozen bags of
imitation sweet'ner into his coffee, I remained silent, stuck in
suspense waiting to hear the rest.

Finally, having concluded the stirring process, he
continued, "I would bet the average age of these Kids is going to
be between the upper teens, and low twenties. They're probably
not going to be well off or flush with cash. Your list included all
their needs, but what about their wants. Besides some souvenirs I
think their biggest want is going to be some cheap entertainment."
Chuckling, he continued "I don't wanna be in the port-a-
potty business, etcetera. If I were you, I would start thinking about
providing the Kids with some kind of entertainment."

I sat there dumb struck, feeling like I'd just been hit by a
truck. I realized after three months of thought, I had overlooked
and missed, the ocean, the pier, and the damn boat. Bill had come
up with the correct answer; provide the Kids with some kind of
entertainment. Once I came back to my senses, I said, "Bill, do
you still have the old office furniture and supplies from when we
moved out after selling the bank?"

"Oh yah," he replied, "I even have our old phone system
with about 20 of the original phone sets."
"Great", I said, "Bill, if I can figure out a way to make
some really good money, big bucks, providing the Kids with some
form of entertainment, will you come out of retirement and work
with me again, on this project?"
"Hell yes!" he replied.

On the drive back home I realized this truly was the answer
to the question of how to make the papal visit profitable. I started
running memory tapes in my mind of people and entertainment
industry related discussions I had in the past. There wasn't much
to work with, regrettably, despite a degree in TV-production and a

very short stint working on the *Dukes of Hazard* and *Perry Mason* sets.

I walked into the house as evening arrived. My older son, Stephen, coming up on his 12th birthday, greeted me with his most adult like greeting, "Hi Dad, how are you today?"

"Fine son, just fine, thanks!" I replied, "And how are you?"

He started down the stairs as he responded, "OK – Fine, but I gotta go downstairs and finish my homework before dinner, so I can go to Anthony's house afterwards, Mom says."

"OK Buddy, you go!" I said as I set my briefcase down and picked up my four-year-old, Christopher, lifting him up in my arms to give him a hug as he squealed in delight over my attention and began to tell me about his adventures. After hearing his story I gave him an extra hug, set him down, and moved into the kitchen. Audrey was busy at the stove preparing dinner, and she turned at the sound of my entrance to smile and say hello. I smiled back, walking up to put my arms around her, gave her a hug and a kiss and said, "I think I have some great news, almost, well sort of…"

"What are you talking about?" She said without missing a step in her dinner preparations.

"Well, I met with Fox this morning about the pope's visit and I think it went very well. I haven't figured it out yet, but I want to tell you about it and see what you think."

As we moved dinner from the stove to the table, she said, "Okay, how about we talk more during dinner?"

"Works for me," I replied.

Later, my wife looked across the table at me with the most perplexed look on her face after hearing the details of my morning meeting, and said, "What exactly is your entertainment idea?"

Looking down at the table, I realized I had to admit, "I really don't know yet."

She said, "JD, it's been almost a year since you've worked. I don't see how we can afford to start a new business or whatever, to do this, whatever this is. I'm so concerned about our finances.

I replied, "Yes, I know full well how serious this is. I know we can't continue financially on your small salary. I'm looking, and trying to get interviews for work. There doesn't seem to be any demand around here and I don't want to relocate somewhere else. But, I do think something involving the papal visit could result in a large enough profit to fill the huge hole in our finances. I'll try to figure something out while I continue to try and find a job. We have to continue to pray and trust in the Lord to help us make it through these seemingly never ending, trying times. But, just say the word and I'll completely forget about the papal visit, because - I won't proceed if you're not with me."

"Snugger," she replied, "I want you to do whatever makes you happy, but don't forget how serious things are. We've made it through some tough times before, and I trust the Good Lord won't abandon us, so I'm behind you, whatever you decide to do."

The next morning, while checking out the want ads, the phone rings and a voice says, "Hi JD, its Chuckles. We met at the fundraiser for the Senator three weeks ago." He pauses.

I don't recognize the caller and remain silent trying to place him when he realizes the pause has to end.

Artfully, he continues. "I was sitting at the Mayor's table. You were with your District Captain, General James Hall, when we were introduced to each other."
"Oh yah, - yah, I remember now, how are you?" I queried.

"Ok, doing well. I wanted to call and invite you and your wife to come over to the Doubletree Hotel Friday night for dinner, as my guest. I was recently promoted to F&B Director, and hired a new chef, and it will be opening night for a new band. The band is led by an incredible female vocalist I would like you to hear. And I am sure you will enjoy her show. She would eventually like to perform in Las Vegas and I thought with your connections there, maybe something might develop. Anyway, can you make it?"

I replied, "Well, Chuckles thank you, we'll be there. Talk to you then." Strange, I thought, as I hung up the phone. My mind had been churning the word entertainment over and over all morning. Is this chance phone call the Good Lord's way of opening the door to a new adventure in my life?

A little later the phone rings again. This time I hear a familiar voice. "Hello, JD, this is Patty Marino with the GAO calling."

"Patty, how are you? How are we doing? You know it's been a while."

Patty replied, "Just fine, JD. I realize it's taken some time to get back to you, but you did bury us in a mountain of paperwork and it's taken over six months to sort through and organize all of it. After a review we've decided to assemble an inquiry team. We need you to come down and meet with the team so we can determine and summarize the facts in order to make a final recommendation as to whether or not we will open an official GAO investigation. We have organized everything we need. We just need you to talk us through all the documentation and the events surrounding it. Can you come down and meet with us next week?"

"When are you thinking?"
"Can you do next Thursday, say 10am?"
"Yah, I'll be there. It'll be good to see you again.

As evening arrived, we sat around the dinner table. Steve and Chris bantered about school events and their experiences of the day until there was a pause indicating they had said all there was to say. I took advantage of the interlude and said, "Lover, I want to take you out to dinner and a little dancing on the 23rd at the Doubletree Hotel. Sound good to you?"

With a stern look she replied, harshly, "No, we can't afford to go out right now!"

Smiling broadly, I answered, "Not to worry, Lover, the whole evening's being comped. A guy I met, called Chuckles is the new food and beverage manager over there, and he called today and invited us to come as his guests. If Steve takes care of Chris while we're gone, then the evening won't cost us a dime. So, what do you think now?"

Taken aback, she responded softly, "Well then, I guess it would be okay. But, why is he doing this and is his name really Chuckles?"

"A two-part question," I replied. "As I recall, I asked him the same question about his name. He explained back in his early 20's, he joined a band as a guitarist. And they already had a band member named Chuck so they started calling him Chuckles instead of Chuck-number 2 and the name stuck. Anyway, he invited us because he wants me to hear this new band he hired. To see if I can help promote them, I think. And when I combine it with the meeting with Fox, in my mind, the sheer coincidence itself makes me curious enough to want to go see what's going to happen."

With a touch of scorn in her voice, she replied, "OK! So, have you suddenly figured out what this entertainment thing is after one phone call and one meeting?"

Suddenly, Steve piped in, "What are you guys talking about?"

Having been caught off guard by her question, I was thankful for Steve's interruption and responded to him, "Well son, your mother and I were talking about the pope's visit. Have you heard about it?"

Excitedly, he replied, "Oh yah, dad. Last week the pastor came to our class and told us all about it. It's really cool! It'll be really exciting to go and see him when he comes."

Interjecting, I said, "Yes, it will be! I'm glad you heard about it. Your mother and I are talking about the possibility of starting a business to provide all the kids that will be coming from around the world some entertainment while they're here."

Astonishingly, he replied, "OH WOW! That sounds great, Dad! What entertainment?"

Looking down at my plate, buying time by moving the food around with my fork, I realized I had no answer to the question they were both asking. Out of time, I looked up at Steve and said, "Well son I haven't figured it out yet, but I'm thinking real hard about it. Do you have any suggestions? In fact, if anyone at the table has a suggestion I'm sure open to look at any of them." Looking at Audrey I asked, "What do you think?"

Lovingly, with a small smile expanding on her lips, she replied, "Do you have any idea of what you're planning?"

"No! I really don't - not yet," as I tried desperately to accelerate my brain matter to formulate a reasonably comprehensible and sensible response. Having dragged her through a number of small business adventures during the past 20 years, which helped us survive, but never became the grand slam home run originally portrayed, and still with no job prospects, I felt I must answer her question carefully. My mind flipped through scenario after scenario as I tried to formulate the perfect response. The pregnant pause in our conversation was way overdue for a response. In sheer desperation, I turned off the scenarios running through my mind and decided I would just have to do the old 'JD-Dance' and ad lib, and pray I could be successful in capturing her interest, and more importantly, her support. I knew in my mind, without her participation and support, this idea was about to die at the dinner table.

A little nervously, the dance began, as I said, "I admit I have no experience in the entertainment business, but I didn't have any experience in the banking industry when I opened the bank back in '74."

"Yes," she quickly retorted, "And after five years we barely got out unscathed." Adding emphatically, "I can't believe you're thinking of starting a business centered on one event."

• • •

I replied, "I was only thinking about providing entertainment for the tourists during the pope's visit, but you never know, I guess it could develop into other things."

Raising her voice, she interjected emphatically, "That's exactly my concern!!"

"Hang on Lover, let's not get the wagon in front of the horse.   I haven't even figured out what 'providing the entertainment for the pope's visit' means. I was hoping you three might throw some ideas out onto the table," looking around, hoping to buy more time, to formulate an idea.

Chris, looking at me as if he knew it was time to step in and bail out his dad, said, "Let's get some singers and dancers, dad!"

"Well yes son, I think you have a good idea, we'll need singers, dancers, musicians, flashing lights, and maybe some magic."

Looking over at Audrey I caught a smile forming on her lips, as Chris responded excitedly, "Magic, dad! Really like a magic show - a real magic show dad?"

Which prompted Steve to chime in, "I think a concert would be better than a magic show."

"Wow, now those are good ideas guys!" I exclaimed with a broad smile. "How about a concert with a magic show during intermission," trying desperately to incorporate the value of both comments equally.

Chris signaling Steve to lean down towards him placed his hand near the side of his face and whispered in Steve's ear. Steve then whispered in Chris's ear, then nodding in the affirmative to each other, they turned to me and said nearly in unison, "That's a really good idea Dad! That's what you should do!"

And that's how the idea to produce a concert for the Pope was born.

CHAPTER 3

Where To Start?

"...I have a very good friend, Tommy Tomato."
As ..., he started to chuckle...

Friday came, and off we went. The hostess led us to a booth on the edge of the dance floor across from center stage where the band equipment was set up. Our names were prominently displayed on the table reservation sign in the center of the table. As we were seated Chuckles walked up. After an introduction to Audrey and some small talk, he said he would introduce us to the vocalist and bandleader, Paula Westerfield, on the band's first break.

Suddenly the stage lights came on and there stood Paula in the center of the spotlight. A guitar slung over her shoulder, dressed in jeans and a long-sleeve red and blue country-western style shirt, which complemented not only her young curvy figure, but also her mane of fiery red hair, styled to perfectly frame her beautiful face. As she looked around the room, she raised her right hand motioning the beat to start her opening number. Her voice filled the room. The background music was at just the right volume so as not to overpower her as my ears began to fill with the sound of an incredibly robust and lovely voice. Man, there was no doubt, this gal could sing!

After dinner and a couple of dances, the band took a break. Shortly thereafter, Chuckles walked up with Paula and did the introductions. She sat down and we began to talk.

I said, "Paula, you have an incredible voice. You can really belt out the songs. We've really enjoyed your show, your music, and of course your singing. Chuckles tells me you would eventually like to play in Vegas."

Paula replied, "Yes, one of my dreams is to be a headliner on the Strip. I hope to get there one day soon."

"Have you got a professional agent helping you to get there?"

"No, I'm hoping to find a good one. I put the band together myself and produced two CDs so far, with songs I've written."

"How long has your band been together and where have you been playing?"

"We've been together for three years now and we play the Denver club circuit. We also tour twice a year, up and down the Midwest states playing at various clubs and bars in the small towns. It keeps us going and together. We hope to get a recording contract one day and play Vegas. Chuckles thought you might be able to help us out. Do you think you can?"

After a brief pause, I responded, "Honestly, Paula, I can't answer your question at the moment. I love your voice. I'm going to ask you to give me some time to look into your situation and see if I can come up with some recommendations. It seems to me, you really need someone very experienced and well-connected in the music industry to help you. I don't think just any agent, or someone like myself with no previous experience, would be of benefit to you. However, I do have some contacts I can get in touch with to see if there are some recommendations I can make to you. Can you give me a little time?"

It seemed she was drowning in disappointment when she answered, "I hoped we would find some answers tonight and someone to help us. I do appreciate your honesty and your being forthright with me. I would appreciate any help or guidance you might be able to provide. And please, I invite you to come hear us play at other venues in the meantime."

"I will." I replied, as she rose and returned to the stage.

The following weekend I went downtown to a local bar where Paula was playing, to hear more and evaluate the audience response to her music. It was evident she had a following of fans cheering her on after each song. The remainder of the audience seemed to really enjoy her music as the sound of many people talking would die down as she started singing each song. The dance floor remained full and everyone appeared to be having a good time. Consequently, I decided she just might be the real thing and concluded I would contact some folks to see if I could help her find a good agent.

Off To Meet The GAO

It had been a couple of months since my last meeting with the GAO and once again I was headed downtown to meet with them on a brisk spring morning. As rush hour traffic reduced my momentum to stop and go, I began reminiscing historical events trying to understand how I ended up in the here and now.

In '84, Denver was a boom town at the peak of trying to become the new oil industry mecca, with oil shale located on the western slope of the Rocky Mountains. The economy was booming, every square foot of office space was rented, and there were jobs for everyone. In July that year, a couple of months after I graduated from Denver University, some rocket scientist finally figured out you couldn't squeeze enough oil out of these rocks to make it profitable and Denver's economy instantly crashed. Every banker and realtor was on the street with resume in hand looking for work, including me. In desperation, I rented a 150 square foot office and opened Boss Corporation, a computer business. With my new IBM-XT PC, purchased during my last semester in school, which could unbelievably hold 10 MB of data on a five pound hard disk drive, business boomed. I engineered and installed the first primitive local-area networks in numerous businesses and government agencies all over the city.

Also in that year, I remember, it was reported that Pope John Paul II was visiting Sorok Island off South Korea, a one-time leper colony where several hundred people with the disfiguring disease were receiving care. After giving his brief speech on the meaning of suffering, he was so overcome by the suffering he saw in the audience, he cast aside his schedule, protocol, and his handlers, and went to work. Touching and caressing them with his hands, he kissed each one, all eight hundred lepers, one by one. One by one!" Pretty incredible I always thought.

Now, halfway to my destination, I started to recall my first job interview with the FDIC (Federal Deposit Insurance Corporation). One day in late October '88, an old friend of mine, who had become a US Ambassador, walked into my office and told me about a new national financial crisis brewing. He gave me a federal government employment application, saying my banking experience and education were perfect for a special job. A month later, I found myself in an unofficial "secret" meeting with a Senator and two Congressmen. They explained to me that the savings-and-loan crisis was creating an alarming increase in fraud, waste, and mismanagement within the FDIC. Consequently, a congressional committee was looking for a handful of people to go into the different regional offices, figure out how it was happening and stop it. And would I have an interest in doing that in the Denver office. They played my love of country and patriotism like master musicians, and I readily agreed, knowing I would be on my own and could not come back to these guys again for help or assistance. I was excited about the prospect of getting out of the computer business and get an opportunity to utilize my dual-degree in finance and real estate.

A couple months later, I went through a series of official job interviews. Then two months later I received a phone call telling me I was hired as a Supervisory Liquidation Specialist and Assistant Specialist in Charge of the Denver office. I sold my business for pennies on the dollar and reported to work. Weeks later I was managing the closing of dozens of banks and savings and loans, as well as the recovered assets worth billions of dollars and their eventual disposal.

It turned out to be a tough gig. I found myself spending eight hours a day doing my "regular job" and later on, another four to eight hours a day doing my "other job," looking for waste and fraud. I did them both successfully, but at a terrible cost - to my reputation, my financial stability, and my family, as I had to fall on my sword in the end. Now, three years later, I'm on my way to a meeting with the GAO – the **US General Accounting Office** to wrap up my "other job" with a big ribbon, my undercover work, for the Inspector General, the agency's internal police department, and surrender my secret identity as "Archibald" once and for all.

It became impossible to sit still while I waited in the reception area. I got up and walked around thinking how in the world does one produce a concert. Then I noticed Patty walking down the hallway in my direction. Smiling, she walked up and said, "JD, it's good to see you again. Thank you for coming."

"You're welcome. Hopefully we're getting close to finishing up. I just want to get this whole thing behind me finally. So I'm all yours."

"Good, we've decided to open an official investigation and have assembled an inquiry team, so let's go back to the conference room, meet the team and get started."

As we turned the corner at the end of the hallway, I was looking at a huge conference room with a table capable of seating at least two dozen people, stacked with very familiar banker boxes up and down the entire length, and more stacked against the walls, with at least 15 people standing around. I thought, without a doubt, this is going to be a really long day.

We entered through the glass doors and Patty announced in a loud voice, "Okay everyone, we're ready to go. This is JD, and JD everyone's wearing name tags, so we'll skip individual introductions and just get started. Everyone please take a seat, thank you. JD, in this, our first meeting together, we need your help. We are about to launch a complete investigation of the Denver FDIC office. We need your guidance on what and where to look for the evidence to support your last report that came with your files," pointing to the array of my banker boxes around the room. "Can you help us out?"

"Yes, I can, where do you want to start?" The answer took up the rest of the day.

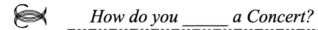 *How do you _____ a Concert?*

Weeks later, I was frustrated and feeling guilty. I'd called just about everyone I knew in LA and Vegas trying unsuccessfully to find a lead to a professional agent for Paula. My frustration was amplified by the fact that I hadn't been able to begin formulating and creating a vision in my mind of a concert or how to do one. I sat there fuming. And then thinking, *Hey Lord, I could use a little help here, I can't seem to find the answers I'm seeking.*

Then suddenly, surprise, I answered the phone to hear, "JD, how yah all doin'?"

I thought I recognized that very Texas Southern drawl, when he continued, "It's Mark Wheeling from Las Vegas. Have you got a second?"

With a bit of laughter, I replied, "Mark, I'm doing great, *how you all doin'?*"

Mark, the only child of a rich Texas oil family, was the epitome of a trust fund baby who had never had a job. He was the most down to earth, nicest guy you could ever meet. His million-dollar home was full of an assortment of expensive treasures, souvenirs, and wall after wall of personalized pictures of very famous people he knew. The bulk of the pictures were of drop-dead gorgeous females, which may have explained why he was still single at age 50. He was always so friendly and unpretentious you just couldn't help but love him.

As the conversation continued, he wanted to know if I could come to Vegas to meet with some friends from Japan. They wanted him to invest in a new LED manufacturing plant they were planning to build. Earlier I had mentioned to Mark that I was considering starting an energy conservation business in Vegas, with an emphasis on trying to integrate LED light technology into a conventional light bulb. I believed the largest concentration of customers burning light bulbs 24 hours a day were all located in Las Vegas.

So I replied to Mark, "You bet, I'll come. What does the schedule look like?"

He responded, "If you can come in early Thursday morning, I'll pick you up at the airport and fill you in. We can meet my friends for lunch, and get acquainted before the meeting. Afterwards, we'll head over to the MGM, play around for a while, and then go to dinner. I want you to stay at my house as my guest."

I answered, "Done deal! Sounds like fun! See you Thursday."

Good Thing I keep the Good Lord on speed dial. I thought, *Amazing, the lead I needed.*

After a late Friday night of casino hopping, we agreed to head over to our favorite breakfast spot on Tropicana Boulevard in the morning. Once our orders of eggs benedict arrived at the table, I opened the conversation with a new topic, the papal visit. He hadn't heard anything about it, so I explained the whole deal to him, including my chance meeting with Paula Westerfield.

I then said, "So Mark, I think maybe I could produce a concert starting out with Paula's band and possibly get a few other bands together and maybe find a large club or possibly an empty warehouse to set up some kind of musical entertainment for the kids.

"Even if I don't follow through with the concert, I'd still like to try and help Paula. She's really a nice gal. If I can figure out some way to help her, I'd like to do that. You have a lot of pictures of people in the entertainment business on your walls at home. Do you have any suggestions or could you recommend someone I might talk to about all this?"

After clearing his throat Mark got a big grin on his face and said, "I sure do buddy, I've got a great friend, Tommy Tomato."

As his grin got even larger, he started to chuckle and continued, "Tomato is not really his name, I just call him that for fun.

"His last name is Amato and yes, the last letter in his name is a vowel. Although he's not in the mob, he probably knows everybody that is, and who is also in the entertainment industry. He's been a 'Personal Agent' for guys like Frank Sinatra, Bobby Darin, I think Frankie Avalon and a bunch of other names you would certainly recognize. It's all he's done all his life. We'll call him when we get back home, and see if I can put you in touch with him before I take you to the airport."

Very surprised, I fumbled my thanks and gratitude as we finished breakfast. When we got back, Mark made the call and introduced me to Tommy. We hit it off. After an in-depth discussion about Paula, he agreed to come to Denver, hear her perform, and see if he might have an interest in taking her on as a client. I agreed to make the arrangements with Paula and get back to him later next week. I thanked Mark all the way to the airport. And to this day I still think the world of Mark and hope we will always be friends.

 # *The Cornerstone*

...Tommy ...just build the project around him.
Simple!

As I pulled up in front of the hotel where Tommy had checked in, I saw a man standing by the curb, impeccably dressed in a suit, tie, and topcoat, looking my way. His salt-and-pepper hair and receding hairline made him appear to be in his early 60s. It was evident from his erect and stout stature he was still in good shape despite his age. There was no doubt he personified the image of a high-level entertainment executive from Chicago, even though he lived in Reno.

As the car door closed, he extended his hand and with a big smile said, "Hi JD, I'm Tommy. Good to meet you!"

As I shook his hand, a spark ignited firing up what would become a long, warm and friendly business relationship. "Tommy, here's the plan," I said, "As you requested, I arranged a meeting with Paula at the Doubletree, where she's playing tonight. We'll arrive in about 20 minutes, and it will only be the three of us, so you can get acquainted with her. After the meeting, I'll bring you back here. Then at 6:30, my wife and I'll pick you up and head to dinner and her show. OK?" Nodding in the affirmative, we pulled up and walked inside.

After introductions and some pleasantries, we were seated in a booth near the dance floor. Tommy got right down to business. For the next hour and a half he quizzed Paula on everything from her youth growing up, her education, and most importantly, an in-depth examination of her musical background and history. Then, out of the clear blue, Tommy asked Paula if she would sing something a cappella. Her face lit up and with a big beaming smile, she nodded, and slid out of the booth and walked to the center of the dance floor.

As she turned back in our direction she asked, "What would you boys like to hear?"

I quickly jumped in and said, "Sing - Me and Bobby McGee." I had heard her sing this song before, and she could really nail it.

Her voice filled the entire restaurant with incredible sounds as she sang the song in its entirety. It was truly awesome. As we applauded, Tommy and I slid out of the booth to walk over and congratulate her. Tommy's final words to Paula were, "You have a magnificent voice and no matter what happens, it will take you to places you can't even imagine. I'll give this some thought and see what I can come up with, and work with JD, and we'll get back to you. I'm looking forward to your show tonight. Break a leg!"

As we headed back to Tommy's hotel, I opened a discussion of the papal visit in earnest. We grabbed a cup of coffee and sat down at a table in the hotel lobby. It was Tommy's turn to talk and leaning back in his chair, thoughtfully, he said, "I think you're on the right track. I think entertainment is the only business gig with the potential to generate some real money during the papal visit. But, I don't think putting together half a dozen bands for a 10 day gig will do the job. If you're going to pursue this I think you need to put on a real, full blown concert. Put the right package together for a two or three night concert. You'll need a minimum of 15,000 to 20,000 people to attend each night, for it to make financial sense. The question is JD, do you really want to produce and promote a concert? It's a big job, and it's not an easy undertaking!"

"Tommy, I really can't answer you at the moment. I don't have a clue as to what would be involved. I don't have any experience related to what you're talking about. Let me ask you, exactly what is needed to put on, produce, a concert?"

Leaning forward, and resting his arms on the table as his hands encircled his coffee cup, he looked me straight on and said, "There are three components of a concert you have to have: 1-the venue, 2-the talent, and - 3rd-a headliner. Then you have to add in a substantial promotional effort to get your target audience to come to the concert. If you correctly assembled the talent with the right headliner, at the right venue, at the right time, and promoted the event sufficiently, you can have a successful and profitable concert."

"That's it, that's all there is to it?"

"Yah JD, that's just about it. However, it's not that simple. Assembling the talent and finding the headliner are the two toughest tasks you face. Then you get into all the issues involved in securing the venue, where you have to consider everything from safety, security, and even the length of lines at the restrooms. It's a big job, but the rewards can be pretty substantial."

"Tommy, if I can put together a plan, a full business plan, to put on a concert for the pope, would you be interested in partnering with me on the project and work with me to make it happen?"

Very intently, he responded, "Yes, JD, I think it is a great idea, a Papal Concert. It's certainly worth taking a look at for sure."

Thoughtfully, I said, "Would you be opposed to including other partners, if they were key players and can make a significant contribution to the project?"

"No I wouldn't be opposed to partners. I think that's a good idea because this will probably turn into a big project in the end, and it will take a lot of talent, and effort, to pull it off."

"OK, I know what I need to do. I'll need as much input from you as possible, as we proceed to put this together. Let's see what develops and make this happen. I'll pick you up at 6:30 for dinner and the show."

My brain raced at the speed of light all the way home, as I began to build a picture in my mind of a Papal Concert and the necessary steps to be taken to pull it off. My excitement level was rising clear off the scale, as I thought about my first hurdle - explaining and selling this idea to my Lover Snugger. Oh boy, this was gonna' be a job. But, the realization of the potential rewards, and what I could do for the family, filled my heart with warmth, and began to instill the confidence necessary to believe I could actually succeed with this project.

The next morning, as I drove Tommy to the airport, I handed him a one-page abstract of the project, which I had thrown together. As he was about to get out of the car, we again shook hands, and agreed to stay in touch and get after this project. All the way home my scrambled brain was trying to make sense of all the data and information stuffed inside during the last few days. Seems the more I thought about it, the more befuddled I became. It then dawned on me to look at this project in the same fashion as if I was constructing a building. Call out all the dignitaries, place the cornerstone, and announce the construction of the new building. I thought, *my cornerstone is Tommy, and now all I have to do is build the project around him. Simple!*

CHAPTER 4

What's Next?

..."Holy smokes! You ain't messing around are you."...

Hmmm, I thought, I've got a number of pieces to the puzzle so maybe it's time to try and put them together and see what it looks like. It's time to develop the business plan; call it PCP for the moment - a papal concert plan. Whoops! That ain't gonna work. Well, we'll name it later. It's gotta be a corporation. We'll need a Board of Directors, some officers, and hopefully, some investors. Must be time to get on the phone and put a team together to make this project a success, so who do I call first.

Two weeks later, after nonstop phone calls and personal meetings, I've assembled 11 people who have agreed to sit on the board and become officers of the new business. I've found an attorney, a CPA, a retired USAF General, some politicians and marketing professionals. It must be time for the next step. My five page business plan has gotten me this far, but it needs a lot of work, and the business needs a home. It's time to find an office and time to bring in the Fox.

Finally, the ringing ends with the word, "Hello." Eagerly I respond, "Hey there Fox, it's time to rock 'n roll! I've got the corporation put together and assembled a really good team of people to work on the pope project with us. So Bill, are you about ready to go back to work?"

"Yah, I've been waiting patiently, thinking maybe you decided to forget about the pope's visit. So tell me what's going on."

"Let's get together tomorrow. I'll buy breakfast, and bring you up-to-date. Then if you've got a little time, we'll go check out a couple of possible offices to rent. Same time, same place as last time?"

"You got it, I'll be there, see you then. Bye!" He replied.

At breakfast the next morning I started to update him on the events that had transpired since our last meeting. He interrupted me, saying, "So what's the name of this thing, the corporation or the event or whatever?"

Thinking for moment, I decided to let the plan speak for itself. So I pulled out what I'd printed so far and said, "Now Bill, don't grab this and jump to the last page, let me take you through it from the beginning." I then set the plan down on the table next to his plate.

ENTERTAINMENT INTERNATIONAL

PRESENTS

A TRIBUTE TO

POPE JOHN PAUL II

THE CHILDREN OF THE WORLD

CONCERT

"So what do you think? Like it?" I asked.

"WOW! I love it! Entertainment International, I assume that's the corporate name and the concert name, that's really cool! Now you've done it JD. You've started my blood pumping again. This looks really exciting. So, can I turn the page now?"

Nodding affirmatively, he turned to the next page.

"Holy smokes! You ain't messing around are you?" Bill exclaimed as he turned another page.

After completing his perusal of the plan Bill uttered, "Geez, JD, how in the world are you gonna get everybody to go along with this deal? I mean, you're gonna have to get the governor, the mayor and only God knows who else to climb on board. How are you going to get all this accomplished?"

Laying the tip money on the table, I answered, "We can talk in the car, let's go!"

Bill had located two office sites for rent in the Denver Tech Center, so off we went to check them out first. We would then go check out my two possible locations. We began walking through the vast expanse of 10,000 square feet on the 14th floor of a gorgeous 30 story office building. Completely barren, and void of any finish work, we listened intently to the leasing agent trying to sell us on the idea that the cost to finish building out the space could be readily justifiable when amortized and added to a five or 10 year lease of only $15,000 per month. Nodding in concert with him, as we stood in the far southwest corner of the space, I noted a beautiful view of the Rocky Mountains including Pikes Peak reaching for the sky to the south. Not wanting to disclose that I was a licensed real estate broker, and fully understanding how costly this space would be, even if I could talk him into letting us have only 2000 square feet, we concluded the tour, thanked him for his time, and departed.

As we set out for Bill's second location. Bill asked, "Well, what do you think of that space?"

It was evident in the tenor of his question that he had no idea how fragile my personal financial situation was currently. Equally important, he hadn't caught on to the concept of the business being a one-shot deal, not a build the business for the next 3 to 5 years undertaking.

Not wanting to go into extensive detail of the plan, only to be interrupted upon our arrival at our next stop, I answered, "Not much Bill. I would estimate to build out that space, put in walls and create the necessary offices and rooms, it would end up being 20 or maybe $30,000. And no matter how cheap the square footage rental rate would be, the landlord's going to add the amortization of the build-out costs to the rent. The shorter the rental term, the higher the rental rate would be. I want to find a place where the landlord will agree to a 14 to 18 month lease, cheap enough so I can afford it, and plan on moving out of by the end of August next year, after the pope leaves.

"I don't want to go bankrupt personally guaranteeing a multiyear lease for a $20,000 a month office. I want everyone involved to make a lot of money helping make this project happen, by spending as little as possible on overhead. You catch'en up with my thinkin'?"

After a moment, in reply, he said, "Yah, I think so. But I think what I'm hearing is that this project isn't funded yet, or ain't got much funding yet. Am I right?

Fortunately, we had been friends for over 20 years, so I didn't have to sugarcoat my answer, and responded quite frankly, "Well, you old water Buffalo, you sure like to get right to the point, don't you. So far, I've been unsuccessful in my attempts to get anyone to write a check to help capitalize the project, but it's still early. If necessary, once we get going, I'll fund it myself by dumping my retirement funds into the project, so long as I can keep the home front afloat in the deal. Right now Bill, honestly, I have no idea how to get this all done, but with your help and everybody else's help, I truly believe we can pull this off." The conversation being forced to a conclusion by our arrival at the second office property, we exited the car and went inside, only to find out that the space advertised had been rented the night before.

Arriving at my first location, it turned out to be too small. 1500 square feet was all that was immediately available. So off we went, headed for our last stop of the day, hopefully, something more amenable to the needs of the project.

As we pulled into the parking lot, I noticed there weren't very many cars, a good sign. Over in the back corner of the parking lot, under the trees, was an old beat up school bus, parked next to an equally old pickup truck. In the first row parking there were only six cars, indicating there might be quite a bit of empty space in this building and a hungry landlord willing to make a deal.

The receptionist escorted us into the back corner office on the second floor to meet the landlord, Mr. David Chung. David explained that he had purchased the property a couple of months ago and only had three tenants at the time. He took pride in telling us that he now had two additional small tenants moving in next month on the second floor, which he had broken up into very small offices. He explained that his largest offices were on the first floor, so we went downstairs to take the tour.

As we walked into the office space I instantly knew this had to be our new home. The entry was just inside the front door and extended all the way to the end of the building, providing about 4500 square feet of office space, including three separate offices and a large work area broken into built-in cubicles. It was perfect. Now the question was could I put a deal together with David and make this work.

Back in David's office, I gave him a copy of the business plan and was taken by surprise at his interest, and the excitement in his voice as we delved into the details of the papal concert. My excitement began to grow as the conversation continued. Skillfully switching roles from tenant negotiator to project pitchman, I started emphasizing the benefit potential of project participation for those involved. Gingerly, I set the stage and transformed David from potential landlord into partner/investor.

I live for this kind of deal making situation. I love the rush and the reward. Two hours later, we were modifying his lease agreement to allow us to take the entire space on a month-to-month rental basis of only $400 per month, plus a carried working interest percentage of any profits from the concert. It was beyond belief. David was now a partner in the project. I could barely contain myself as we worked out the details. I was truly excited to have made this deal and have David on board with us. Wow!

As we drove back to Bill's car with the keys to our new office in hand, we worked out the details to have Bill move all our old office furniture and equipment out of storage and into the office. This would provide a dozen desks and chairs, as well as the reception area furnishings, and most importantly, a complete phone system for every desk. Bill would get a hold of the phone company and set up new phone lines for the desks and fax machines. We were in business. We were underway. During the next week our business plan expanded to 30 pages.

We ended up filling every desk. Initially, we had three people working on just logistics planning, two on marketing and public relations, and four dedicated to finding the talent. Needless to say, three weeks later, it was time to meet the first payroll and I remained unable to raise any cash from outside investors. Consequently, I had to liquidate my retirement plan to fund the enterprise. By the end of the month, the office was looking great. We had checked out some artwork from the library to decorate the walls. Our crew was now organized and becoming productive. Tommy was working from Reno, with what I'll call our talent scouts, contacting agents for all kinds of entertainers. The fax machines had started going off incessantly with communications back and forth between the talent agents and ourselves. It seemed this was the agents' preferred way to communicate. I was busy exploring all kinds of governmental organizations trying to find out the correct persons to talk to about the papal visit.

I grabbed a bottle of water from the fridge on my way to my office and saw Bill coming back in the door, saying, "JD, I almost forgot, some guy, Ron - Thomas or Thompson with the UPI newswire service called for you this afternoon."

I interjected, "Really, what did he want? Don't tell me they're going to start publishing our press releases."

"No, he wouldn't tell me anything. He said he wanted to talk to you personally. He wouldn't leave a number."

"Thanks, Bill. He'll call back if it's important. You go ahead and head on home, good night.

"Morning Becky," I said to our receptionist, and fast becoming my secretary and assistant, "how you doin'?"

As I walked into the office, she replied, "Fine! JD, I've got a guy from the UPI newswire service holding on line three. He wants to talk only to you, and he won't tell me what it's about. Do you want to take the call?"

"Yah, sure, what the hell, go ahead and put him through.
"This is JD, how can I help you?"

"Hello, JD, my name is Ron Thompson. I'm a reporter for the UPI newswire services and I would like to talk to you about a story I'm working on. Do you have a few minutes to visit with me?"

"Yah, okay, maybe, what's your story about, and how am I involved?"

"A few months back I got a tip on some serious problems going on at the Denver FDIC office, and during my investigation recently, your name came up. I wanted to see if you would be willing to talk to me about your activities at the agency."

"Ron, I signed a 10 year confidentiality agreement when I took the job, so I'm not certain how much help I can be, but let me ask if I may, how did you get my name, and who did you get your tip from?"

"Sorry, JD, I can't divulge my sources, but the good thing about that is, if what you tell me is confidential, then I won't divulge your identity either. So let's start there and I'll agree to keep your identity as a source confidential until you're willing or authorize me to use your name and what you tell me in the story, if

I decide to publish it. I really need some information from you, and your help to determine whether or not I really have a story here, or I'm just wasting my time. I would appreciate it if you could help me out. Can we talk for a few minutes?"

Seems harmless, but who is this guy really? Sounds awfully young, let's test the waters and see who this guy really is, I thought.

"Okay, I'll talk to you on a purely confidential basis, if you agree not to write one word of what I tell you until I give you a written okay to do so. Fair enough?"

"Agreed!"

"Ok, put it in writing on your letterhead and fax it to me, here's the number. In the meantime, let's see if this conversation's worth pursuing, what'd ya got?"

"Let me start by telling you what I know. Just interrupt me if what I'm saying is incorrect or if you want to add something."

Thinking, *this kid's either very naïve or just dumber than a rock if he thinks I can completely trust his verbal assurances. I'll have to be extra careful and watch what I say.*

After disclosing numerous facts and details regarding his findings so far, Ron then asked, "While you were employed as a Supervisory Liquidation Specialist, somewhere along the line you began working for the Inspectors General's Office undercover, with the codename Archibald. Is that correct, and how did that come about?"

Now, my internal early warning radar system was sounding alarm bells. *This guy has way too much information and too many details. I got to figure out a way to check this guy out,* I thought.

"Ron, can I put you on hold for a moment? Someone just stepped into my office."

"Yah, that's fine."

"Okay - I'll get right back to you. Hey Ron, give me your number, in case we get disconnected, I'll call you right back as soon as I'm done... Got it! Hold on."

I hollered into the intercom, "Becky, I need you!
"Becky, call this number. It should be busy, if so, change the last digit to another number and try again. I need to find out the name of the company that answers - let me know ASAP, thanks.

"Ron, you there? Good! Well, let me say, it sounds like you have some pretty good sources. The answer to your question is yes. And the genesis took place during my final job interview with the Specialist in Charge of the Denver office."

Becky slipped a note on my desk that read, "UPI newswire services." At least he's for real, but I gotta keep my guard up.

"At the end of my interview he asked if I had any questions and I responded, 'What exactly would be my job, and exactly what would you need me to do for you?' And permanently etched in my mind, are both the moment and his response. As he slid his chair back from the table, he stood up and walked over to the window, looking out as if either making a decision, or only formulating a response. He then turned, looked at me and said, 'JD, you'll be my assistant, the Assistant Specialist in Charge of the Denver office.
'You'll answer to me and together we will expand this office to meet the demands that will be made upon the agency in this region. Right now we have 120 employees scheduled to close approximately 10 banks and savings and loans next month. We're forecasting in 90 days the number will increase to 30 or 40 per month. I'm planning on increasing our staff to 300 or more to meet the anticipated workload.

'We're at least five to seven years behind the technology curve. One of your functions will be to help us improve the automation of our operations, from institutional closings to final liquidation of the assets, which at this time is done mostly by hand.

Washington has decided to decentralize the asset management and liquidation process by delegating that authority to each office.

'Consequently, we'll be receiving new delegations of authority for which you will formulate a plan on how to implement this new authority, and once I've approved it you'll help me implement it. Lastly, the agency is very concerned about fraud and waste during this period of extreme growth. Your most important duty and responsibility will be to help ferret out any fraud, and eliminate any waste of taxpayer dollars. The agency needs our help and it needs leadership with action. Literally you will have to saddle up your white horse, and ride in with guns blazing, and make shit happen. So if you can do all that - you've got the job, if you want it.'

"Ron, those were his exact words, and I accepted the job.

"You and I probably wouldn't even be talking now if it weren't for the lapse of time between that interview, and the first day I reported for work. It took about four weeks for me to fire-sale my computer business and turn it over to the new owners. Then it took nearly two months to go through the agency's HR process and finally receive my notice to report for work.

"Sometime during that three-month period, the guy who hired me was promoted and transferred to a new agency called the Resolution Trust Corporation, RTC. At the same time they appointed this young gal, Caroline, to be the acting supervisor in charge before my arrival, and by default, she became my boss. It was apparent during my initial meeting with Caroline that I was a threat to her keeping that position, and her hopes of making it permanent. It was evident she had no knowledge of the discussions during my interview, and really had no clue as to what to do with me, and I had no idea whatsoever as to how to proceed. So I just turned the interviewer's words into my mission statement, grabbed a shovel, and started to work.

"Ron, can you hold on a minute, someone just came into my office. Becky, what is it?"

"The Governor's office is on line 4. Do you want to take the call? I didn't want the intercom to go off."

"Yes, tell them I'll be right with them, thanks."

"Ron, gotta take this call. I'll call you back in a couple of days, when I have more time."

"Well, OK, please get back to me as soon as you can, thanks."

"Talk to you soon – bye."

The Governor's office provided me with a host of names and phone numbers of state agencies and contact info to pursue, which consumed the remainder of the day, as I made call after call in pursuit of interest and help in finding a venue to hold the concert.

I had fast become accustomed to going out on the front steps of the building around 5 PM every evening after we shut down to just sit with a cold drink, in the shade of the building, and contemplate the day's events, while enjoying the view of the sun setting behind the mountains to the south and west. It was just a nice opportunity to have some quiet time as I waited for rush-hour traffic to die down before heading home. It also gave me an opportunity to meet a couple of the other tenants as they left. Except for this one guy, who always seemed to be coming in rather than leaving at days end. He would pull up in his old pickup truck, parking next to the old school bus, and sometimes go inside the school bus, and then lock everything up as he headed into the building. A tall lanky gentleman about 45, my age I guessed, always dressed in jeans, western shirt, cowboy boots and hat. It seemed like the bigger and the shinier the belt-buckle, the nicer and fancier the cowboy hat became, as he came and went. We would nod and/or exchange greetings from time to time as he passed by.

One evening I was running late. Night had settled in and I decided to stay at the office to finish up. It was time to take a break, so I headed over to the convenience store behind the building to get a cold soda and munchies. There was a nice moon out and the streetlights made the short walk pleasant. Returning, walking on the shoulder of the road, after passing a small grove of trees that separated the building from the store, movement up on the second floor balcony on the back side of the building caught my eye. I hadn't noticed before, but apparently each office on the second floor of the building had a small patio. There on the corner patio closest to the street stood a man, buck naked, holding a pail over his head, pouring water over himself as he stood in a larger steel pail about two foot deep. Mesmerized by the sight, I had to stop for a moment just to ensure my eyes weren't playing tricks on me. Lo and behold, he apparently had a bar of soap in his hand and was washing himself down, then picking up one of two smaller pails to pour water over himself to rinse off. Just amazing, I thought. We must have some pretty crazy tenants in this building.

I decided to sit out on the steps and enjoy the cool evening as I ate my sandwich and downed the soda. It was about 9pm, the stars were out and the air was still, when I heard the building door open behind me. I turned to see the cowboy coming out with a gallon jug of wine and a large plastic cup.

"Mind if I join you?" He said, smiling.
"Sure, pull up a seat, make yourself at home." I replied, wondering if this was the nutcase taking a shower in a bucket on the building patio. He unscrewed the cap on his jug of wine. Holding the plastic cup between his knees, and the jug with both hands, he began to fill his cup. Once the cap was screwed back on the jug, he extended his hand to me and said, "Hi there, my name's TP, but my friends call me Doug."

Setting my drink down, I reached out and shook his hand. "Hi, my name's JD, and my friends call me Joe. How did you get a handle like Doug from a name like TP?"
He replied, "Picked it out when I joined the service, didn't like my middle name, so Douglas I became. Good to meet you.
"You work in the office with the lights on? The sign on the door says Entertainment International, what'd you guys do?"

Thinking for a moment, as I took a drink from my soda, which question should I answer first, and more importantly, I just gotta find out if this is the shower guy. I replied, "Yah, I work for Entertainment International. We're here to set up and promote a concert for the papal visit."

Interrupting me before I could continue, he interjected, "Really! That's why I'm here. I came up to Denver from my ranch down in Castillo County to put a deal together to sell T-shirts to the tourists when they come."

Caught off guard by his comment, I just had to know if this guy was for real, so I said, "Do you mind if I ask you a question? When I was walking back from the store a little while ago, I noticed someone up on the second floor balcony taking a shower in a bucket. Was that you?"

Surprised, he started to chuckle and then said, "Yah, that was me. I didn't know anyone could see me. I learned how to do that in Vietnam. I haven't found an apartment yet, so I've been sleeping in the office or in my bus until I can find something affordable." Smiling broadly, he added, "So was it a good show?"

Laughingly, I replied, "Yah, it was a great show! Actually you couldn't see much. So you spent some time in country," I inquired. This was like a coded question, to determine whether or not he had just been in the service during the war, or was actually on the ground in 'Nam.

He responded instantly, recognizing from the question that I had probably been there as well, "I was a Lieutenant in the Marines stationed in I Corp, and you?"

I answered, "Yes, I was in the Navy, and in country from February '66 until November '68. I was an air traffic controller for the bombing missions and search and rescue operations in North Vietnam on my first two tours. Then I was assigned to river patrol boats, Swift boats, for my last three tours, based out of DaNang, KheSon, and ChuLai. How about you?"

He responded, "I can't believe it! I rode with the Swifty's a bunch of times. Sometimes they would take us up river and drop us off, and other times, come in and pick us up after we completed our patrol. I wonder if we ever met. One time I remember so well, during the battle of Hue, we were pinned down on the river's edge when two Swift boats came around the bend and opened fire. They literally saved our asses. We were running out of ammo and about to be overrun when the Swifty's arrived. A few minutes of heavy fire from the boats was all it took for the gooks to hightail it into the jungle. Wouldn't that be something, if I had ridden on your boat?"

Memories started to flash through my mind. Thinking about all the different combatants we had hauled on our boat. I just could not place this guy. Until he added, "Fourteen of my men climbed aboard one of the boats, three were wounded, one had a stomach wound and we took him down inside the cabin of the boat and laid him down on the bunk. The other two wounded, we sat down leaning up against the ammo locker on the back of the boat. There was so little room for all of us I ended up sitting on the bow resting against the pilot house. Man I can still remember the ride, racing for the coast. Anyway, that was a long time ago."

Taken aback by what he had just said, I replied, "I remember the wounded guy on the bunk. When we pulled up alongside the Coast Guard cutter to transport him to the hospital ship out in the gulf I helped lift the stretcher the cutter had given us, up through the rear hatch onto the deck, so they could hoist him up the side of the cutter. I don't remember meeting you specifically because there were just so many of you guys. I was the guy behind the twin 50s, in the gun tub on top of the pilot house. Man, I can hardly believe this - I finally get to meet a passenger who took a ride on my boat, pretty incredible!"

He responded, saying, "Man, it's a small world! I was just a second 'louie' at the time, but I remember the battle of Hue very well. The VC really kicked our butts in that operation.

"How long were you there?" I queried.
"Two tours, a year, seemed like forever at the time. Looking back on it, it was a pretty incredible time in my life. It seemed like I was cramming the reality of the entire spectrum of

life itself, from being alive one minute to possibly dead the next, into every single day. You know what I mean?"

I did, and replied, "Yah, I know exactly what you mean."

We both knew it was a different kind of war. For the first time in the history of man and warfare there were no battle-lines. No line drawn on some commander's map that we would know as the ridge, the tree line, or the river where everybody on one side of the line was the enemy and everybody on our side of the line were the good guys. And if you were far enough away from that line you were safe and sound.

Nam was different. In the North we had the air war. We fly over and bomb their industrial complexes while they try to shoot our planes down. Then in the South, we had the ground war, which I never understood. Officially we weren't allowed to pursue the enemy if they fled across the DMZ and went back into North Vietnam. We couldn't shoot down their helicopters resupplying their troops on the North side of the DMZ; it just wasn't permitted. But we could conduct black ops -- take special boats painted all-black flying a Jolly Roger flag, dressed in civilian clothes with no ID or dog-tags, and run up the rivers in North Vietnam blowing up or killing anything we came across.

It seemed like the command plan in the South was simply pick a spot, any spot, set up a camp or build a base, and wait for the enemy to come, which they did. Oh and by the way, hire the enemy, disguised as civilians, and put them on your payroll, to cook, clean, and maintain the camp or base. In this manner, you don't have to worry about battle-lines, you're simply surrounded by the enemy 24/7. And also, by the way, the enemy will kill you every time they get a chance, so stay on your toes, 24/7. Take your weapons everywhere. In the can, into the shower, into the mess hall, even to bed because you never know when the maid, the cook, or the laundry lady will pull out a gun or grenade and try to kill you. For me, it was simply an insane place to live for three years, 24 on 24 off, and whoopee, 5 days R&R every six months.

TP continued, "It was insane! What drove me crazy were the special orders during the 'bombing halts.' You remember, every time they sent that politician to Paris to negotiate a peace treaty, the US would declare a bombing halt and we would get special orders that said, while we were out on patrol, we could not attack or engage the enemy; we could only return fire, if fired upon.

"The first time that happened to me, I thought, why are we even going out on patrol? Aren't we just sitting ducks in a shooting gallery? Then, off we go, out there in a field of rice paddies, or one-time, I'll never forget. Coming around the curve on a dirt road, we ran right into a platoon of North Vietnamese Army and VietCong soldiers marching in the opposite direction. Surprise! It's the enemy! Fully armed, carrying all kinds of supplies down the road in the opposite direction. I can't even explain the crazy thoughts that raced through my mind. The leader, with his machine gun slung over his shoulder, raised his right hand and waved and smiled, without missing a step as he closed the gap between us. Caught completely off-guard and dumbfounded, I unconsciously released my grip on my piece and waved - and even smiled back. Then coming to my senses, I turned to the guy behind me and said, 'Take the lead and keep going.' I stepped to the side and did an about-face, nodding to my guys as they passed by, keeping a close eye on the fricken enemy as they continued on around the bend. They never even looked back! They just kept on going! It was like they knew what our orders were and knew they were perfectly safe. Nam was so unbelievable. It was absolute craziness.

"I ended up doing 20 and retired as a major, then went to work for the CIA. Later, working in black ops, I just barely got out of that deal with my hide. However, that's another story for later. Now I own some land in the mountains, just trying to figure out how to stay financially alive. Then I heard about the pope coming to Denver and figured I better get my ass up here and figure out how to make some money on this deal."

We spent the next couple of hours exchanging stories about NAM, getting acquainted and becoming fast friends. And to this day, TP remains a good and close friend.

. . .

CHAPTER 5

The Ace of Clubs is Lost
and
The Queen of Hearts Found

... I had imagined him as a partner, my Ace of Clubs,
to match up with my Ace of Spades, ...
With a pair of Aces like that...

My desk was buried under a mountain of faxes from agents representing entertainers of all makes and models, most of whom I had never heard of, but that didn't mean much either. Included were many immediately recognizable. Musicians and groups I had grown up listening to, bringing familiar tunes to my mind, making me feel warm and fuzzy. It also made me realize how little I knew about what I was involved in. Doubt was trying to sneak in the back door of my mind as I reflected upon the possibility of failure due to my lack of experience in the concert production business. It truly was lonely at the top.

In an effort to find someone experienced in such matters to join me and help out, I had high hopes of talking to Barry Fey. Fey was the world-renowned concert producer and promoter who happened to live in Denver. I called him several times last week without success and finally left a message asking him to call. All weekend I had imagined him as a partner, my Ace of Clubs, to match up with my Ace of Spades, Tommy. With a pair of Aces like that, I knew I could win the game, and we would be successful.

Suddenly I noticed Becky, standing silently in front of me. Looking up to meet her gaze, I said, "Good grief, Becky, how do you move so quietly? I'm going to start calling you Becky the ninja warrior. What can I do for you?"

"Well, JD, there is a lady out front who wants to talk to you."

"Did she give her name or say what she wants?"

"No - she just said she'd like to talk with you."

At that moment we were interrupted by the intercom, "Mr. D, a Mr. Barry Fey is returning your call on line 5."

This was the call I had been waiting for. I picked up the phone and said, "Tell him I'll be right with him." Nodding to Becky, I said, "Tell her we're fully staffed and I just don't have time right now to meet with her." Nodding affirmatively Becky turned and left.

I answered, "Barry, thank you for returning my call. I know very little about putting on a concert, but I have a concept for a concert in Denver that I think is worthy of your consideration during the Pope's upcoming visit. I wanted to see if I could interest you in participating with us in producing this event together."

For the next ten minutes we discussed the concept, our efforts so far, and our need for his expertise to help ensure the success of the concert. At the same time, Becky had returned to my doorway, pointing to a business card in her hand, trying to signal me with a message that I couldn't make out. I tried to wave her off, while continuing my conversation.

"Barry, are you certain I can't interest you in this project?" hoping to keep the conversation alive.

He responded graciously, "JD, I think you have a great concept. You've got some good people involved. I think you have a good shot at success. However, my upcoming schedule precludes me from being able to participate in your project. I wish you the best, and thank you for your call and your invitation."

And with that the ace of clubs I had hoped to acquire for the deck vaporized. As I hung up the phone Becky stepped through the doorway and said, "JD, I think you need to meet with this lady. Her name is Haley Henderson, here's her card. I'll bring her back."

I stood as a large black woman about 5'3" walked through the doorway, smiling. She extended her hand, and as I shook it said, "Thank you for seeing me. My name is Haley and I was a community liaison director for Mayor Webb's campaign. I heard about your concert and I wanted to talk to you about how I could help you. I'm just assuming that since the Pope's visit and activities will be in Denver, so will your concert. If that's correct, I could be your liaison with the mayor's office."

Unbelievable, I thought, I could really use this lady on our team, the new queen of my heart. I responded, "Haley, it's nice to meet you and I'm glad you stopped by. Your assumptions are pretty much dead on. Let's pursue this and see where it goes." Simultaneously, thinking to myself, as one-door closes, another opens.

For the next 45 minutes, we discussed her history and relationship with the mayor and his staff. She assured me that she would be able to set up a meeting with the mayor himself. She was unable to work full-time and wanted a consulting gig. We cut a deal, a $1000 retainer and a percentage of the concert profits. She left, promising to get me a meeting with the mayor the following week.

Later that afternoon, I finally got a return call from the governor's office instructing me to contact the State's Economic Development Commission Director. My preliminary discussion with him was sufficient to warrant a meeting at 10 AM tomorrow.

Then Bill walked in and said, "JD, Tommy's doing an incredible job with the entertainers' agents. The word's getting out and we're just buried in faxes. I finally reached the point where we've had to designate one fax machine for just outbound responses and we can't keep up. Me and a couple of the guys are going to stay late tonight and try to catch up. You need to call Tommy when you have a minute - he wants to talk to you."

I replied, "Geez Bill, that sounds great. Sounds like we're really moving along."

Rolling his eyes, he responded, "Yah, easy for you to say. You don't have to figure out what to say to all these people. You have to start getting us some answers fast, or were gonna lose our credibility. I just can't keep answering every question with 'I don't know'. Every one of these faxes is filled with questions that I have no answers for. The two biggest questions are where's the venue and how much performance time do they get. We have got to get after our logistics or we're gonna be toast."

Immediately, I answered, "I get it Bill. You have to continue to hold everyone at bay a little longer. I can't answer any of the questions until I can find the venue. Possibly Monday or Tuesday, I'll meet with the mayor and hopefully, have some answers." He rose to leave, as I continued, "Please try to hold everything together for a little longer."

"Tommy my friend, Bill tells me you're doing an incredible job." I bellowed into the phone.

"Well, thanks for that, but I've got other news. I spoke to Steve and Melanie Dawson last night. You recognize the name?"

"No, I don't."

"Did you ever watch Frontier Sheriff when you were a kid?"

"Oh Yah! Every Saturday, Sheriff Mark Robertson was one of my favorite heroes, along with the Lone Ranger, of course," smiling to myself, good memories.

"Well, Steve was Sheriff Robertson. He and his wife would like to meet with us in Los Angeles. They're very interested in possibly funding the concert. After he left the studios he got involved in real estate and did very well, building small shopping centers all over California. What'da ya think, shall we go meet with them?"

"Wow! I love your sense of humor Tommy - of course I want to meet them! When?"

"How's your schedule look?"

"My schedule doesn't matter.   I'll work around their schedule. You set it up and we'll both fly out to meet with them. Sound good?"

"I'll take care of it, Joe."

"Thanks Tommy, let me know - talk to you later."

Unbeknownst to me, across town in Littleton, a suburb south of Denver, TP was just asked to take a seat in the reception area of a company called Hong Kong Trading Limited. After several minutes, a gentleman, Kwon Xang, approached and introduced himself.

TP responded, "Nice to meet you, Kwon, just call me Doug."

Kwon then escorted TP down the hallway to a conference room where he was introduced to the other three gentlemen at the table.

TP opened his portfolio case, setting aside the cardboard protectors of the original artwork he removed, and gently set each one of the four layouts in the center of the table. Each full-color illustration was his own creative design celebrating the Pope's visit to Denver and World Youth Day Eight.

After an extensive discussion regarding the design and processing that would be required to produce each of these drawings on an individual T-shirt, it was time to get down to the meat and potatoes of the deal.

TP said, "Kwon, I get it. I have to buy a 20 foot container of T-shirts and pay the freight to get them here. Now the question is how much is it gonna cost me?"

After a somewhat short conversation in Chinese between the four gentlemen, Kwon responded, "Doug, our best price will be $80,000 for the T-shirts and you'll have to pay us separately, and in addition, for the freight. This is our lowest possible price. We cannot go any lower. If you like the price, you will have to pay us $25,000 up front, as I mentioned in our last phone conversation, for us to be able to get started. You will then have to pay another $25,000, once you approve the samples. You then have to pay the balance and freight charges when the container is loaded on the ship. Are these arrangements satisfactory?"

After a pause, TP looked over at Kwon, while removing a white envelope from his portfolio case, and said, "I am pleased that everything is as we agreed earlier, and yes, the arrangements are satisfactory. Did you prepare the purchase agreement and bill of sale?"

"Yes we did," he replied, as one of the other gentlemen slid two documents across the table.

After perusing the documents, TP opened the envelope and handed the contents to Kwon as he said, "Here is my PO and a cashier's check for $25,000. If this meets with your approval, let's sign the purchase agreement and call this a done deal. What'da ya say?"

Smiling, Kwon replied, "That is fine. Let us do that."

 ## _Back at the Ranch_

It was time to call Ron at UPI back. "Ron, JD. I've got a little time to continue our conversation. How about you?"

"Yah, I do. Thanks for calling back. Let me get my notes. Ok, you left off when you first reported for work. What was your assignment, what happened?"

"Well, at first there was no assignment. They concluded I needed to learn how to close down a bank. So I decided I should include observing and looking for excessive waste and ways to reduce costs wherever I could as each day passed. For example, at my first bank closing in Colorado Springs, we arrived with a semi-trailer truck of supplies, carrying 50 portable Compaq computers. We called 'em barely luggables, as they weighed about 20 pounds each, one for each data entry clerk. Their job was to take each paper loan file and extract all the data and enter it into their portable computers. This included all of the data from the loan applications on each borrower, bank officers involved, and then all the loan data itself, including every payment made over the life of the loan. Then each evening, all the computers were hooked up to a special bank of phone modems and the data entered that day would be uploaded throughout the night to the agency's mainframe in Washington. This had to be done, not only for every current loan, but for all the closed loans for the past five years. Depending on the size of the bank, this process could take 4 to 6 weeks.

"I had only been with the agency about three weeks at the time, and I must admit, Caroline told me to just go down and observe. But, as I sat and watched one of the clerks process a single loan file for more than two hours I just couldn't stand it, as we had a couple of thousand current loans, in addition to the old closed loans. I'd been in the computer business way too long and knew this process was just arcane and unnecessary. So after checking with Jackie, the supervisor in charge of the bank closing, and finding out she had no specific assignments for me, I went to work on correcting the data entry system.

"I contacted the IT department in Washington and had them fax me the storage data array criteria, and mainframe data transfer protocols, for a tape to tape transfer of data. I went over to one of the empty Compaq computers and copied the data file the clerk was working on, onto a floppy disk, and then contacted the bank's computer system service provider.

"I immediately left and went over to their offices, where I met with a handful of their programmers. Four hours later I had a reel of tape in my hands with a recording of all of the bank's computer data, including all the data that was being entered by the clerks, and a new floppy disk with the software necessary for Washington to transfer all the data to the agency's mainframe. I stopped at FedEx on my way back to the bank and overnighted it to Washington.

"The next day at the bank was spent just watching, observing, and learning about the process of closing a bank. Then the following morning, Wednesday, I got the call from Washington. They had successfully transferred the data yesterday, and had since completed an audit of the data, and found it to be complete. The correct number of items, the total dollar amounts, and the ancillary data all matched up perfectly with the bank's monthly reports on file. I confirmed there would be no further necessity to continue the data clerk entry systems for this bank, and asked them to fax me a confirmation to terminate our data entry process.

"As I waited for the fax to come in, I was thinking, wow, it worked! I just saved the agency a boatload of dough, tens or hundreds of thousands of dollars on just this one bank closing. I wondered how much money that would be system-wide, and when they give the same technology to RTC they would double the savings amount. Wow, now that's a lot of money. Maybe they'll give me the employee of the month award.

"Once the fax arrived, I took it to Jackie, explaining what was going on, expecting an expression of her joy and happiness. Instead, she began to rant and rave about my interfering with her bank closing.

"A short time later Caroline is on the phone instructing me to leave immediately, return to Denver, and meet with her first thing in the morning. Well, needless to say, I didn't get the employee of the month award. Instead I was berated extensively. She was furious, telling me I did not have the delegations of authority necessary to do such a thing. That I should've written up a report, and put it through the chain of command, to get approval first. And continuing, said she had just gotten off the phone with the head of the agency's employees union, who was mad as hell, because this means we're gonna have to lay off at least half of our data entry clerks, maybe as many as 40 individuals. Who, by the way, have all filed complaints, because their work at bank closings doubles their paychecks, with the overtime, per diem, and travel allowances they receive. Now suddenly that income is lost, and possibly their jobs as well.

"Without so much as a pause in her tirade, Caroline continued, angrily letting me know that everybody in the entire chain of command was pissed at me, as well as every employee in the entire office. Bottom line, she said, I had seriously failed to consider the impact and ramifications of my actions, and completely disregarded the chain of command, so she was going to have to write me up.

* * *

"At that point she finally stopped to catch her breath, so I interjected, write me up – for what exactly?

"She retorted with a sneer, 'Because you didn't have approval to spend all the money to do this, and when I get the bills totaled up, I can tell you - if it's in the thousands of dollars, you probably won't be working here any longer. I'm sure the computer company bill for all this is going to be huge. We're done and you're probably done. You can go now.'

"Then Ron, actually one of the greatest moments in my life took place. As I rose and headed to the door, I turned and smiled and said, 'Well Boss Lady, one thing I know for certain is that you can solve any problem on the face of this planet, if you're just willing to throw enough money at it, which I did, but you won't be getting the bill. -- I charged everything to my agency credit card. The computer company charged me $35 for the reel of tape I sent to Washington, $350 for their programming services, and they didn't even charge me for the floppy disk. Oh, and by the way, I charged $12.50 at FedEx to get it to Washington. That's all I spent on the entire undertaking.' I remember shutting the door extremely firmly, before she could reply, to let her know I was as pissed at her as she was at me, thinking to myself, proof positive, no good deed shall ever go unpunished.

"Understandably, Ron, she just didn't have enough real-world experience to deal with me, or the situation. Instantly, the agency and the RTC began using my data transfer system for all future bank closings and I never heard another word about it. That's how my career with the agency began, and it seems it just went downhill from there."

Ron replied, "Incredible story, I'd really like to use it in my article."

"I don't have any problem with that, but let's first see how this all turns out in the end. We are agreed that we'll take a look at the whole story before I agree to release it, right?"

"Yes, but I want to let you know what parts I want to include as we proceed.

"So, when and how did the investigation with the Inspector General start?"

"Ron, can you hold on a minute, someone just came into my office. Bill, what is it?"

"JD, it's Tommy, he needs you right away."

"Ok, tell him to hold for a minute."

"Ron, sorry to do this again, but I gotta take this other call. I'll get back to you soon."

"Alright, I understand. Be sure to call. Bye."

"Tommy, how we doin'?"

"Great JD, we're on. We meet with Steve and Melanie at 10am next Thursday at the Beverly Hills Hilton."

"Oh that's just terrific Tommy. It'll be good to see you again. Shall we meet Wednesday afternoon or evening?"

"Yah, we need to spend some time together to sync up. Also, I'm going to arrange for us to meet with a couple of other folks we need to talk with about the concert. So don't plan on leaving until late Friday afternoon."

"Got it. I'll have Becky coordinate our travel arrangements with you. See ya soon."

 Day's End

What a day it had been, I thought, as I opened the fridge, grabbed a cold soda, the sack lunch my lover snugger had made for me, and headed out to the front steps. It was ten after seven, my first opportunity to step outside the building since my 7:30 arrival this morning. I was really looking forward to some quiet time, finally.

Halfway through my sandwich, I saw TP's pickup truck pull in and park alongside the bus. Knowing he would want to chat, it was decision time, fight or flight. Sit and wait for him to come by or head back into my office and finish dinner at my desk?

Tired and worn out, I decided it was just too much trouble to go back inside. So I remained seated while awaiting his arrival.

As TP approached the stairs, I exclaimed, "Evening! Nice hat!"

"Thanks!" as he brushed the brim of his hat and continued smiling. "And a big howdy to you. Hey, have you got a few minutes to visit?"

"Yah, sure," I replied.

"Great! Give me five minutes to go up and change into something comfortable and I'll be right back down."

"No problem, I'll be waiting right here."

I finished my sandwich and downed my drink, just as TP came through the door and sat down. Plastic cup in one hand and in the other, one finger curled through the small circular handle of a brand-new gallon jug of wine. He began the process of filling his cup and began to tell me about trying to find a place to store his T-shirts when they arrive. Then, out of the blue, he asked, "Do you know anything about the Pope? I mean, are you even Catholic?"

With a quirky smile and a look of chagrin, I replied, "Oh boy, TP, one thing I learned in the Navy and was even true in the Army..."

Immediately he interrupted me and inquired, "You were in the Army too?"

"Yah, I flew helicopters for about 18 months, until they discovered I had been exposed to Agent Orange and had a bad case of PTSD, so after they removed a tumor they rifted me out with a medical discharge, but that's another story for another time. Anyway, what I was about to say, was that I learned if you're gonna talk politics or religion you need to be prepared for a long and somewhat argumentative conversation. So let me get a fresh bottle of water and I'll come back out and answer your question."

Upon my return, I sat down and said, "In answer to the first part of your question, no, I don't know much about this Pope, other than his name and a few news stories I've read. And yes, I'm Catholic. I could even say mass in Latin when I was an altar boy. I went to parochial school through eighth grade, which was the last time I went to church until I got married. My wife joined the church, just before we married. I started attending mass again, and have done so ever since, to set an example for my kids, who also attend parochial school. However, just between you and me, I've always had a problem with the Catholic Church as a bureaucracy, and its leaders, the Popes, but not the teachings of Jesus Christ or my belief in God. It tore me apart inside for years, love or hate the church? I couldn't resolve the conflict until one day in Nam. I know it may sound weird, but let me explain.

"While I was in DaNang, I used to take the unused cases of C&K-rations that we didn't use on patrol over to the orphanage near our base. Going over there and giving those kids food, and getting a chance to spend time with them was really the only time I enjoyed while I was in Nam. I always looked forward to going over there, but there was a sad part to the visits. It wasn't just seeing and witnessing their suffering it was participating in, and sharing their suffering. So many, nearly all had been wounded. Many were missing limbs, eyes, and hearing. Disfigurement was everywhere you turned. Yet those kids remained full of life, searching and reaching out for just a moment of happiness in the midst of the misery they were engulfed in. I loved those kids, but they broke my heart every time I had to leave. Until the next time, when I could snag some supplies to take over to them - then I'd be all happy again. Anyway, at the time I was 17-18 years old, and it seemed that every day, everywhere I went, and everywhere I turned, there were the children of the war, suffering so terribly. Starving, orphaned, injured, maimed, and a couple of times even dying in my arms. It just tore me up, and it created memories that never go away.

"Now that you have an idea of where my head was at, you may be able to appreciate how one afternoon as we were headed out on patrol, I had grabbed a copy of the Stars & Stripes newspaper. I was sitting on top of the pilothouse in front of the gun tub reading as we cruised along the coast. I came across an article about Pope Paul VI visiting South America. Describing his visits to various cities, it included descriptions of overpopulated cities suffering from raging and relentless poverty, and how the starving children in the cities suffered the most. At point in the story, I thought at least they weren't in the middle of a war zone at the same time, like my kids at the orphanage.

"Then the article went on to highlight the Pope's message. That's when I went ballistic.   I couldn't believe what I was reading. I can't quote it, but the gist of the Pope's message was go out and create more babies; you will go straight to hell if you use contraception.   Don't think about becoming a responsible adult before making babies, just go out there and make more babies. Don't worry about all the children starving in the streets, just go out and make more babies. I got so upset I tore up the newspaper into little bitty pieces and threw them in the air as I continued to fume over what I had just read.   When I heard a voice say 'Hey asshole what are you doing? Get down here and clean up the mess you made,' I had to go down on the fantail and sweep up all the little pieces of newspaper that the wind trapped.

"About a week later, I was still very upset about the article. I was leaving the orphanage one afternoon after trying to help treat a little girl who had been burned by napalm, and I just broke down. I stopped outside the gate and sat down against the wall and just cried. The only time I ever did that, I just couldn't deal with what I had been through. That's when the events in the orphanage and the article collided in my mind.

"I looked up in the sky and said – Hey God, You and I need to have a talk. I love You, I love Your son Jesus Christ, and I love the Holy Ghost. I trust in You, and I believe in You, without exception. But, I hate Your Son's church, the bureaucracy of the church, I want nothing more to do with it. It's run by a bunch of old men who haven't got a clue, and who haven't had any experience outside the church. You and I both know the only way to lead is by example and you can't demonstrate an example if you've never done it, or experienced it yourself. Not one of those old farts leading the church has ever been the leader of a family, raised a child to adulthood, or been responsible for the economic planning and welfare of a family unit. So how can they possibly understand the enormous impact of the "church's doctrine" they invent and try to force down everybody's throat, claiming it's Your will and word. God, if this pisses you off, I'm really sorry. But, I have to be honest with you, and tell you this is the way it's going to have to be until somebody cleans up that toilet bowl. I'm done. And one more thing, please send an extra Angel or two, to help that little girl in there, to stop her suffering and help her heal. Thank You.

"And that was it, the end of my relationship with the Catholic Church. From that point on my house of worship became anywhere and everywhere outside a structure, when I'm alone, surrounded by nature itself, and the beauty of God's creation. It's then and there that I pray, commune and talk to God. Ever since then it's worked for me. I feel very comfortable in my relationship with my Creator. He looks out for me, he keeps me out of trouble most of the time, and He keeps me alive, despite the fact that I burn the candle at both ends, and I love Him in return.

"The only reason I'm involved in this Pope's visit to Denver is to make money, plain and simple. That's it. How about you, are you Catholic?"

TP replied, "No, I believe there is a God, but I don't believe in any particular religion. For a lot of the same reasons you just mentioned."

"Well, you know, looking back TP, that little talk I had with God extinguished the flames of my conflict with and between God and Church, which had raged for so long within my mind and heart. I guess it was the result of having been brought up in a catholic environment, where so much is centered on the church itself and its teachings force fed to me throughout my childhood. However, my little talk with God that day really brought me peace, peace of mind. And ever since that day, I've never again been torn up by my inability to understand or explain the distinction between God and the church or, more importantly, that it's okay to accept or reject the church's teachings, based upon your own determinations and conclusions.

"I really want my sons to experience, learn, and understand the Catholic Church. So when they become adults they can then

* * *

make their own decisions and determinations as to how they want to relate and interact with the church, and still love, and be in love with their Creator."

After a few moments of silence, TP responded, "Yah, it always seemed to me that churches, religious organizations are more interested in ruling and controlling their congregations with their teachings for political purposes, than they are trying to teach people how to build a relationship and love for their Creator. That may have been what was necessary back in the dark ages when the only entertainment around was going to church, but in this day and age, as people become more knowledgeable, the old system ain't gonna continue to work."

"Exactly!   Churches, religions themselves, are going to have to start changing with the times and quickly." I responded, and continued, "They are going to have to eventually come to the realization that the stories and writings they rely upon for credibility and justification were not etched in stone by God. But hand written by man, sometimes translated hundreds of years later, losing the tenor, innuendos and actual purpose of the words as they were spoken at the time, for the audience at the time.

"What I mean is based upon a conversation I remember having on the fantail of the USS Chicago in the middle of the Gulf of Tonkin in '66, I'll never forget.

"It was a beautiful evening. The water looked like glass all the way to the horizon. There wasn't enough of a breeze to even move the flag hanging on the stern mast as the sky began to take on color from the setting sun. I leaned up against the rear railing with my cup of coffee, enjoying the sunset and waiting for my shift to begin. Then this engine rat walked up next to me, disheveled, covered in oil, grease and sweat, and said hello. Turned out he got off his shift in the engine room a half hour early, and decided to grab a cold drink, and came up to get some fresh air on the fantail. We began to chat and somehow after a while the conversation turned to religion. Turns out he was a Muslim. I'd never met one before and knew nothing about his religion. He talked about his

Bible, a book he called the Koran. Somewhere along the way, during the conversation, he tells me that according to his prophet Mohammed and the Koran, he is supposed to kill anybody or everybody who refuses to believe in Mohammed and the Koran.

"Taken aback by such an extreme statement, I had to ask, 'Since I don't believe in either Mohammed or the Koran, does that mean you're going to kill me now, or some other time?'

"He looked at me with a quirky smile and said, 'Well I'm supposed to, but no, I'm not going to kill you now.'

"'Well, that's good to hear! But, how I am I supposed to believe you're not going to kill me later as I lie awake in my bunk all night waiting for you to come?   Never-mind!   More importantly! How can you believe in a religion that wants you to kill everybody who doesn't agree with your beliefs?   I don't understand'

"He looked over at me with a very strange look on his face, and said, 'I don't know how to answer your question. We would have to talk for a very long time for me to explain. I'm tired, it was a tough shift today. I need to go hit the head, take a shower, and get to the mess deck before it closes. Maybe we'll meet up again, and I'll try to answer your questions, see you later.'

"And with that he turned and left.

"Now, TP, you explain to me, how any religion or religious leader can take a religious command like that, written a thousand or 1500 years ago, when such a statement, law, or rule may have been necessary for their survival at that time, and continue to claim, now today, that this commandment from the Koran is still valid. Their Allah is the same Deity as my Creator, who at this point in time would never command me or anyone else for that matter, to go out and kill everybody who disagrees with my religious beliefs. It seems like complete insanity. Times change! Why can't religions?

"I respect their right to believe in their Creator any way they want to, so why can't they respect my right to do the same? I don't get it. I don't get the all-encompassing desire of religious leaders to control everything and everyone. It just doesn't sound like the Creator nor does it seem to me to be a part of His plan for mankind."

With a loud sigh, TP uttered, "Amen Brother!"

CHAPTER 6

A Good Plan – For A Busy Week

...the number of kids coming is going to be 40 to 50,000
and this number may grow larger.

"Good morning everyone. As always, I thank each of you for your timely arrival to our Monday morning staff meeting. First thing, any unresolved problems or complaints from last week?"

Becky was the first to speak up, "Yes boss. Last week people calling were constantly complaining when I answered the phone, that our phone lines are always busy, requiring them to call back repeatedly. *Sorry!* Doesn't seem to cut it much anymore. Is there anything we can do about it? Some of our callers are really pissed."

"Well, I had no idea we had such a problem. Thanks for pointing it out. Bill, any thoughts?" I asked.

"Not off the top of my head JD. I know the phones are all lit up - all day long, but I didn't think about the consequences."

After a few seconds of thought I inquired, "Do we have call forwarding on our last line in rotation?

"Anybody? -- Okay Becky, go over and pick up the last line in rotation and dial *71 and see if you get a tone, and then another dial-tone."

Moments later she sat back down, and said, "No boss, nothing happened."

"Okay, Bill, call the phone company after the meeting and have them add call forwarding to that line as soon as possible. Becky, once it's set up - forward it to our answering service. Tell them what we're doing and ask them to call in the messages every 20 or 30 minutes as they build up.

"Okay, problem solved. Anybody else with a problem?"

Kathy interjected, "Yes sir. We're still pretty much at square one with the logistics team. Other than one old barn that doesn't sound very big, we've been unable to find any farmers or ranchers outside the city limits willing to discuss allowing us to use, or renting some of their land for the concert. They all seem to remember Woodstock and are scared to death their property will be destroyed. The title company you hooked us up with has been very helpful and is continuing to provide us more names and phone numbers of property owners, and I guess we'll just keep on trying, but is there any other solution on the horizon for a venue? Without the venue, we can't even begin to conceptualize a stage, to determine how much actual stage time we'll have for entertainers, so any kind of planning can't even begin."

Nodding in understanding, I sympathetically replied, "Kathy I understand your dilemma and I appreciate your comments. So let's talk about logistics for a few minutes. Friday afternoon, I finally met with a Secret Service agent who would at least talk to me. He told me that the estimates regarding the number of kids coming to Denver has been raised significantly since the original estimate of 20,000. Currently, they think the number is going to be 40 to 50,000 and this number may grow larger. Their biggest problem is trying to decide whether to include additions for the possibility of parents traveling with them, and they haven't determined yet how to quantify that possibility.

"So, if you believe that X% of the say 50,000 kids coming - will have one or possibly two parents in tow, then the total number of people coming to Denver increases substantially.

"Now the good part, for us anyway, is that the last thing 50,000 kids are going to want to do is drag their parents to a concert.

"For conceptual planning, think about 200 or 300 acres of open land, 100 acres for entertainment and the rest for parking and concessions. I know the city has a couple of venues that will hold a crowd that size, but only two that come to mind have roofs - are fully enclosed. I'll talk to the mayor about them this afternoon, but my concern is that in the end they won't be large enough to handle the crowd that may show up. Because we haven't been including the local kids in our estimates, we could have 100,000 people show up, or maybe more. So for right now, let's anticipate 50,000 tourists and 50,000 locals attending the concert, without their parents, and find a suitable venue.

"As for the stages and stage time for the entertainers, for the moment, imagine our venue is a 100 acres square and we build a separate stage in each corner. Or, alternatively imagine a big X built in the middle of the square, out of 15 foot tall soundproof walls with a separate stage in each of the angles in the X. It's a start, something to use as a base to develop some possible scenarios for the moment. Be sure and get a couple of electrical contractors involved this week to start planning for a bid proposal for electricity. That's going to be one of our most critical factors."

I took a breath and looked around the room and instantly realized that I didn't have the time to resolve every little problem that was going to arise. I had failed to provide my staff with the leadership necessary to take care of business. How do I teach these kids, these young men and women with no in-depth management experiences - how to manage this business. I've got to think of something, and I have to figure it out right now.

I stood up, came to attention, and said, "All right, everybody listen up. Fortunately, you and I, we all, live in a capitalistic society. If we lived in a socialist society or form of government, we wouldn't be sitting here now, together, developing a business. A business, the business of taking a thought - an idea, and then turning it into reality for fun and profit, and in our case, to create a wonderful and joyous concert to honor, and in honor of, Pope John Paul II.

"The profit we hope for will reimburse me for the wages you earn each day, and your share of the profits, once earned, will financially help you and your families afterwards, as you proceed to your next adventure on your journey through life.

"In order to make this all happen, we not only have to work together as a team, but each and every one of us, individually, has to make shit happen every day!

"How do you do that? You take your assigned tasks and duty assignments and own them. They are yours; they're all yours, and only yours. Take title and ownership of them. Then show me, and everyone else on the team, what a good job you did taking care of them.

"Now, while I continue just nod if you agree or disagree on what I'm about to say. You're concerned about keeping your job. You're concerned that if you make a mistake you won't be forgiven and will lose your job. You're concerned that if you make a decision, it might be the wrong one and you'll lose your job.

"Well, I see, finally, everyone is nodding in agreement. That's Good! That means there's hope!

"Basically, there are only two types of economies, quasi-socialist, and capitalistic societies. In a socialist society, there is no hope! Hope cannot survive, or even exist in a socialist environment, because everything is shared, and not necessarily equally, until productivity sinks to zero. No matter how much natural resource wealth may exist, the socialist society will collapse, at some point. Case in point, look at Communist Russia. It's gone, and more importantly, look at China. They figured it out. They are beginning to change their economy to capitalism.

"Capitalism on the other hand, a capitalistic society, thrives on, is fueled by hope and productivity. Hope of the individual to make life better is the energy nucleus, the nuclear power that drives the individual to be productive and even more productive each day, for the rewards received for their productivity. Simply stated, be productive, make it happen, and you will be rewarded.

"There are two kinds of rewards. Eternal rewards, defined and provided by your Creator, based upon your spiritual productivity with Him while you're here. Earthly rewards, on the other hand, are man-made, defined by man, and created by mutual agreement.

• • •

"In a socialistic society, your reward is defined by the current ruler, and based not on productivity, but sheer existence.

"In a capitalistic society, your reward is based solely upon your productivity, the value of which is freely agreed upon by and between two or more persons.   Each of you met with me, individually, and agreed to provide your productivity to the production of this concert in exchange for the reward we agreed upon.

"I in turn, will ask each concert attendee for a reward to watch and enjoy the fruits of what I've produced with your help. Will they pay a reward?   And will they pay a fair and sufficient reward?   I don't know the answers, but that's my risk.   And to a certain extent, from a profit-sharing standpoint it's your risk as well.   If my productivity was insufficient and no one is willing to reward me for the concert I produced, then no one will show up and I will receive nothing.   But, it is the risk that both you and I accepted at the onset.

"Fairness and/or reward equality was not one of God's gifts to man.   Nor was it guaranteed in the Constitution.   It comes from and can only exist in a free market, based solely upon productivity.

"And yes, there are, and there always will be inequalities, and disputes as to value.   But a free capitalistic market will always automatically adjust itself, and correct itself regarding value.   It's the inequalities that the participants are required to resolve to ensure every human being has an equal opportunity to participate in the market.   This includes the requirement of charity as a moral obligation for the benefit of persons precluded from participating in the market, by reason of physical and/or mental disability.   For those who elect to be nonproductive, to sit at home and watch reruns on TV, they have to be left aside and not allowed to become a burden to those who wish to be productive.   Eventually, they will either turn off the TV and become productive, or rely on charitable handouts.   It's their choice.

"The crowning jewel of capitalism is that if the reward is insufficient or unfair, an individual can take his or her productivity elsewhere, and find a greater reward, or create their own enterprise and let a free market determine the value and reward for their productivity.

"Such things can never happen in a socialistic state and no civilization can survive, or even exist without productivity. The greater the productivity, the greater the nation, the greater the productivity, the greater the civilization, and the greater the productivity, the greater the peace and happiness the populace will experience.

"Economic equality and economic fairness can only be found in a self-regulated free market. Outside regulation has to be limited to only ensuring honesty of exchange and the environment of the marketplace. Any other regulatory burden will only skew the market.

"I say all this, not to provide you with an economics 101 lesson, but to clarify my expectations of your job performance. I expect you to be productive each and every day. You can do that by simply taking ownership and possession of your tasks and assignments. Collect the data you need, evaluate all your options and draw your conclusions. If necessary, collaborate with others, including me, make your best decision, and then make it happen. Try to avoid doing or saying something that will require you to say I'm Sorry! Never say I'm afraid, and no matter what, never - never say, I can't.

"You will make mistakes, which is why we have erasers. All your decisions will not be the right one every time. Correct your mistakes, and try to make the right decision at least fifty-one percent of the time, and you should be fine. Just keep in mind that someone has to pay for each mistake and each wrong decision, and that someone is me.

"Bring your brain and your productivity to work every day. The only thing I want you to be sure and leave at home, folded nicely in a dresser drawer, is your trepidation, your fear of performance failure, and most importantly, your fear of success. I want each of you to come to work every morning knowing and believing that everyone, including you, is going to have a good time and a lot of fun helping you be successful in making this project an incredible and wonderful success. So let's join together, be productive, and make it happen."

"Now let's take a look at this week's agenda. Everything is pretty much self-explanatory and I have included my itinerary for the week. As you can see I have a meeting with the State's Economic Development Commissioner later this morning and with the Mayor this afternoon. Tuesday, I have several meetings with individual investors and Wednesday evening, I fly to LA to meet up with Tommy. We have a number of meetings scheduled for both Thursday and Friday. After which I'll fly back to Denver. Bill's in command while I'm gone, see him if you have any problems.

"Any questions?   None, okay until our next Monday morning meeting, let's rock 'n roll."

"Bill, have you got a minute? Let's go to your office. I've got a couple more things I want to go over with you."

 ## _Time to meet the Mayor_

The Denver City and County building, built in the early 1930s, is a huge four story, two block long half circle facing the state capital to the east, divided in two by a wide hallway in the center, running from one end to the other. It always seemed somewhat dark and foreboding to me as daylight had a difficult time penetrating the tunnel-like hallway. The mayor's office, with the city seal etched in the frosted glass of its double doors, is centered on the east side of the second floor. I saw Haley sitting on an old wooden bench beside the entrance as I approached. Seeing me, she rose and I said, "Haley, good to see you, looks like we're on time."

"Hi, JD, we've got a couple of minutes before we have to go in. How did it go with the State this morning? Anything new?"

"No, nothing that affects us. It was a strange meeting and I'm not sure what to make of it yet. I'll fill you in on the details after our meeting. You ready? Shall we go in?" I asked as I held the door open for her to enter.

After introductions and exchanging a few pleasantries, the three of us sat down in a very small meeting room adjacent to the mayor's formal office.

I began, "Mister Mayor, did you have an opportunity to examine our proposal for the concert?"

"Yes, I did. On the surface, it sounds like a good idea. However, it was not clear regarding the venue or exactly how the city, would be involved. Can you expand on that?"

"Yes sir. We believe, with the tourists and the local kids, we have a combined total of about 80 to 100,000 possible attendees. We are currently contemplating two, maybe three nights of entertainment, starting at 7PM and running until possibly 1AM each night. We believe there may be three facilities in Denver that could handle this type of event. One of them, Bears Stadium, we understand from the Secret Service, will be the central hub for the papal events and therefore we've eliminated it from consideration. Leaving us with the possibility of the coliseum, and the city auditorium - we believe the city auditorium is too small and its downtown location a crowd control nightmare. Leaving us with only the Coliseum as a candidate for an indoor venue and it too is problematic, but if this is where you would prefer to have it held we can overcome the problems

.

"Our preference, the best possible venue for us, and which may also provide some ancillary benefits to the city in handling this event, is the old and vacant Stapleton Airport property. Stapleton is the perfect venue for this event! Its immense size would allow us to create a center stage and divide the property up into different mini-venues by genre. We have received requests to participate from entertainers of every genre from all over the world. The old airport is the perfect venue for us. It's also the perfect site to set up tents and commissary services to house and provide for tourists unable to find suitable housing. We could set up a tent city on both of the old north runways to provide a safe and secure place for the kids coming with nothing but a backpack."

The mayor interjected, "Well, we have already recognized that problem and have a plan in place to accommodate that situation."

I responded, "May I ask what your contingency plan is going to be."

He replied, "The plan isn't finalized, but presently we're considering shutting down all of the parking lot structures downtown to allow the kids to stay in the parking garages, so they are close to the papal events."

"Okay, that sounds like a good housing idea, we weren't aware of your plan. We were just thinking we could possibly help out. Actually that makes our proposition a much simpler proposal. If we're not housing any of the kids at the airport, we can better control security by opening the grounds in the late afternoon and completely vacate the property each night at the conclusion of the entertainment.

"Mayor, if we have the necessary space this event could be bigger than Woodstock. We literally have top entertainers from around the world, ready to come to perform for the Pope and his kids. This concert could be so beneficial. It can bring millions of dollars to Denver. It could be historic. We are willing to meet any and all requirements the city may have to allow us to rent this facility. It's perfect! We're willing to put up temporary fencing to restrict access to only the venue. We'll provide security guards to secure the existing buildings and will pay for use of the existing parking garages as well. And most importantly, we're prepared to pay a flat fee plus a percentage of the gate, if there is a gate charge. It may turn out in the end that the concert is free."

"Excuse me? Did you say that the concert may be free?" The mayor inquired sternly, leaning forward and resting his arms on the table.

I answered, "Let me explain, it is a possibility. So far during our negotiations with the entertainers, almost every single one of them has stated that they're not interested in compensation; they simply want to be able to perform three or four pieces for the Pope and be a part of this event. A free gate is a possibility, but my initial discussions with our potential investors won't take place until later this week, so I can't say for certain. But, if the city wants a gate charge as part of the rental package, we may be able to give you possibly as much as 100% of the gate depending on how things work out."

Leaning back as far as his chair would go, the mayor looked at me and said, "This has to be the strangest proposal I've ever heard. The city receives proposals every day and nearly all are about the money and you're sitting here telling me it's not about the money. That's not exactly what I understood from Haley. In fact, she told me that she would be sharing in the profits from the concert. Now what am I supposed to believe?"

After pausing for a moment, I replied, "Well sir I didn't mean to imply that this would be a nonprofit proposition. I believe the profitability lies in the corporate sponsorships, advertising and most importantly, possible broadcasting rights. If the entertainers are going to perform for free, I don't want to insult them by charging their audience unless it's required to compensate the city for the venue. This event will be profitable and I have no problem sharing those profits with the city."

The mayor replied, "Okay, I get it. Have you talked to the State yet?"

For the next few minutes I explained that I had met with the State Economic Development Commission and was unable to find state property within the city that could be considered as a venue.

Concluding by paraphrasing, "Mayor, the bottom line for the State to get involved, is they want us to put together a $100 million industrial development revenue bond package to build a film and recording studio as part of the package. I wasn't real thrilled with their idea. Consequently, I have no reason to believe that the State has any interest in our project."

The mayor looked at his wristwatch, telling me that the meeting was about to come to an end as he said, "Okay, I have to admit I'm very intrigued. So I'm going to meet with some of my department heads and other city officials who will have to be involved. In the meantime, I want to make it perfectly clear and I want your personal assurances that should the city approve your proposal and provide you with this venue, that you will take the very best care of Haley. Haley is a dear and longtime friend. She has worked for me for years and worked relentlessly to help get me elected. I want to know that she will be properly taken care of, because you wouldn't be sitting here if it wasn't for her. Is that clearly understood?"

"Yes sir, and I thank you for taking the time to visit with us today."

"All right then, you're welcome."

We all stood, and as we shook hands the mayor added, "All communications with my office go through Haley. I'll let her know our decision week after next. Have a good day." And with that he turned and left the room.

As we walked down the hall headed out of the building, I said to Haley, "Nice job Haley! For a while there, I was feeling bad that you didn't get an opportunity to speak. But then I realized in order for us to be there in the meeting, you must've had some extensive conversations with him already. So I just want to know if you're okay with how the meeting went. Do you think it went well?"

Haley replied, "Oh yes, I think it went very well. Wellington is always very serious and direct during work time, so don't worry about there not being more friendly chatter in the meeting. When he's not working, he's very warm and friendly with everyone. I really think the world of him."

"Well that's good to know. He did seem a bit cold, but I figured he's just a busy man, with a lot on his mind, so I didn't draw any conclusions from his demeanor. But what I want to know is do you think there's any hope for his approval of our plan?"

As we waited for the elevator, she looked up at me and replied, "Oh yes, I think he left the meeting, a proponent. I think he will make every effort to try and get the deal done for us. I feel really good about it."

"Great! If anything comes up, be sure and let me know. I'd like you to attend next Monday's staff meeting, to fill everybody in on the meeting and provide us with any update."

Upon my return to the office, I found the Fox in his office. I sat down, saying, "Why are you still here? It's after six."

"I've got to reword our response to the entertainers. I'm trying to change the wording so they'll wait for us to contact them, rather than faxing us another inquiry every couple of days. We're bordering on being completely out of control. How about you, how did it go today?"

"Overall, I think it went very well," I said, and then continued to give him a blow-by-blow description of the meetings.

Bill then said, "I agree with your take on the meeting with the State and I sincerely hope you're not going to spend a lot of time trying to sell an IDRB (Industrial Development Revenue Bond) investment package. I'm really more concerned about having to wait two weeks to find out what the mayor's going to do. We can't just sit here and do nothing for the next two weeks, just waiting. I hope you understand that *time* is about to become public enemy number one. We're about four months away. Just what are we supposed to do for the next two weeks?"

"Bill, I understand the time issue. I'm doing everything I can to get the venue as soon as possible. I'm not going to lose two weeks waiting for the mayor. I'll be on the phone tomorrow, and again on Wednesday with only one objective, to find us a venue.

"Have you and the team been able to develop any numbers regarding performances and the entertainers?"

"Well, let me tell ya, without taking into account the time necessary to set up their equipment and instruments, and if we had four stages. Limiting each entertainer to 10 minutes of stage time, and open the gates from 2 PM to 2 AM every day, and if only a third of the entertainers show up, we need the venue for a month. And, if they all show up, make it two or three months of continuous nonstop music. Are you beginning to understand the insanity I'm faced with dealing with the entertainers?"

"Wow," I exclaimed. "I had no idea it had reached these proportions. I assume you and the team are categorizing and rating the entertainers by genre and fame or something, because they all can't come and perform."

"Well, of course, but once we have the venue, the dates, and times of performances, we're going to be faced with some serious decisions and will have to disappoint a whole lot of people. I'm not happy about it, but I see the handwriting on the wall and it's coming. Anyway, I've had enough for today. See you tomorrow. I'm gonna head on home. Good night."

Another Evening with TP

Checking my watch, it was evident I wouldn't make it home in time for dinner. So I headed over to the convenience store to grab a sandwich. Upon my return, whom should I find sitting on the steps next to a half a jug of wine?

TP bellowed, "JD, how the hell are yah? If that's dinner in your bag, why don't you pull up a seat and join me."

It had been a long busy day. I was worn out, but what the hell, maybe a visit with TP would help me ignite my afterburners so I could get some work done later. It became readily apparent TP was in a talkative mood. I sat down on the steps and opened up my sandwich wrapper. I hadn't got a word in edgewise yet, as he was concluding his opening remarks regarding his morning activities.

Finally, as he paused to refill his wine cup, I asked, "So how's your T-shirt project going?"

"Well, that's what I really wanted to tell you about. You know, our government has gotten completely out of control. I'm so pissed I can't see straight."

"So what else is new?" I replied.

"Well, I spent all day last Thursday and Friday on the phone with the city trying to find out how I go about getting a vendor's license so I can sell my T-shirts. Nobody had any answers and no one returned my phone calls. So, I decided to go down to their offices and talk to them in person. I got there at 1 PM and was forced to leave at 4:30 when they closed. I spent the entire afternoon trying to find out how to get a vendor's license. Nobody would give me a straight answer. The only thing they told me, for certain, was that if I was caught selling anything to do with the papal visit without a license, I would be ticketed and my merchandise seized.

"They've created the perfect Catch-22, you can't sell anything during the papal visit without a vendor's license and they won't tell you how to get a vendor's license. When I put all the different conversations together, it seems like there's some company from Israel that has an exclusive license for selling anything and everything that might have something to do with the papal visit. However, they won't even tell you who the company is or even say so officially.

"Can you believe this shit! There's some company in Israel that has enough political clout to get the City to refuse to issue street vendor licenses to give them a monopoly on everything sold. I've already made my second payment on the T-shirts, so they're coming. I plan to go back down there tomorrow and try again, but when I saw you coming, I thought maybe I should talk to you and see if you had any recommendations?"

"Good grief Charlie Brown! Didn't you think to get your license before you purchased the T-shirts?"

"Hell yes, but back then, the city was even less helpful and said I would have to wait until they formalized the special regulations for this event, and I couldn't wait. The T-shirts wouldn't arrive in time. So, do you have any suggestions?"

"Not at the moment, but I too was downtown today, and met with the mayor with Haley. I'll ask her to look into the matter and see what she comes up with. I'll let you know."

"Thanks my friend, I'd appreciate any help I can get."

CHAPTER 7

California Here We Come!

...there are a number of great entertainers that could be
designated the headliner on the list. But, ...

"Tommy, so good to see you." I said as we shook hands at the entrance to the restaurant.

Smiling broadly, Tommy replied, "And it's good to see you as well. The hostess said she will be seating us shortly. I assume you had no problem with the reservation I made for you."

"No, everything is fine and I got a great room. Believe it or not, I stayed here at the Bonaventure for a week back in '76, when it first opened. I really enjoy this hotel and I'm glad you picked it. Riding the glass elevators up and down the outside of the building is really cool, and this rotating restaurant caps it off."

"Yah, I always stay here when I'm in LA, and I like it better than the Beverly Hills Hilton, which is where we have our meeting tomorrow morning at 11. You ready for it?"

"You bet I am."

After placing our orders for dinner, I asked, "Tommy, do you know Richard Markett?"

"No, doesn't ring a bell." He replied.

"Well, the reason I ask is he showed up at my office yesterday afternoon. It was really weird. As he walked into my office, there stood a giant of a man, a black man. I'd say at least 6 foot 6, with shoulders as broad as a walk-in refrigerator door, smiling, and extending a hand, as big as a catcher's mitt, for me to shake. I felt certain I knew him, but I couldn't place him. So I said, 'Do we know each other, you seem very familiar.' He started to chuckle and said, 'I get that a lot. You've probably seen me in a movie or on TV.' As soon as he said that, I instantly recalled that he was the starring police captain on one of those east coast police shows. You know who I'm talking about now?"

"Oh sure, but I didn't know he was that big. I've never met him."

"Well, let me tell you he is a big guy. Anyway, he sits down at my desk and tells me that he's going to be in town for a while, until after the pope leaves, and has some downtime and heard about our concert. He wants to know if he can help us out with the concert, because he has a lot of entertainment industry contacts. He thought he might be able to give us a hand. Now, ain't that something, but more intriguing is how and why did he show up at my office? We spent about half an hour talking and it turns out he's a really nice guy. At the end of the meeting, he invited my wife and me to his house for dinner next weekend. What do you make of that?"

As our dinner arrived, Tommy replied, "For the most part I'm not surprised. Most people in the entertainment business who are between gigs are always looking around for the next one, or another one. I think as we progress and get closer to success a lot more of that kind of thing is going to happen. Have you got something for him to do?"

"No, I don't and I really haven't figured out what to do with him. Have you got any ideas? Is there anything that he can do to help you out?"

"No JD, there really isn't anything I need assistance with. I'm in good shape and we're making good progress together.

"I think tomorrow morning's meeting is critical. You have to find the capital to fund this thing or we're dead ducks, but all that may be resolved in our meeting tomorrow. I feel really good about it."

"Man, Tommy, I'm so relieved to hear you say that."

"JD, the most important issue we have to talk about tomorrow is the venue. Any indication yet, from the mayor's office?"

"No, but I've had a number of conversations and a couple of meetings about possible backup solutions. However, it's really premature to go into details. Hopefully, we'll hear something very soon."

"Okay, but be prepared to be thoroughly grilled on that issue tomorrow."

"I will. I'm ready!" With that, we wrapped up the evening and headed to our rooms.

   Finally! Morning!

I was really having trouble mentally processing the fact that I was standing in the lobby of the Beverly Hills Hilton Hotel, shaking hands with Steve Dawson, one of my favorite TV wild west cowboy heroes, who I watched religiously every Saturday as a child growing up. He still looked a lot like he did back then, lean, handsome, with a warm smile that put you at ease. Finally, my tongue became fully engaged, and I said, "This is such a thrill and honor for me personally to get to meet you, Steve. I watched you, I swear, every Saturday morning catching the bad guys and riding that beautiful horse of yours across the screen."

"Thank you for those kind words. I'm glad to hear you enjoyed the series. It was a good show, and I really enjoyed the role. Please allow me to introduce my wife, Melanie."

I took her extended hand and held it gently, as I said smiling, to this very lovely woman who appeared to be about the same age as her husband, "Good morning Melanie. It's such a delight to meet you."

We all sat down in the overstuffed chairs circling a small glass top table in the lobby and began to discuss the concert. It was evident as the discussions progressed that even though the Dawsons were gentle, soft-spoken people, they were very astute when it came to business matters. They were truly delightful people to visit with and I was really enjoying myself. I pulled out a file folder I had brought along, containing examples of the faxes we had received from both agents and entertainers themselves. They recognized many of the big-name entertainers from the US and expressed surprise at the number of different genres we had received from other countries.

Twenty minutes later Steve said, "Well, Tommy, I'm sure glad we got together to see this. Neither Melanie nor I understood the magnitude of the entertainment side of this project. It's somewhat overwhelming, but now I think we both appreciate your reassurances that the entertainment was handled."

Turning toward me he continued, "And, JD, I'm really impressed with what you've gotten done. This project is really something, and we're thankful for the invitation from you both to participate. You see, we're Catholic and we are both great fans of Pope John Paul II. We believe he is one of the world's great leaders today. We just wish there were more like him. So let's order some coffee and continue on."

While waiting for the coffee to arrive, Tommy chatted with the Dawsons about old times. I sat and worried about how to handle the venue issue. I had called Bill before leaving the hotel to see if Haley had called in yet with an update from the mayor's office. She hadn't, so I asked Bill to be sure and page me if she called during the meeting. Which made me think to check my pager and make sure it was still on. It was and that was a good thing. I was starting to get antsy. I was excited about how well it was going so far, and I wanted to get back into the discussion.

Finally, the waitress showed up and set a silver tray with a pot of coffee, four cups, and a fancy creamer and sugar dispenser on the table, and with an experienced flair, commenced filling each cup, and placing it on a saucer in front of each of us, one after the other.

Upon her departure, Steve reignited the conversation, saying, "JD, assuming the entertainment is in place, what are your plans for the venue?"

"Steve, Melanie, we have been working diligently on this issue. We have talked to hundreds of farmers and ranchers trying to find a suitable field without success. We have discussed this with the State of Colorado and the city of Denver. Our first choice is the old Stapleton International Airport facility, which has been closed down for a couple of years. It would be perfect. If we get the nod from the city, our concert will make Woodstock look like a small picnic. It's what we're hoping for. But, should that not work out, I'm in discussions with the University of Colorado regarding the use of Folsom Field arena which seats 52,000, and we may be able to get another 10 or 15,000 people inside. So far we've had a very positive response from them. They understand they're our backup venue. They presented our project to the Board of Trustees yesterday. I just haven't heard back yet.

"It's a much smaller venue with two advantages, it's less costly, and more manageable, but we're holding out for the city of Denver. This gives rise to the most important question facing us. As of this moment, you folks are the only individuals expressing an interest in bankrolling this project. If the city of Denver or Folsom Field wants the rent in advance, neither Tommy nor I have the personal resources to finance this project or advance rental payments. I don't have enough data yet to provide you with the firm fixed figure, but if we end up at Folsom Field, the cost could be as high as $1 million, and if Denver approves the project, that amount could double or even be a little more. Are these sums something you and Melanie would be comfortable with and consider? I know Tommy has had discussions with you regarding the potential revenue streams for this project, but there are no guarantees that I can offer. My primary concern is that if we put on the concert, and when all is said and done, there's little or no profit left, let alone the recapture of the costs invested. Would that financially harm you in any way?"

"No, the loss of our investment would not cause us any harm or concern. Of course, if it is profitable, we would most certainly expect a fair share of any profits."

Melanie interjected, "You see, JD, we are more interested in supporting and helping Pope John Paul II on his first visit to the US. That is far more important to us than the money."

Addressing both Steve and Melanie, I replied, "I understand. You folks are really incredible. It's evident your feelings for this pope run very deep. So let me make this promise. The first revenue dollars received from the concert shall be the return of your capital investment, and only then shall the remainder be divided accordingly. Tommy, do you agree?"

Tommy responded, "Absolutely! I agree. Very well said. That's the way it should be."

As everyone began smiling and nodding positively the moment of quiet was broken by the sound of my pager going off. I had forgotten to set it on vibrate. Recognizing the number was the office, I looked up and said, "Can everyone excuse me for a minute, please. I need to return this call. I won't be very long."

As I turned the corner and headed for the front desk in search of a phone, I walked up to one of the lobby hostesses and said, "Excuse me, ma'am. Can you tell me where the nearest payphone is? Thank you."

Reaching a large bank of payphones in the back hallway, I said, "Yes operator, collect please.

"Bill, it's me. What is it, did Haley call?"

"No, haven't heard from her, but the University called - we got Folsom Field - the trustees approved the project late yesterday afternoon and I just got the call and thought you needed to know."

"Are you serious? We got it?! Bill, that's incredible news. At least we have a backup plan now. Hopefully, we won't need it. Let's just keep praying for Haley to corral the mayor and get Stapleton for us. I'm still in the middle of this meeting; it's going very well. I'll call you when I get back to the hotel – OK – Bye – gotta go."

As I approached the table, Tommy concluded whatever he was saying and asked, "Everything okay?"

"Oh yah, I'm so glad I got the page. I've got news. The University called our office just a little bit ago and notified us that the Board of Trustees has approved our project and we will be able to utilize Folsom Field if we want it. So our backup plan is now locked in."

Tommy replied, "Oh, Joe, that's fabulous. Congratulations on a job well done."

Melanie interjected, "Yes, yes, congratulations - this is getting exciting."

Steve added, "Well, pardner, looks like it's time to saddle up, as I might have once said to my sidekick years ago – well done.

"So Tommy, according to what you've told us in the past, that leaves us with only one last component, the headliner. It seems like there are quite a few candidates to choose from. There are a number of entertainers on JDs list that could be headliners, what are your thoughts?"

Tommy replied, "What you're saying is accurate, there are a number of great entertainers that could be designated the headliner on the list. But, just before we left the hotel this morning, I called Florida to make another follow-up call to an old friend of mine, and finally got a favorable response. So I also have news that I think all three of you will appreciate. But please understand it is still tentative and will depend on some conditional requirements that will be provided to me this weekend. My friend, Frank, Frank Sinatra has agreed to be not the headliner, but a co-headliner with someone else he's speaking with. He wants to be a co-headliner because he feels our target audience is too young. He believes we need another name to headline with him for our

● ● ●

audience. He hasn't disclosed who that is yet, but he said he's had several conversations with him. Frank's definitely in, but this other party has to agree to come as well and Frank tells me their conversations are very positive. So even though it's not a done deal, I felt it was time to inform you of this development. My backup plan is to use one or more of the entertainers on JD's list, especially if we are opening on multiple nights. But, I've got to get the corporate sponsors and media companies to go along with our final choices. It's all up to them, because without revenue, there's no sense in proceeding."

Steve replied, "Good answer Tommy. I agree and I trust your judgment to make the right call. Unfortunately, as exciting as this is, Melanie and I have another scheduled event to attend. So let me close by saying, we're in. I'll have my attorneys draw up a letter of intent and draft an agreement to fund the project, for your review and consideration. How does that sound? Will that work for you guys in the interim?"

As everyone stood, I replied, "You bet. That's perfect, and not only do I thank you for the funding, but more importantly, I thank you for meeting with us this morning, and the incredible opportunity to shake hands with one of my oldest and most favorite heroes. You folks have a really good weekend."

     Two Days Later . . .

"**W**ell JD, looks like we're going to get you to the airport on time. You should have a good 20, maybe 30 minutes before takeoff."

"Yep, it's perfect timing. And, by the way Tommy - thanks for lunch."

"You should be feeling really good about all the good news you have to take home."

"I am Tommy, I really am! This is one of the most incredibly successful business trips I've ever been on. Consider what we accomplished in just three meetings in two days. I mean, just think about it. We got all the capital funding we need. So I don't have to go to any more meetings with possible investors. And like WOW, what happened at IBC today, that was just bodacious, the icing on the cake. We no longer have to worry about finding enough corporate sponsors and advertisers for the project. Whatever else may come along is just fine."

"You know, JD, I've been thinking in the back of my mind ever since we left International Broadcasting Corporation's offices what a truly unusual meeting it turned out to be. In my wildest dreams I could've never predicted what took place and the final outcome."

"Me either, I know exactly what you're saying. I never imagined what actually happened.

"Yesterday afternoon after the meeting with Media Distribution, I was ecstatic. When they offered us $2.5 million, for the North American distribution rights, to all recordings they would produce during the event. I was dancing in tall cotton all night long. Finally, my mind got overwhelmed crunching the numbers and I fell asleep.

"Then today's meeting! I'm not sure I even need to bother getting on an airplane to get home. I'm so high on adrenaline right now I think I could just flap my arms and make it all the way home. Even with my suitcase."

"Yah, I got that feeling myself. I'm actually glad I decided to stay over to meet with some friends this evening and tomorrow. So I have a chance to calm down before I get on my plane and head for home."

"Tommy, you know, when I mentioned the Media Distribution offer in the meeting with IBC, I was just trying to be honest and forthright with them. I really wasn't certain yet where they were headed in the conversation, but I found it interesting when the chief honcho reacted by writing something very brief on his notepad, and double underlining it. I would give almost anything to know if it was a new dollar amount to offer to us. To me it seemed their intent was to get Media Distribution out of the game.

"Later on, I couldn't believe the look on their faces, after you dropped the Sinatra Bomb in answer to their question as to who was going to be the headliner. It was like time stopped, or slowed down so we could watch what was happening in slow motion. I would almost swear I thought I saw Tinkerbell flying around their end of the table making magic dust come out of her wand, when the boss inhaled, folded his arms across his chest and leaned back in his chair as far as it would tilt and said . . ., You remember the words, don't you?

> He said, and I quote, *as I tried to mimic him*:
> -- I think Media Distribution is trying to steal this deal from you. Not that they're bad people or anything. It's just I know Tobias over there, and he's one cheap-ass SOB! So we're prepared to offer you $7 million for the worldwide distribution rights of any and all entertainment performances at the concert. Our offer is subject to our final approval of the headliner, as well as the other performers and their schedules. How does that sound to you gentlemen?

"The look on your face Tommy, at that exact moment, it was priceless. I wish I would've had a Polaroid camera."

"Well JD, you were looking pretty strange at that moment as well. You turned so pale I thought you were about to have a heart attack."

We were both laughing heartily at ourselves at the moment. It felt good. It felt joyous and delightful. It certainly must be what success is supposed to feel like, when success can be measured on such a grand scale.

But the magic moment suddenly ended, and it was back to business when Tommy said, "But let's set the euphoria aside for a moment. We have two offers on the table. What we need to do is just lie still in the tall grass, and wait until we find out what Frank's plan for the other headliner is all about. If it's as big a deal as he has been leading me to believe for the last three weeks, it may be really worthwhile. If we play this right, we might be able to get another million or two out of this deal. You agree?"

"The first thing that comes to mind is an old saying my grandmother used to say to me, a bird in the hand is worth two in the bush. But, I agree, I think you're right. The only question is, can you stall them long enough to find out, without losing the deal."

"Yah, I believe I can."

As we stood at the curb at the airport terminal, I said, "Tommy, I've learned to trust you, without question. Use your best judgment and handle the deal anyway you want. Keep me posted as it progresses.

"Talk to you Monday - give my regards to your lovely wife when you get home. Luv ya, buddy, adios."

"Anche a me! Addio amico mio!" Tommy replied.

CHAPTER 8

Pope John Paul, I Need Your Help

...I don't see how I'm going to find a 50 piece orchestra and ...

Wednesday morning proved to be very busy. We'd received the final artwork for the logo, 18 cassette tapes with possible theme songs, poster artwork, and three ad agency proposals, all needing review. Right after lunch, I hear the magic words on the intercom, JD, Haley's on line five for you. "Haley, how are you and how are we doing?"

"I'm fine JD, but I have bad news. I met with the mayor last night for about half an hour and then again late this morning. Bottom line, the city will not let us have the airport as a venue. They feel there are too many complex issues that need to be addressed and they're stretched really thin just trying to deal with all the related papal activities. They simply don't have the personnel necessary to get involved with our project. They see the same problem for any of the possible city venues. So they asked me to convey their apologies and regrets. JD, I gave it my very best effort. I feel really bad, and I don't know what else to do."

I could hear the deep disappointment in her voice and gently replied, "Haley, don't take it so personally. If it was supposed to be, the Good Lord would've made it happen. Fortunately, we have Folsom Field as a backup, so were gonna just keep on truckin', okay?"

"Okay, JD, thanks, I'll give you a call next week"

I immediately hung up the phone and called CU.

After the call, I had Bill join me, and explained the outcome of the two phone calls.

"So Bill, the University is still willing to let us have the arena. They've agreed to give us a letter of intent to start the ball rolling. However, they want to meet with us next week and requested a treatment with details."

Bill's responded, "Well I guess that means were going to be working Saturday, huh?"

"I don't know how else we're going to get it done. See if you can find two volunteers for Saturday and in the meantime, let's get started. Why don't we make a list of both what we've got and what we need to get the job done . . ."

Interrupted by the intercom announcing, "JD, it's Tommy on line one."

"Tommy, how we doing?"

"I'm fine JD. But we have a problem."

"What's that?"

"I just got off the phone with Sinatra. He wants a 50 piece orchestra behind him. Not 40 pieces, not 49 pieces, it has to be a minimum 50 piece orchestra. Can we handle that?"

"Where in the hell am I supposed to get a 50 piece orchestra, Tommy? You've got to be kidding me! Please tell me you're just making every effort to get my blood pressure up a little bit to see if my head will explode, right?"

"No, JD, I'm as serious as a hit-man with a really big gun! It's a deal-breaker. I tried everything, I tried to sell him on a small band or even a medium-sized one with some added musicians to provide whatever instrumentation he needed, but he remained steadfast. He wants an orchestra, period. So what are we going to do?"

"Tommy, I have no idea at the moment. I've never even thought about trying to find or hire an orchestra before. I need some time to try and figure this out. I also have other news I want to share with you. Bottom line is, our venue's going to be Folsom Field. Stapleton Airport is a dead deal. I'll explain everything to you later, after I call my bookie and make a wager on whether or not I can come up with a 50 piece orchestra. Talk to you later.

● ● ●

"Becky, I need you!" I hollered into the intercom.

My thoughts became chaotic, as I looked at Bill silently, while waiting for Becky to walk through the door. "Becky, get with Jack. Have him help you. I need you guys to get on the phone and find out everything you can for me about the Denver Symphony Orchestra. Most important is the name and phone number of whoever is in charge of the orchestra and what sort of gigs it does. I need some historical backup data so I can formulate a presentation. Tommy just called and Sinatra will not perform unless we get him an orchestra. This is now your number one priority. Got it?"

"Yes, I understand. Jack and I will get right on it." She replied as she turned and left the office.

Bill, taken aback, said, "Well I guess that means we're done?"

"What do you mean? It's just a stumbling block, an obstacle. We have to figure out how to resolve it or get around it."

"JD, over the years, I've always been amazed by some of the things you've done, but there ain't no way you're going to get a 50 piece orchestra. Ain't gonna happen!"

As he stood to leave, I looked up and said, "You may be absolutely right, Bill. But it ain't over, and we're not done, until the fat lady sings. Don't go negative on me. And, more importantly, don't say anything to anyone else out there, and tell Becky and Jack the same thing. Let's play this hand out and see what happens, okay?"

Visibly dejected, he turned in the doorway, and said, "Okay, let's see what happens."

I leaned back in my chair, gazing out the window trying desperately to assemble, in some order, all the thoughts going through my mind. Thankfully, I hadn't yet mentioned Sinatra's name to anyone involved in the Folsom deal. Words began to form in my mind and I heard myself silently say, *Lord, John Paul, it seems I've gotten myself in a bit of a pickle here. I really need your help to find an orchestra. I have to agree with Bill, I don't*

*see how I'm going to find a 50 piece orchestra and pull this off,
please help. Thanks for listening. Amen!*

Hmmm, I thought, *did I just pray to the Pope? He's still
alive! Gee, I wonder, can you do that? Is there some kind of
heavenly communication system that will deliver the message to
him? Oh well, let's see what happens. It's a much larger
conundrum than I have time for right now.*

Strangely, I felt relieved and managed to put the chaos in
my mind aside, and returned to the mountain of work on my desk
when the intercom sounded. "JD, it's Richard Markett. He would
like to talk to you."
"Fine, what line?"
"No, he's standing here in front of my desk."
"Oh, okay, send him in, thanks.

"Richard, nice of you to stop by, how are you? Please have
a seat."
"Good JD, I wanted to stop by and formalize my invite to
you and your wife to come over to our house for dinner. Would
Friday night, say about six, work and would you still like to join
us?"
"Richard, actually I'm honored, yes, of course, my wife
and I will be there. Where do you live?"
"Great! Let me put my address on the back of my business
card and we'll plan on seeing you at six. How's things going?
Well I hope."
"Funny, you should ask. The day was going pretty well
until moments ago, when I was notified that we won't be able to
use Stapleton Airport as our venue, but it looks like we've got
Folsom Field wrapped up. Then I got a call from Tommy just
now, and he informed me that Frank Sinatra won't come unless I
find him a 50 piece orchestra. And of course, I don't even have a
clue on how to hire a 50 piece orchestra. You don't happen to
have one in your back pocket, do you?"

As this giant of a man stood up and chuckled lightly, he
said, "No - I don't carry one of those around with me. Sounds like

a real problem, but I'll make a couple of calls and see if I can help you out. I'll let you know on Friday if I come up with anything."

"Terrific, and thanks Richard, I'd appreciate anything you can do." I said, as he smiled and turned to exit through the doorway.

Moments later the intercom sounded, "JD, it's the GAO on line three."

"Patty, what can I do for you?"

"We really need to meet with you again. Can you come back tomorrow?"

"Man, Patty, I've got a business to run. I can't spend another entire day with you guys. Tell you what, I'll give you three hours tomorrow, from 1 to 4, but that has to be just about it, okay?"

"Okay, JD, we'll try and wrap it up tomorrow. Thank you, see you then – bye."

I had no more than hung up, when Becky's voice came over the intercom again, and said, "JD, it's that Ron from the newswire, you want the call?"

"Got it. Ron, how are you? Well I hope."

"I'm fine, JD. I apologize if I'm interrupting you, but I haven't heard from you in a while and I really need to keep after this story."

"I understand. I'm just slammed. But it should be quiet around here for a little while. I have a meeting soon, but if you want to talk some more, we can give it a whirl for a while."

"That would be great, JD. We left off last time when I asked you - how did the investigation with the Inspector General begin?"

"The answer to that question is complex and convoluted. I'm trying to think of how to answer in summary, without all the details, and still have it make sense.

"Technically Ron, it all started during an upper management staff meeting in Denver when the discussion turned to an examination of an asset management report out of the Irvine,

California office. Bottom line, the statistics involving the number of assets and the related returns were way off the mark. At the conclusion of the meeting our office would send a report to the Regional Director recommending a preliminary investigation. About a week later I was informed that I'd been assigned TDY (Temporary Duty Assignment) to the Irvine office for the next two to possibly three weeks to look around and see if I could determine the cause of the erratic statistics being reported. My cover would be that I was training in procedures and processes in the Irvine asset management department and nothing to do with the Inspector General's office, yet.

"Every Monday I flew to Irvine and returned home each Friday evening. I was assigned to a section chief with a portfolio of assets to manage. As I tended to business each day I began developing a rapport with more and more of my fellow asset managers.

"About two months after the Colorado Springs bank closing incident, while working in Irvine, I got a call from the Regional Director in California, telling me that he had decided to promote my acting boss, Caroline, from GG-10 to GG-15, above my pay grade of GG-14.6, and thereby making her the highest pay grade individual in the office, and therefore, the new permanent Specialist in Charge of the Denver office. But he also told me that after completing my TDY assignment, I would keep my position as Chairman of the Credit Review Committee, which controlled the execution of all delegations of authority from Washington in the Denver office. And of course Caroline constantly reminded me of her disdain for the Regional Director's decision to leave me as the Chairman. It seems she didn't like having a rooster in her henhouse. Later I would learn that it was she who had finally convinced the Regional Director to send me out to California in hopes that my absence would provide her with the justification to step in and replace me as Chairman of CRC.

"Although dejected by the Regional Director's call, I just continued on trying to fulfill my self-derived mission, and do the best job possible. Then during my third week in Irvine, I was invited to join a group of asset managers for drinks after work. My co-workers were unaware I had made arrangements with our waitress to keep me supplied with Perrier and a twist of lime as the evening wore on. After a couple of hours and a huge bar tab later, someone mentioned partnerships buying assets, and then the keywords 'silent partner.' As the conversation continued on, it became evident at least two and probably more of my companions had experience in helping friends and relatives to set up General Partnerships, wherein they could remain completely invisible, as a Secret Silent Partner. The asset manager would then advise the General Partners which asset packages contained the most valuable assets and what the agency's reserve price and appraised price were. Then during the bidding process they would advise the General Partners of the sealed bid prices received prior to bid closing, so they could submit a slightly higher price just before the closing bell.

"After I reported this to the Regional office, my assignment was continued for about another three months, during which time I identified four asset managers who were participating in these types of schemes.

"During my third month, I also learned that I had been relieved as Chairman of CRC.

"Then one afternoon while I was out of the Irvine office on an asset inspection, I received a call from the assistant office manager. He informed me that when he went into my office to retrieve a file I was working on, he noticed a brown manila envelope on my chair marked 'JD Urgent.' Thinking it might be important he opened it, and found one piece of paper, a handwritten note that said, 'You're Dead!' And on the next line, 'We Will KILL You!' He explained that the Justice Department had been notified, and instructed me to contact the agent in charge, who then met with me. He and another agent then took me to an out of state hotel where they kept me for the next four days.

"On the fifth day the agent walked in and said simply, 'We got the guy who left the note. Your boss said to tell you that your assignment in Irvine is completed. You are to return home tonight, and you are off duty for 10 days. Report to work in Denver a week from next Monday. Good luck!' And that was it. I thought.

"Anyway, thinking back Ron, you know, it turns out timing is everything. On the first day I returned to work back in Denver, who should be the first person to drop by to say hello and invite me to lunch?   A former section chief of mine and premier asset manager, Charlie, that's not his real name, I just called him that. With his scruffy curly brown hair, black rimmed glasses, and a quirky smile, he was somewhat of a geek, and an unbelievable math wizard. He could make a spreadsheet dance right before your eyes.

"He looked in the open door to my office, and knocked a couple of times on the doorjamb while saying, 'JD I'm so glad you're back, I've been waiting. I have something really important to talk to you about, but I don't want to talk about it in the office. Can we do lunch?'

"I answered, 'Charlie, good to see you, I was planning to stop by and see everyone later today, and yes, it would be a pleasure to go to lunch with you. Stop by around 12:30 and we'll go.'

"And Ron, that's the moment I became, let's say, sorta, a little bit, pregnant with Archibald. But, at the time, I really had no clue that it might be something important or consequential coming from a former section chief.

"Later, Charlie stopped by at the appointed time and off we went to a small quiet restaurant a couple of blocks away. After exchanging a few pleasantries and the arrival of lunch, Charlie reached down beside his chair, picked up the small briefcase he brought with him, and pulled out a brown paper wrapped package, about four inches thick, and handed it to me.

"As I reached out for it, he let it go in my grasp, and said, 'Finally, this is officially out of my hands!' With a sense of great relief in his voice he continued, 'I finished this almost six weeks ago. I was afraid to turn it over to anyone else in the office. JD, you're the only person I trust to protect me.'

"With the heavy sealed package firmly in both hands, I looked across the table and said, 'Charlie, what in the hell is this?'

"Looking very serious, he replied, 'You have to read it! You must read it.'

"I answered him in serious disbelief, 'Do you want me to open this, and read it here, and now? It'll probably take the rest of the day and possibly all night.'

"He shot back, 'No, absolutely not here, take it home and read it. In fact, I wish you wouldn't take it back into the office. Let's stop in the parking lot on the way back, and put it in your trunk.'

"Looking away from his intense gaze, I set the envelope down on an empty corner of the table, picked up my fork and took a couple of bites, as I tried to figure out what was going on.

"Ron, the silence became foreboding as we both finished more of our meals. Finally, I laid my fork down, leaned back in the chair, and said, 'Charlie, what's going on? Why were you afraid to give this to anyone else? What in God's name, do you need protection from?'

"After a long pause, he answered, 'JD, I uncovered a huge fraud that's been going on for some time and the problem is it goes right inside the Chairman's office in Washington. It seems like there are at least two people in his office involved, and possibly more. I don't know if the Chairman himself is involved or even knows about it. This is so far above my pay grade I am literally scared to death to know about it. You have to promise me you'll never tell anybody where you got this information. You know, I have a wife, a son, and a new baby on the way. I need this job and more importantly, after hearing about the death threats against you in California, I'm just downright scared. So I'm turning everything over to you.

'What you'll find in the envelope are the documents involving my last asset sale where the $70 million high bid was discarded and the asset portfolio sold to the ninth highest bidder out of 14 bidders, for just over $30 million, less than one third its appraised value.

'Once I discovered this, because that portfolio was worth well over $100 million, I started checking a few older asset sales, and found the smoking gun. My sale and the others I looked into were not awarded to the highest bidder. Two different people in the Chairman's office issued sale orders to other lower bidders.

'In seven separate sales I tracked down the companies who were awarded the portfolios even though they weren't the high bidders. I checked the Secretary of State's records on each company. At first I didn't see anything unusual, but upon closer examination, I discovered five of those companies had one name as a director or officer that was the same in each company. Once I saw this, I decided I was done investigating. I tried real hard to just forget about it. Finally I decided I couldn't just forget about it, and eventually decided you are the one and only person I could trust, to turn this over to.'

"Absolutely dumbstruck, I leaned forward and looked Charlie straight in the eye and said, 'Charlie I appreciate your faith and trust in me, and I'm even honored by it. But, if everything you've said is supported by the evidence, I have no way, to guarantee you protection of any kind. I don't have such authority. What I can do, and what I will do is this. If you want me to proceed and read the contents of this envelope, and look at your other evidence, I promise you, I will do the very best I can to keep your name out of this for as long as possible.

"'Hopefully, that means until you or I are under subpoena on a witness stand. Until then, I will keep your identity secret. You, in turn, are going to have to help me dissect all of this, and then write up the final report. You cannot work on this during normal work hours. You have to agree, here and now, to put in whatever time it takes to get this fully documented and neither of us will be able to do it at the office. We will have to do everything off the clock at my house. Do you fully understand everything I'm saying, and do you agree to this bargain?'

"Instantly Charlie responded, 'Yes and yes, I've thought this over extensively and it's the right thing to do.'

"As I extended my hand across the table I said, 'Do you have any questions Charlie?' He nodded negatively, as he shook my hand and I said, 'OK Charlie, you got yourself a deal. Let's head back to the office.'

"And Ron, that's what started me on the journey to the Inspector General's office and my foray with the "IG" began. I was completely committed. I had an absolute duty to take appropriate action. There was just no way for me to walk away from what I had learned, and I had no means or authority to protect Charlie. I had no alternative, I had to step in and take Charlie's place in order to protect him.

"For months and months, Charlie and I would photocopy the documents necessary to support our investigation and take them home. Then, every Tuesday and Thursday night from 7 to 9:30 and every Saturday from 10 AM to 4 PM, we would work at my house pursuing the investigation, until it was completed.

"My problem right now Ron, is that I'm out of time. I have to get to my meeting. So if you want to know how Archibald was actually born, we'll have to talk later."

"I understand. How about next week?"

"Yah, Sounds good – talk to you then."

By the time Bill and I had met with each team, going over every phase of the project in detail the afternoon had turned into early evening. Finally, only Bill and I remained, as TP walked in to say hello. Twenty minutes later, we agreed to have a pizza delivered and go outside to chat and try to relax.

TP and I headed for the convenience store to pick up sodas to go with our pizzas. As we walked out the door, sodas in hand, an old black man approached me, disheveled, his clothing worn and dirty. He smiled and said, very politely, "Excuse me sir, can you spare a quarter? I'm sorry to bother you, but I haven't eaten for some time."

I reached in my pocket and grabbed the first bill that touched my hand, ignoring the pocket full of change, and handed him what turned out to be a $10 bill. His eyes widened in disbelief, as he reached for the money, and with a huge smile, said, "Oh, thank you, sir! Thank you so very, very much!"

Smiling, I said gently, "Don't thank me, thank the **Good Lord**! He's the One looking out for you!"

As we turned the corner, TP said, "Why in the world, did you give him $10, he only asked for a quarter?"

I just love it when I get this question. I replied, "Well, TP, it's because I believe that as he walks around each day panhandling, he's praying silently, 'Oh Lord, please help me find someone to help me out!' Or something like that. Now I also believe, there are few billion people walking around every day saying the same prayer, including me. That makes God a pretty busy fella! So if I get the opportunity to lighten His load by answering the guy's prayer, then that'll give the Good Lord a little extra time to answer someone else's prayer, maybe even mine.

"Think of it this way. He was praying for a quarter, probably hoping for a dollar, a somewhat small request, and if I take care of it, tenfold, then maybe it will free up enough time for God to deal with my really big monsters. So I pray for help with the hope for a tenfold response.

"Maybe I only save God a second. But honestly, it's about the giving, the helping, it makes me feel warm and fuzzy. I just wish I had a pocket full of hundred dollar bills and could have given him one of those. Now that would've been something!"

As we sat out on the front steps munching pizza I terminated the small-talk with the question, "So, TP, how's the T-shirt business doin'?"

"Not good! I'm up against a brick wall, a big one. I can't seem to find a way around it. If I can't get a license, I'm a dead duck, I'm gonna lose everything. I had to make the final payment on the T-shirts, which took my last dollar. I'm totally out of money and out of answers."

Bill inquired, "What in the world are you gonna do with the container load of T-shirts if you can't sell 'em?"

TP answered, "I don't know, I really haven't thought about it. If I don't get my license, I guess, -- I'll have to check around and see what the value might be as scrap rags."

Bill replied, "Well, you could donate them to charity for a tax deduction. That might be more valuable than the scrap value."

Chuckling lightly and sarcastically, TP responded, "How do you spend a tax deduction? I need cash, I have none right now. Thankfully, JD paid for the pizza. I invested everything I had trying to do this deal. I've got my product, a small army of street salespeople lined up and waiting, waiting with me, for just one final stinking piece of paper, a license."

Smiling broadly, Bill replied gently, "Sounds like you need a miracle."

Chuckling again, TP looked over at Bill, and said, "Yah! A miracle - that's what I left out of my business plan - a miracle!"

Trying to be sympathetic, I interjected, "Yah, me too!" Recognizing the question mark now on TP's face, I added, "Sinatra wants a 50 piece orchestra or he ain't comin'. And not only do I not have any idea where to find one, I'm scared to death to even think about how much it would cost to hire one. So I may need a couple of miracles as well."

Bill exclaimed, "Boy, that's for sure! I don't think we have a chance in hell of finding an orchestra, let alone hiring one."

TP answered, "I don't know how to get one either! If it's anything like gettin' a license from the city of Denver, - it's no wonder you seldom ever hear about a miracle. I wonder if there's a form - a request for a miracle form?"

Beginning to laugh at his own remark, TP continued, "Come to think of it, I've never seen a miracle. If I did, I sure didn't know it was a miracle at the time. I mean - maybe I did and I just didn't know it was a miracle. My point I guess, is how do you know what a miracle is; how do you define it? Exactly what is a miracle by definition?"

Bill interposed, "While I was in the Navy, there were a couple of times, things happened, and afterwards, it seemed like it must've been a miracle. But, I can't say for sure. Like you, TP,

I'm not certain I can give you the correct definition of a miracle. To me it seems like something that God did, or that only God could do - that would be my definition of a miracle."

TP thoughtfully replied, "Yah, that sounds like a pretty good description, good enough for me anyway. So what do you think JD?"

"I was afraid this conversation was gonna get around to me," I replied. "I've seen a couple of miracles in my lifetime, especially in 'Nam. But, in concert with both of you, I think it's how you define the word miracle.

What is A Miracle?

"To me, seeing what happened, a miracle, right before your eyes is one thing, like Lazarus rising from the dead. But, then there are the ones that the only thing you see is the result of the Hand of God touching us -- touching something, touching someone. I think it's an expression of God's joy in participating in our lives. But, because he gave us free will -- He only participates if we ask! And only if it's part of His plan, for our tomorrow - our journey through life, to reach Him.

"So, it's not so much filling out a request form. It's the answer to the question -- is the miracle we seek a part of His plan for us and our tomorrow? Is our love for, and belief in Him, strong enough to withstand the impact of his miracles on our lives? Those are the questions, the answers to which result in the response, 'request approved or denied'.

"Too many times, we all, everyone, asks for a miracle. When in fact it's nothing more than a request for help to pound a square peg into a round hole, which I think – well, is akin to filling out the wrong form at the local government office.

"To me, I think a miracle is defined by the person or persons witnessing or affected by the event. It's what they comprehend and/or perceive to have happened.

"I think there are two reasons for God creating a miracle. One being, something that was necessary to take place to allow God's plan for us to continue. The other being God's way of smacking us upside the head with a 2 x 4 to remind us that the actions of one or more persons can either enhance or destroy the lives and dreams of many. So we have to be reminded every now and again to use our free will judiciously."

Bill inquired, "What did you mean about God reminding us? I don't ever remember gettin' hit upside the head, especially with a 2 x 4."

TP joined in, "Yah, what did you mean?"

After a few moments of silence, I responded, "Well, I can't think of a good metaphor, so let me try to give you an example. Today, I believe the creation of the United States of America was a miracle. Years ago, when I was just learning about it, and later, intrigued, and studying more closely its creation, I never perceived its creation as a miracle. It wasn't until I was old enough, and had experienced our government from both inside and out, had watched closely how it functioned, was I finally able to correlate all the data, and come to the conclusion that it was truly a miracle.

"When you look back at the country's founders, so many individuals coming together and accomplishing so much, for so many. Two hundred years later, we still benefit from their actions. Never before in the history of the world, and probably never again, will so few do so much, for so many, as did our forefathers. I think they knew, and believed, that what they had done was a miracle. And I think I can prove it." I reached into my pocket and pulled out a quarter, saying, "They gave us a permanent reminder, and their perpetual thanks to their Maker, of the miracle, by stamping it, and engraving it on almost everything that would last in perpetuity and be seen by all, the words, "In God We Trust." It was their mantra, and they became united in their efforts to create a place where mankind could enjoy and exercise God's two greatest gifts to each and every person ever born: life, and free-will, in peace and harmony.   God looked down and smiled at their undertaking, and miraculously guided them through to completion.

"Now you both may totally disagree with me, but that's the beauty of sitting here on these steps in the USofA. You have the free will, the God-given right, and now the Constitutional right, to not only disagree with me, but to express that disagreement verbally without retribution. And that's the best way I can come up with an explanation and define miracles and one of the greatest miracles - freedom.

"I didn't join the Navy and the Army because I was bored, or thought of it as an adventure.   I didn't join up because a congressman or the president called me and asked me to join. I did so because I had concluded that the evil of socialism - communism must be stopped.   It was and is a deadly threat to our freedom and the country, our country, where the miracle of freedom lives and reigns.   I believed in my heart, after comparing our country to every other country, and the freedom available elsewhere, that the USA was a miraculous gift of God to me personally.   And if it needed to be protected, I would, and still will, follow in the footsteps of my forefathers and fight.   And if necessary, die to protect it, at all costs and without reservation.   And if you really want to know what I was thinking, as I started melting down the barrels on my twin 50's in a firefight, **that** was what I was thinking about. I had to protect God's great gift to me – to us, -- no matter what, for the benefit of everyone.

"And with that, gentlemen, let's call it a night. What da-ya say?"

CHAPTER 9

Life: can be - Just Crazy sometimes!

*...working for the Inspectors General's Office undercover, with the
codename Archibald ...
Maybe it does pay to pray*

For a Monday morning, still swimming in the success of the California trip, I felt really good about our progress and where we were at the moment. As I began to sift through all the work piled up on my desk, Becky's voice came over the intercom. "JD, it's Ron from UPI, you want to take the call?"

"Got it. Ron, how are you?"
"I'm fine, JD.
"You were going to tell me when and how you ended up working for the Inspectors General's Office undercover, with the codename Archibald. How did that come about?"

"Well Ron, it started the night I took Charlie's package home. I spent the night reading his report, and the next several weeks collecting documentation to support the report. He had definitely found the smoking gun.

"Charlie's package meticulously laid out and documented, from front to back, asset sales transactions evidencing millions of dollars of assets being sold for pennies on the dollar to buyers with agency employees hidden in their corporate structure. The sales were then approved by senior officials working in the Chairman's office.

"Now the question was what was I supposed to do with it? For the next several weeks I remained perplexed and troubled as I tried to formulate a plan of action. Finally, I recalled having met a lady named Mary Durrant at an FDIC function out in California who actually was on the Board of Directors of the agency. She was a really nice lady. At first I was concerned about compromising her in this deal, but then I concluded that I didn't know anyone else to speak with. So I picked up the phone and gave her a call.

"I explained the situation to her in hypotheticals, without ever presenting the actual facts to her. I didn't want to put her in the same position I was in. And with the smoking gun pointed directly at the chairman's office I didn't want to set off any alarm bells. For several days, we spoke on and off again as she tried to guide me in determining the appropriate actions for me to take. In my last conversation with her, she explained she'd met unofficially with Jack Bowman, a Deputy Director at the IG's office, and alluded to my situation. He instructed her to have me call him directly and have no further contact with her.

"I hadn't been able to figure out any other course of action, so I called him. Once I had informed him of the extent of the information and evidence I had my possession, he told me to speak with no one else but him, within the agency. I was never again to use my real name in any communications with his office or with anything to do with what he was now calling an open IG investigation. From that moment on, my name was Archibald, a name he just pulled out of the air in midsentence, as he gave me instructions on how to proceed. That was the moment Archibald was born, and for the next six or seven months, I reported to Jack on an almost daily basis. I never disclosed Charlie's identity to him or anyone else.

The intercom barked, "JD, it's Tommy. I've got him on hold on line five. It's the third time he's called and he asked me to interrupt you. He says it's very important."

"Okay, tell him I'll be right with him. Ron, I have to take this call. I'm gonna put you on hold for a minute.

"OK, I'll hold." He replied.

"Tommy, how are you?"

"JD, Sinatra's waiting for me to call him back with your approval of the co-headliner. Sorry to interrupt you, do you have a moment?"

"Absolutely Tommy, go ahead."

"I have incredible news! Are you sitting down?"

"Actually, yes I am.

"You ain't gonna believe this - no, actually, you gotta believe it. I need you to approve - Michael Jackson as the co-headliner with Sinatra. What do you think of that pile of jelly beans!?"

Trying desperately to inhale again, I retorted, "Are you shittin' me? THE Michael Jackson, are you serious?

"I am JD, I'm serious as a man standing in the rain with no clothes on! I got off the phone with Sinatra about half an hour ago, and I have to call him back and let him know your answer. There is a caveat to the deal, Jackson wants Whitney Houston and Bill Strosby as part of his act, and on the billing. I told Sinatra that shouldn't be a problem. Please tell me I have your approval to proceed."

"Of course, you have my approval. And Tommy, I would've backed you up, even if you'd already approved the deal. Congratulations on a job well done, way to go guy!"

"Thanks for them nice words JD, but, gotta go, I gotta call Frank back – bye."

Suddenly, I realized that the blinking light I was staring at on the phone was my call with Ron that I had put on hold. It was like I was in some kind of stupor from having my mind explode into a million little pieces. Finally, I stammered, "Ron, you still there? I'm so sorry I left you on hold so long, where were we?

"Oh yah, I remember. It wasn't until Charlie and I finished the final report that I told Charlie about the existence of Archibald.

"It was quite a time. I'd spend each day doing my regular job, and then I spent half the night working on Archibald. I did everything Jack asked me to do. I did it exactly as he instructed, with no idea whatsoever as to what was happening in Washington.

● ● ●

"For the next 6-8 months I worked feverishly on the job, and on Archibald. I thought all the while that I was doing a good job and helping out the agency. Then one morning, a couple of months after I'd submitted the final Archibald report, the boss lady walked into my office with an assistant carrying an empty cardboard box, with two uniformed Denver police officers in tow. Smiling broadly, she announced, "Put your personal belongings in the cardboard box. You're fired, Mister Archibald. These police officers will escort you to the door."

"It was an unbelievable experience, being escorted through the office, cardboard box and briefcase in hand, by two armed uniformed cops. I could hardly believe it - what an exit! But it was her words, 'Mister Archibald' that echoed over and over in my head as I stepped out of the elevator and exited the building.

"Ron, can you hold a moment?"

"Of course."

"Yes Becky, what is it?" I asked, as she stood in front of my desk with an outstretched hand full of call message slips.

"I've got eight messages for you, and some of them are very important. You've got to start returning calls soon, because you've got that appointment with the GAO after lunch. You have to leave, like really soon!

"Yes, I understand. Let me have the messages and I'll get after them shortly. Thanks.

"Ron, you there?"

"Yah. I'm still here."

"Good. Ron, I've run out of time. I have to get back to work, I'll call you. Let's talk next week. Call me Tuesday if you don't hear from me before."

Ron's tone of voice suddenly changed to doubt as he was saying, "I understand. But, we have to move this along more quickly."

"I know, but I'm doing the best I can for you right now."

His voice still overlaid with doubt, replied, "From the tone of your voice, I'm concerned your return call might not be a very high priority. So let me ask you one last question. Do you know who exposed your identity as Archibald to your superiors?"

"No, I don't and the GAO claims they don't know either. It really bothers me, and I wish I knew who did."

"Well I know who did it and you'll be very surprised. I'll explain everything when you call me back. Okay?"

"Really, you got my attention now Ron. I will call you back. Talk to you later - bye for now."

His last comment really made me stop in my tracks. *If he knows who leaked my cover so they could fire me, why doesn't the GAO? I better ask again this afternoon and see if they have found out for themselves.*

Pressing the intercom button, I said, "Bill, can you step into my office for a minute, please.

"Close the door and pull up a chair, we need to talk for a minute.

"What I'm about to tell you has got to remain just between us until after we sign the letter of intent for Folsom field. This news just can't leak out. You can't tell a soul. Tommy's in the process of finalizing a deal for Michael Jackson to be the co-headliner with Frank Sinatra for our concert. I'm very concerned that if this news leaks out, it may scare CU to death because of the potential crowds, and they may refuse to let us have the venue. Or, on the other hand, they may look at it as a cash bonanza and make the venue so expensive, we can't afford it."

I'd known Bill for nearly 20 years. We'd spent a great deal of time together over the years, but I'd never seen him at a loss for words or so completely shaken. As the silence continued, I was beginning to wonder if maybe he was having a heart attack.

Then suddenly, he replied, "I don't know what to say. I know what I heard, you said Michael Jackson, right? Don't answer! Give me a second to try and find some words. I'm absolutely blown away, and I will keep it to myself, but I really need some time before I try to talk to you about this. Let's talk later, after you get back from your meeting this afternoon."

As he stood up to leave, I was happy he was not having a heart attack, and, trying not to grin like a Cheshire cat, I replied nonchalantly, "Works for me. Will you make sure that the draft for the letter of intent is completed while I'm gone this afternoon, and please send Jack in - I need to talk with him." Nodding affirmatively, he turned and left.

"Jack, how are you guys doing with the symphony project?"
"So far, it's not going too well. The people who answer the phones down there seem to know very little about the management of the symphony. And it seems every time we get a name of someone to talk to, they aren't there. They're either on vacation or they only work on Mondays and Tuesdays or only on Thursday, or some such thing. But, don't worry about it yet, we're on it. We'll get it done."

"Okay, keep after it Jack, we gotta get this handled, thanks."

 Off to GAO, Again

Fortunately, Becky threw me out of the office in time to make my meeting with Patty and her gang on time. Thinking, as I maneuvered through lunch hour traffic, the only good thing is, Patty has some real talent on her team. So there is hope she will succeed with the investigation. But today is the day, I have to confront her and find out exactly where I stand in all this; it's been over a year. Let's see what she has to say.

"Patty, we've been at this for over five hours nonstop. It's after six, and I need to go home. We really need to stop here. And I've got a couple of questions and concerns that I would like to go over with you personally."
Double checking her watch, she replied, "Yah, you're right JD, let's call it quits. Okay everyone, let's wrap it up and call it a

night. Let's just leave everything where it is and we'll start fresh in the morning. Come on JD, let's go to my office to visit.

"Have a seat. What's on your mind?"

"My first question, Patty, is - have you determined who compromised my undercover identity yet?"

"No - we haven't figured that out yet. But, it's possible we may find out during our investigation of the Denver office."

"Patty, I don't think you'll find the source in the Denver office. I'm certain it came from Washington, and I believe from the IG's office. Will you be investigating the Washington DC office?"

"That's under consideration, but it depends upon what we find in the Denver office. Are you prepared to divulge the identity of the person, or persons, who helped you with Archibald yet?"

"We've addressed that a number times in the past, Patty, and I just can't do it. But, I will check with him again next week, and see if he's willing to talk to you. That's all I can do.

"Now I want to talk about my chief concern based on my last conversation with the IG's office. From the moment the IG's office called and asked me to become Archibald and work undercover to follow through on my findings in my initial report, I did each and every thing that they asked, and followed their instructions to the letter. Granted, they didn't know, and I didn't know, that in the end Archibald would end up inside the Chairman of the Board's office in Washington.

"When my undercover identity was compromised and I was fired, the IG's office asked me to stay in the game and fight the termination. So I did. I went to court in Washington DC and won my job back. As you know, the court found that I was wrongfully terminated, but it cost me $140,000 in legal fees, which they told me that they cannot reimburse me for. Then during the second week after I returned to work, they called and informed me that they had become aware of a plan by the California Regional Director to get rid of me once and for all.

"They said the plan called for a special supervisor to be sent from California to Denver for the express purpose of making sure that I was terminated again.   This time, with sufficient documentation to ensure that I could not overcome the termination. But, the good news was that the plan called for terminating me in such a way as to prevent my access to the courts in Washington, leaving my only recourse to receive an administrative hearing in Denver, which they will be able to control and orchestrate. So all I had to do was go through the process, and once the administrative hearing officer ruled against me, then the IG's office could arrange to have that ruling overturned internally in Washington.

"So far, everything they said has come to pass, and even though it's cost another $30,000 in attorney fees, I'm still hanging in there. The administrative hearing is scheduled for the first week in September and the question my attorneys have asked me to address with you is - would you be willing to be a witness on my behalf, and testify regarding my work with you and your findings. Will you do that for me, Patty?"

"What I can and will do for you JD, is take your request up my chain of command. But honestly, I don't think there's any chance it can happen. And, I want to be the one to explain to you why.

"We have spent thousands of man-hours following through on your investigation and before we're done, we will have to spend thousands more. This investigation has become just huge. I can't give you any details, but just in the Denver office, we will be conducting a formidable and thorough investigation of every aspect of the operations in that office, and based on our findings, we may be doing the same in other offices. Our investigation will be nowhere near complete by September. If I were to be on a witness stand, subject to examination by the very agency officials we're investigating, there is simply too great a risk that I could be asked for details regarding this investigation, and end up jeopardizing, or possibly destroying all our work. There is just too much risk that if it became known what we were looking for, it would get buried so deep, we'd never be able to find it. I would like nothing more than to be able to help you for what you've done.   It truly is a great service you have provided to your government, but there is no way for the GAO to step in and help you out. Our agency simply does not have the authority or the capability to help or protect you. All I can do is thank you so very much for your service and what you've done."

"Well Patty, that's not exactly what I was hoping to hear. I thank you for being open and honest with me, and I do appreciate your thanks for what I've done. It's the only thanks I've ever received. But, it doesn't help me out. I feel like I'm a lamb being led to slaughter. I truly believe someone in the IG's office compromised my identity. So I'm not sure I fully trust them. Consequently, you leave me no choice. I have to try and protect myself. So when you talk to your chain of command, let them know that if I'm forced to - I will go public with the Archibald story, because you are leaving me with no other alternative. And with that, I'll say good night and hope you can get your chain of command to pony up to the bar, and step in."

"All right, I'll pass your message along. But JD, think very carefully before you take any action that you can't undo. Good night."

Friday Night has arrived!

"**M**y, my, don't you look just drop-dead gorgeous!" I said to the beautiful lady, my lovely wife, as she walked into the living room.

"Oh, stop that. Do you have the wine?" she replied, smiling.

"Yah, you ready to go?" Adding, "Good - let's rock 'n roll," as she nodded in the affirmative.

As we headed over to the Markett's for dinner, I was feeling some excitement building up and was beginning to enjoy the thrill of the moment. After the introductions, Richard opened the wine we brought and we spent about 15 minutes chatting in the living room, until Michelle, Richard's wife, returned from the kitchen, announcing that dinner was ready.

Dinner was terrific. And throughout the meal, Richard told us interesting snippets and stories and about movie and TV roles he had played in over the years. While Michelle told us what it was like being married to a recognized actor, some of the good parts and some of the bad parts. It was really quite interesting and we both enjoyed their stories.

Once dinner was concluded, Richard said, "JD, why don't we go back to my office and let the gals chat for a while."

"Okay," I replied, as we rose and headed toward the back of the house.

Pointing to one of the two chairs adjacent to a small table, Richard said, "Have a seat. Make yourself comfortable. I know you don't drink, but I'm going to have a little brandy, and if you'd like, I'll pour you a snifter. It'll go great with one of these." And he picked up two aluminum tubes sitting in the center of his desk, extending one in my direction.

As I reached for the tube I said, "What the hell, go ahead. I'll try the brandy, but only give me half of what you're having."

As he poured the drinks, I began to unscrew the top of the unmarked aluminum tube in my hand, smelling the aroma of a fine cigar. As I tilted the tube to allow the cigar to fall into my other hand, I saw the little paper band near the top. I positioned it so I could read the inscription on the band, 'Hand - Rolled – Cuban – Extraordinaire.' "Oh Wow! A Cuban and it's fresh! Man, I haven't had one of these since I was down in the Cayman Islands back in '73. What an incredible gift, thank you, Richard. But I just gotta ask, how in the world did you get this to Denver, Colorado?"

Smiling slyly, he replied, "Diplomatic passport, which I'll explain in a moment, and you're welcome. And here's a cutter to open it properly," as he handed me a cutting tool with a glass of brandy in his other hand. "Go ahead and light up," he added, as I took the brandy snifter from his extended hand.

As he sat down, I said, "You mean light it up in here? That's one thing I'm not allowed to do. My wife would kill me if I lit up a cigar in the house."

"Go ahead, Michelle actually likes the smell of cigar smoke, so we're fine."

As I lifted my snifter in his direction and tilted it, I exclaimed, "This is such a treat, and here's to you and your lovely wife, and may you both live happily ever after."

After we both sipped our brandy, I had to add, "I am in no way a judge or connoisseur of brandy, but I have to say, this stuff must be what people mean when they say, 'the nectar of the gods,' this brandy is golden! I'm glad I decided to try it."

"Good - it's actually very old and very special.

"And, I appreciate your toast. But, I actually invited you here tonight to meet with me in private, and without interruption, so I could tell you some things that you need to know, and which must remain confidential between you and me. Will you keep our conversation this evening confidential and use your discretion even in what you may say to your wife?"

"Yes, of course. Anything we talk about tonight will just remain between you and me." My brain suddenly switched gears and went to full alert. What in the world is this all about?

"Well first, let me ask, have you resolved your orchestra issue?"

"No, I haven't. I'm actually quite concerned; it may be a hurdle I can't overcome."

"Good! That means I have one more gift for you."

Richard stood up, walked over to his desk, and picked up a business card. Turning, he handed it to me, and said, "Here you go, I've taken care of the problem."

As I took the card, I replied, "I don't get it, it's your business card. You already gave me one."

Smiling broadly, and with a slight chuckle, he responded, "The other side. It's the 50 piece orchestra you're trying to find. I took care of it for you. Call that number Monday and speak to the gentleman named on the card to formalize the arrangements. He's expecting your call. I spoke to him earlier this week and met with him today. They're actually very excited about your project, and will make sure that the instrumentation meets Mister Sinatra's requirements. The best part, of course, is that they will perform free of charge. All they want is credits for the orchestra to be included in any billing or media materials and announcements. Problem solved."

"Holy smokes! Richard, I don't even know what to say. This is beyond incredible. How in the world did you do this? My people couldn't even find this name, let alone the phone number."

Leaning back fully in his chair and smiling, he answered, "Let's just say I know some people, the right people in the right places. I made a couple of calls and took care of it. Like I said, it's a done deal. You don't have to sell 'em, just listen and let them guide you through the process to set this up."

"Richard, I'm speechless! I really don't know what to say, this is so incredible - thank you, thank you so very much."

Suddenly I heard a large bell ring in my mind, followed by the thought, my prayer was answered. Maybe it does pay to pray to the Pope, even if he is still alive!? I'll have to give that more thought later.

"I'm glad I could help, because what I'm about to tell you, I don't want you to take the wrong way. I like you, and I'm impressed by what you're trying to do, but I haven't been honest or forthright with you until now. I finally received permission to have this meeting with you.

"You see, for years, I've worked for a government agency that takes care of international affairs for our country, since shortly after I got into the acting business. My extensive travels as an actor made me a perfect asset for the agency, and sometimes I even travel under a diplomatic passport, which comes with a few perks, like these cigars.

"Anyway, I was assigned TDY, to the NSA (National Security Agency) to help with security for the pope's visit. His Secret Service code name, by the way, is Halo. And when your name and your concert popped up on the radar I got called in to help assess the situation. Because of your interest in the entertainment industry, your past activities in Hollywood working on the Dukes of Hazard production set, trying to get into SAG (Screen Actors Guild) while you were an extra in those Perry Mason shows, your undercover work with the FDIC, and now your efforts to produce and promote this concert, you got everybody's attention. It was decided that I was the perfect person to try and get close enough to you to complete a risk assessment, and ascertain whether or not you posed any threat to Halo or his visit. It is the government's most important priority right now, which is why I showed up at your office the first time and began building a friendship with you. That's why my wife and I moved to Denver and rented this house for a while.

"Let me continue, before you draw any conclusions to what I'm saying. Under normal circumstances, we would have never had this discussion. You would've never known that I was involved with the government. The reason I'm making these disclosures is because we were concerned you might find out what we were doing on your own. And when we found out the UPI newswire service was looking for you, we became very concerned about the possible outcomes. I convinced my superiors that I could trust you to keep this meeting confidential. We felt it was paramount to protect the GAO investigation, and our activities regarding Halo's visit, in any conversations you may have with UPI. I'm not, we're not, telling you or asking you not to talk to UPI. You just have to wait until the GAO investigation is completed, and, of course, honor your confidentiality agreement. What we're saying is our investigation has determined that you pose no threat to Halo or his visit. In fact we're all kind of rooting for you and hope you pull off the concert. But you need to continue to protect the GAO investigation. I truly hope my trust in you has not been misplaced."

I sat there in shock and disbelief of what had just been said. I was having great difficulty trying to formulate a response, as the silence in the room continued to get louder.

Finally, still not certain of exactly what I wanted to say, I asked, "Are my phones tapped?"

"No, they're not tapped, but the NSA has authority to monitor all phone lines involved in overseas calls as necessary to insure the safety and protection of Halo.   And you, and your company, are talking to entertainers from all over the world every day.   So your calls are monitored, but they're not tapped."

Still not certain of what I wanted to say, I replied, "Boy, I'd sure like to see the details of that fine line of distinction."   And then added, "Is there anything you don't know about me, or what I do every day?"

"Not really, not since you received that first overseas phone call," he casually replied.

My mind was completely consumed by the echoes of the meeting as I drove home.   Should I mention anything about the meeting?   Will it cause her to worry or scare her to death?   Then suddenly I heard, "What is that terrible smell?"

My train of thought was shattered as the silence was broken.   I had to chuckle, knowing full well the answer to the question, and replied, as I pulled the remaining half of the cigar from my inside coat pocket, "Lookie there.   Richard gave it to me. It's a real honest-to-goodness Cuban cigar."

As we pulled into the driveway, she retorted, "Don't you dare bring that nasty thing into the house.   It stinks!"

CHAPTER 10

Reaching For The Stars

Got A Couple!

*... a grand finale with Michael, Frank, Whitney and Bill
performing the closing song.*

"Tommy, how's it going this early on a beautiful Monday morning?" I queried, as he answered the phone.

"Good, JD! I've got some great news!"

I interjected, "Me too. Friday afternoon I picked up the contract for the venue. Becky's faxing it over to you now."

"Go pull the contract off your fax machine and we'll go over it."

"Okay, hold on a minute."

"Oh, this is terrific, JD. Do you mind if I ask what that set us back?"

"No, not at all. Actually, I'm only out-of-pocket $10, so far."

"Are you serious? You only paid $10 and you have a signed contract?"

"Yep! Pretty cool, huh? Based on the agreement, I think we will end up spending about $500,000 for the venue.

"This is good news JD. I'm really relieved we finally have it in black and white. I'll fax it over to IBC shortly.

LETTER OF AGREEMENT

This agreement, made and entered into this 21st day of June, 1993 at Boulder Colorado, by and between CU Program Council and Entertainment International Inc. is to serve as a confirmation of The Children of the World Concert in Folsom Field on August 15, 1993.

It is to be understood that until a formal contract is approved through our Contract and Buying department, this agreement will serve to commit the University of Colorado Program Council and the Entertainment International Inc. to an agreement of good faith that The Children of the World Concert will occur in Folsom Field on August 15, 1993.

Whereas; Entertainment International Inc., Hereinafter referred to as EII, desires to lease the facility known as "Folsom Field" for a musical television production called, "Children of The World A Tribute to Pope John Paul II" on August 15, 1993, from 3:00pm until 10:30pm, and further:

Whereas: The University of Colorado, Program Council, hereinafter referred to as CUPC, has or can obtain the rights to lease the aforementioned facility and desires to do so in accordance with the terms and conditions set forth herein.

Now therefore; It is mutually agreed by and between the parties, to exercise their best efforts to execute a lease of the aforementioned facility to EII in acordance with the following:

1. CUPC shall convey a right to tenancy to EII, upon satisfactory resolution of all support concerns.

2. All rights as to facility access on August 15, 1993 shall be mutually agreed upon, with final approval from EII. This is to include the right to ban all photography and audio equipment of any kind without the advance specific written authority of EII.

3. All Press and Media access shall be mutually agreed upon, with final approval from EII.

4. EII shall have exclusive rights to control all negotioations, bidding and contracting for World Wide and National Broadcast and/or re-broadcast via any media form.

5. Any filming, television production and/or audio recording to take place at Folsom Field on the date at issue and approved in writing by EII shall remain the sole and exclusive property of EII, after all commitments to the University have been met.

6. The University of Colorado and its affiliates agree not to permit any broadcast from Folsom Field via any media for 72 hours prior to August 15, 1993 and 24 hours after the show closes.

Furthermore:

1. EII, hereby guarantees CUPC, that payments for expences including, rent and staffing will be received prior to August 5, 1993. An additional $1.00 service charge, per ticket, will be provided for the Athletic department on the day of show.

1. Eli, hereby guarantees CUPC, that within 72 hours of completion of the production, payment, over and above the lease parameters for fees, in the amount of $100,000 or 1% of the gross proceeds, whichever is greater.

2. Eli hereby guarantees $200,000 or 15% of the gross proceeds, whichever is greater, shall be paid over to charity, with the first $200,000 ear-marked for the benefit of St. Pius X Catholic Church Family Center Building Fund.

3. Eli, hereby guarentees CUPC, that payments for the cancellation of the Colorado Snakespear Festival's performance will be received prior to July 2, 1993, in the amount of $23, 000.

4. The term of this agreement shall be binding upon both parties in conjuction with said facility lease, once executed, and shall no longer be binding after 5:00pm MST, July 2, 1993 in the event Eli shall fail prior thereto, to execute said lease.

5. In consideration of this agreement Eli hereby conveys and CUPC hereby receipts the payment of $10.00 and other considerations.

6. A faxed signature and an original signature shall bind the two parties to this agreement.

Wherefore the parties in mutual agreement hereby and hereon affix their hand and seals by and through their respective authorized representatives on this _2/_ day of June, 1993.

Executed this 18th day of June, 1993

CU PROGRAM COUNCIL

BY _____

DATE _6/21/93_

BOSS CORPORATION

BY _____

DATE _6/21/93_

"Saturday I got everything worked out with Bill and Whitney's agents. They have agreed to perform with Michael. Michael and his agent are on board and Sinatra was thrilled. Everybody in both camps is working on a plan for both Jackson and Sinatra to be on stage at the same time. They'll do a couple of songs together. Conceptually, each of them will do their own individual sets. At the conclusion, we have a grand finale with Michael, Frank, Whitney and Bill performing the closing song. Planning is underway, and I'll keep you posted.

"Everyone is in agreement that the show date has to be Friday, August 13, with Michael's show beginning at 8 PM."

I replied, "That should work. We were anticipating Friday or Saturday, and since we have no clue yet as to what the Pope's agenda is for Saturday, I think Friday night is the correct call. Can we etch it in stone and call it a done deal?"

Tommy answered, "Yah, let's do it. I can make that happen. August 13, it's Done!

"I also spoke with the Dawsons. They're pleased with our progress and are ready to pull the trigger anytime."

"Good grief, Tommy, I can't get over the fact that this thing's coming together. I'm relieved you've spoken with the Dawsons, and they're still with us. I know we still have a lot of details to work out, but the fact that we have a date set is such incredible news."

"Well, if you think that's good news, wait 'til you hear what's next. This morning, just before I called you, I had hung up from renegotiating our deal with International Broadcasting. I felt that adding Michael Jackson's name to the playbill had definitely increased the value of the deal and the price of poker should go up. Once they have all the paperwork drawn up, they'll fax it over to you sometime tomorrow, and here's what you're going to read in the new deal. We are responsible for all local promotional and venue costs. That's it, but it has to be a free gate. They want to make sure the stadium's full to overflowing.

"IBC will be responsible for all promotional costs outside the Denver Metroplex, and any and all expenses related to the recording of the event, and they retain all rights to the recordings and distribution on any media worldwide. They also retain all rights to any sponsorships and advertising revenues. For which, get this, I hope you're sittin' down, we receive 20 million buckaroos! Can you believe it? It's so much more than I ever imagined we might get when we first met, after hearing Paula. You remember?"

I exclaimed, "WOW! Unbelievable! Tommy, you're amazing! I would've never had the hutzpah to ask for that kind of money. Man, some quick math tells me if we spend $2 million for the venue and expenses, that means we're splittin' $18 million three ways. That's $6 million apiece, you, me and the Dawsons. Incredible! Man oh man, who'd-a-thought!"

"It is incredible JD!   One more thing, IBC set a "Drop Dead Date," August 4.   Everything has to be completed, signed, and agreed upon by that date period.

"Listen, I got a lot to do to follow up. So let's talk later!"

I jumped in and said, "Wait, one last thing, I still want to let Paula open for the headliners. That's not a problem is it?"

"No, I don't think so, but I'll check into it. And you're going to have to give some thought as to how long she's going to play, if you're going to open the stadium at 4 PM.   My recommendation is you have her sing the last three songs, with the orchestra, just before the curtain opens for Jackson.   She can handle that even with her lack of big-time experience. I just don't want to be any further involved in production management. You take care of that part, talk to you later – bye."

I sat in silence, staring out the window at absolutely nothing, trying to process the conversation that had just taken place. I can't even say for certain that I was still firmly grounded on this planet. I was having a terrible time trying to wrap my brain around what had just been said. In my wildest dreams, I had really never envisioned the magnitude of what I found myself standing in the middle of. Could this really be happening, and when time played the story out, would everything work out as planned? It just seemed too easy. Throughout my life, I always had to work so hard for every achievement, large or small, for every little success, and for every step forward. How could this be? No huge battles, no swordfights with anyone, or everyone, and no casualties lying on the battlefield. Can this be happening - have I really reached the stars?

My thoughts vaporized as I heard Bill's voice say, "JD, everybody's ready for the staff meeting. It's time."

To say the staff meeting was pure bedlam would be an understatement.   After announcing the news, it took a full 20 minutes to return to order. Everyone was thrilled with the developments. Everything was very upbeat and positive until Jack took center stage and said, "I see a bit of a problem boss. If our 50,000 fans are camped out in their sleeping bags in the parking garages downtown, how in the hell will they get to Folsom Field to see the show?"

The silence was deafening, as everyone looked around the table at each other, dumbstruck. Then the chatter between individuals began to crescendo. I finally recognized that the only solution to this situation would be found within the Regional Transportation District (RTD), the public agency responsible for providing public bus transportation services throughout the metroplex. So I raised my voice and said, "Okay, everybody, I got it. I'll take care of it.

"In the meantime, Jack, being the bright fellow you are, I want you to grab a notepad, talk to everyone individually, and make notes about their ideas. I'll get hold of somebody I know who probably has just the answer we need. Then we'll reconvene, examine everyone's individual ideas, strategic options, and make a determination on how to proceed to resolve the situation. Meeting adjourned!"

It was time to call in the General! James Hall, General, USAF, Retired, Jim was one of my closest and dearest friends. I once told him I had officially adopted him as my second father, because no matter the problem, he always responded and helped me out as best he could whenever I asked. Starting out as a noncom during World War II, he became one of the forefathers of parachuting and eventually an Air Force General. He starred in a TV series in the mid-50s about parachuting called Ripcord. He was a formidable driving force in the political arena, helping many pursuing an elected office. We worked together on various political projects over the years. Consequently, he was highly regarded and respected throughout the political community in Denver.

So I picked up the phone, and when he answered began, "Jim, my friend, I have a problem. Have you got a minute?"

"Of course JD, what's up?" He replied.

After delivering a full explanation of our transportation quandary and the possible implications and impact it might have on the concert, he responded, "Sounds like we need to have lunch with John Martinez again. I don't know if you remember, but we had lunch with him about three years ago when he decided to run for the RTD board and you ended up contributing to his campaign."

"Vaguely Jim, there've been so many over the years, I lose track. But, if he's our guy -let's do it."

"Let me make the call, and I'll get back to you."
"You got it, my friend. I'll be standing by."

Jim called me back a short time later and told me John didn't have time for lunch, but would meet with us at 1:30 PM at his office. It was evident during the meeting that Jim had been instrumental in getting John elected to the RTD board. He was extremely helpful and went out of his way to accommodate us and our situation. The following day he faxed over a complete plan to provide bus transportation to and from downtown to the concert beginning at 4 PM and running continuously until the venue was empty. It turned out that because it involved the papal visit the rates we would be charged were unbelievably inexpensive.

Another problem solved, this time thanks to the General.

Two weeks later ...

CHAPTER 11

Crises Abound...

...JD, we have a problem I don't think we can overcome...

"Ron, your timing is impeccable.   I was thinking about you earlier this week and was planning to give you a call.   How you doin'?"

"Fine, JD. The reason I'm calling is to see if you have time to talk further about Archibald?"

"Yah, right now is as good a time as any. However, I can't talk right now in the office. There are too many people around, and too much going on. I need to go somewhere quiet and call you back. Are you at your office number?"

"Yes, I am."

"Okay, give me 10 minutes, and I'll call you back – later, bye.

"Becky, I'm gonna run over to the convenience store. I'll be back in little bit."

Walking around the corner on my way to the store I started fuming. I was going to have to stand out in the hot sun, talking on a pay phone hanging on the wall, because the government had its nose so far up my butt I could no longer talk freely on my own phones. I began to feel trepidation as I weighed all the factors surrounding my involvement with the newswire. On the one hand, I knew the government was going to hang me out to dry. On the other hand, it seemed like the newswire interest was a gift. If timed right, it might be just the weapon I needed to win this battle with the feds. But, in the back of my mind were the echoes of sage advice I'd given to others, on occasion in the past. You can sword

● ● ●

fight with the State, you can sword fight with the City, and there's a possibility you might win the battle. But, never sword fight with the feds. The US government, your adversary, has an unlimited checkbook and no accountability for their actions whatsoever, so don't even bother, just roll over and play dead. It was good advice when I gave it to others, so maybe I should take it myself.

How am I going to keep this opportunity alive and control the publishing date? Man, I gotta be careful. Gotta figure this out.

"Ron, I'm calling from a payphone. Don't ask me how I know, but I found out my phones are tapped. The government knows all about our conversations. So if you need to talk to me in the future, when you call me, you'll have to give me time to call you back from a payphone. So where do you want to start?"

"Are you certain your phones are tapped JD? Are you comfortable proceeding?"
"Trust me Ron, I'm absolutely certain! I need to find out if you are actually going to write the story. Then the issue will be, when will you publish it. Can you answer the first question?
"No, I can't I don't have enough of your story yet, and my bosses control the publishing date."

"OK, let's proceed under our agreement and see if you even want to write the story. Then we can discuss changing our agreement.
"In our last conversation you said you knew who exposed my undercover identity, Archibald, to the FDIC. Who was it?

A moment of silence passed and then Ron said, "JD, this will blow you away. It was the IG himself who disclosed your undercover identity to the Chairman, who then forewarned your entire chain of command of what was happening and about to happen.

"That was what I was going to tell you. I have a copy of the memo from the Inspector General himself to the Chairman disclosing your identity as Archibald and the outcome of your investigation. Just so you know, the Chairman selected and hired the IG. It turns out they have been extremely close friends since college. You never had a chance. You were set up from the beginning. They wanted to know what you knew so they could cover it up and bury you and the evidence together, once and for all. They had no intention of making this right for you. In fact they have your second termination completely planned from get to go.

"Once the administrative law clerk makes his ruling you will be disgraced to ensure you have no credibility should anything come up in the future. And don't think for one minute that they're going to rehire you. It ain't gonna happen. You're done. The Archibald affair is a much bigger thing and goes deeper than anything you ever imagined. You've been royally screwed! The only hope you have of having any kind of reputation after the smoke settles is to tell your story before everything goes public, not afterwards.

"Work with me - let me tell your story. I can come to Denver on July 27 or 28. I want to see and talk with you. At least meet and talk with me before you make any decisions."

It took a few moments for everything Ron had said to sink in. I was truly blown away. It made me feel really sick to my stomach. To think I had been that gullible, to have been sucked in so completely, and manipulated like a puppet on a string. The more I thought about it, the more furious I became. I was fully outraged by the time I heard Ron say, "JD, you still there?"

Now seething, I retorted "Yah, I'm still here. I'm so pissed off I can barely talk. Let's do it. Can we make it the 28th?"

"You got it. Let's make it firm the 28th at 7pm at the Marriott Hotel on Hampden and I-25 in Denver."

"Done deal, give me a call once you get checked in and let me know your room number. Talk to you later."

I was still very apprehensive as I hung up, thinking I really don't need to have my mug plastered in newspapers all across the country. At least it won't hit the stands until after the concert's over. I can't let anything jeopardize the concert.

"JD, Tommy's on line 2." The intercom announced.

I answered, "Tommy, what's happenin'?"

The chagrin in his voice nearly melted the phone in my hand, "JD, we have a problem I don't think we can overcome. It's Jackson. Now he's demanding an audience with the Pope, for him and his family, Whitney, and Bill. I've been fighting with his agent nearly all last night, and again this morning, trying to get this demand off the table, without success. Jackson's adamant he ain't coming unless he gets to meet the Pope. Is there any way to accommodate him?"

"Jesus, Tommy, yah maybe, if he had said something two months ago. We're close to 30 days away, and it's so damn difficult trying to deal with the Vatican people. I don't think there's any chance in hell to get this set up on such short notice. This a-hole is nothing but a prima donna. We've had what, a dozen or more special requests or demands during the last three weeks from him? Based on our experience with him, I'm surprised he was ever successful holding a concert. I'd like to fly out to LA and strangle the little SOB with my bare hands."

After pausing for a second or two, I continued, "Tommy, I need some time, I need to make some calls to see what I can do. Don't hold your breath, this may be a hurdle we can't get over. I'll call you back, as soon as I know something."

We've made it so far. The entire show is all but done. Now we get this bullshit. How in God's name am I going to get this resolved?

After two days and two dozen phone calls and being stonewalled by the church itself, the local archdiocese, and the Vatican representatives, I'm just about ready to throw in the towel. I just can't seem to find the right person or make any headway whatsoever at all. *Lord, I thought, how in the hell am I supposed to fix this?*

Then Becky walked into my office and said, "There's a gentleman, Jim Hall, out front. He would like to talk to you."

"Bring him back, thanks, Becky," I replied.

After a few pleasantries, Jim said, "Seems pretty quiet out front. Where's all your staff?"

"Ran out of money, Jim. I had to lay-off everyone but Becky, until we get Jackson's signature, which triggers the Dawsons funding. For whatever reason, which remains a complete mystery, Jackson still refuses to sign the contract. For the last three weeks, he's made one demand after another that we had to address, and purportedly, he'll sign the contract if we agree to just one more demand."

"Well, are you going to make it happen?"
"I honestly don't know, Jim. His last demand that I got two days ago seems to be more than I can say grace over. I've called everybody on the planet with absolutely no success whatsoever at all. You see, Jackson waited until now to demand to meet the Pope, along with Whitney Houston and Bill Strosby. I think this may be the straw that breaks the camel's back. I'm just about ready to call it quits. I just can't find anyone to even talk to about this request."
"Can I use your phone?"
"Of course," I said, as I picked up the phone-set and placed it in front of him.

After dialing, I heard Jim say, "May I speak with Xe (pronounced 'say') Truong, please. Tell him it's General Hall, calling.

"Xe, it's Jim Hall. Do you have time to visit with me and a friend in about 30 minutes? We have a problem you may be able to help us with and I would sure appreciate any assistance you may be able to provide. -- Okay, and thanks, we're on our way."

As we pulled out of the parking lot, I asked, "Where we headed, Jim?"

"Little Vietnam, they call it. You know the place at the intersection of Alameda and Federal. There's a two square block area that is almost entirely all Vietnamese businesses and Xe has his office there in one of the office buildings. Xe was a colonel in the South Vietnamese Army. I served with him for a while and helped him and his family to get their citizenship after they escaped in '75. It's quite a story. They left in the middle of the night on a broken down old boat that was filled to capacity, and were at sea for two months before the old boat sank. Fortunately they were rescued by a US cargo ship that was headed back to the states. When he landed in Long Beach, he asked the customs people to contact me and the rest is history. Now he's like the mayor of Little Vietnam. He's helped everyone in his community to assimilate, find work, and in many cases, helped them start their businesses. I called him because he once told me that his nearest and dearest friend he grew up with had been made the Archbishop of Vietnam. If anybody can help you solve your problem, it's going to be Xe. Just tell him what you need and let's see what he can do."

After concluding an explanation of the concert I explained to Xe that the only thing holding us up was Michael Jackson's demand to have an audience with the Pope.

Xe lit up a cigarette, leaned back in his chair, and smiled, saying, "The general spoke well of you and your endeavor, and as his friend, I will try to help you, because I owe this man everything. The Vatican has set aside two hours for the Vietnamese community in Denver to meet privately with the Pope. I'll reach out and see if we can accommodate your needs. Communications within Vietnam are still very difficult. It's going to take a couple of weeks, but I'll let you know what happens as soon as I can."

Extending my hand across his desk as I stood up, I said,"Xe, I can't thank you enough. I really appreciate any effort you can make on my behalf. There is only one issue. I will need something in writing, and before our drop-dead date of August 4."

As he shook my hand, Xe replied, "I understand. I can't make any promises, but I'll do the very best I can for you.

"General, it's always so good to see you. You need to stop by more often. You gentlemen have a good day."

 ## *T-23 Days and Counting ...*

Sitting on the steps once again, I was in a real funk, having just calculated August 4, 1993, was only 23 days away and there was literally nothing left to do. I kept thinking over and over there must be something else that needs to be done. There must be someone else I need to call. There must be something I need to do. But, for the life of me, I couldn't come up with a single thing.

Suddenly, the silence and my thoughts were shattered by the familiar voice behind me, saying, "Hey there, JD, how you doing?"

It was TP and I wasn't sure if I was even in the mood to visit with him. Sitting down, he continued, "Boy, things have sure gotten quiet around here since you laid everybody off. Seems like this place has become a morgue. Talked to my attorney today and he tells me there ain't no way I'm gonna get a vendor license. So I gotta figure out some way to get rid of a container full of T-shirts. You got any ideas?"

"Not today, TP. I've got problems of my own and I can't seem to come up with any answers. Everything is done with the exception of one signature on one piece of paper. I can't figure out how to get that horse's ass, Michael Jackson, to sign his damn name to the contract. He screwed around with us for over a month, I guess to show us how important he is, and now he wants to meet the pope. I even called Rome thinking the Pope must have a secretary or ten or twelve of 'em, and if I could just find one and explain my situation, maybe I could get some help. That turned out to be a complete waste of a couple hundred bucks in long distance charges.

"My entire project hinges on one guy who happens to be a childhood friend of the Archbishop of Vietnam, and I can't do anything to help him out. More importantly, I'm truly afraid, even if he is successful, Jackson will just come up with some more weird demands until there's no time left. The concert only has 23 days left to live, then it's dead. It just dies for the lack of a headliner.

"On top of that, I've decided to go public with the FDIC story after the Pope leaves town. I have a meeting with the UPI reporter on the 28th here in Denver. And I'm still not sure I'm doing the right thing. I have a lot of apprehension because I can't foresee all the ramifications. I have to protect the concert, no matter what. You know what I mean?"

"Well, sort of. Kind of like going into battle, you never know how it's going to turn out, until it's over. You really sure you want to tell your story to the press?"

"No, I'm not. But I'm gonna get screwed by the government anyway, so why not."

Smiling broadly with raised eyebrows, TP replied wryly, "So it's all about revenge then?"

"No! No, not really, it's about credibility. It seems they want to trash me, trash my reputation, so my testimony against them will be worthless. The government will always have the upper hand, but I'm hoping that having my side of the story out there will offset the two black eyes they're planning to leave me with."

"Well, I'm not sure it will necessarily come out the way you think it will. You won't have any control over what the reporter or the newspaper ends up printing. It's a double-edged sword. It could blow up in your face.

"Even if they could write the whole story, based upon what you told me, I'm not sure many of the readers have a chance in hell of even understanding the complex and convoluted financial transactions you were investigating. Your story is not the simple 'John Doe walked into the government office building, and at gun point, stole all the money and ran away.' I mean, you almost have to have a degree in finance just to understand what you are talking about sometimes. It just gets so complicated I don't think people will make it past the first paragraph.

"My only recommendation is that you think this through completely and be certain that this is what you want to do."

"Thanks, TP, that's good advice and I'll take it. By the way, I'm sorry to hear about your vendor license. I really don't have any advice or recommendations. I wish there was something I could do to help you out."

 T-18 Days and Counting ...

CHAPTER 12

Blindsided!

…Them good old boys were drinking whiskey and rye …

 T-16 Days and Counting …

"**T**ommy, I still haven't heard anything about the meeting for Jackson with the Pope."

"Well, Sinatra's not very happy with the delay, but I think I've got him satisfied for the moment. IBC's having a coronary and the Dawsons are extremely nervous."

"All we can do Tommy, is sit and wait. I simply can't call Xe every day, and ask how things are going. It turns out that the church in Nam, the Archbishop, doesn't even have a phone in his building. He has to go somewhere else to make or receive a call. So it's very difficult. Let's touch base on Friday, if I don't call you with news before then."

Friday came, and as promised, I called Tommy. He sounded very depressed after I told him we still had no news. Bill, who was normally jovial and just happy to be alive for another day, had been quiet and reserved all week. The monotony of the waiting, with absolutely nothing to do was like a vacuum sucking all the energy out of the room. The question in everybody's mind seemed to be; when is JD going to accept the fact the horse died, and finally bury it. Many times great ideas and great projects don't succeed, no matter how hard you try to bring them to life.

The hardest question facing any visionary or leader is when do you give up and pull the plug. It was the question that had been haunting me all week. Was it time to give up and throw in the towel? The stubborn streak that courses through my entire body always gets in the way of my better judgment. I just hated to quit and have to admit that all the time, effort, and money I had spent on something was wrong, bad judgment and/or just plain stupidity.

As I sat there and dwelled in this quagmire of thoughts I had lost track of time when Bill came into the office to say good night.

"JD, I wanted to let you know I have a doctor's appointment at nine Monday. So I won't get in until 1030 or 11. Have a nice weekend."

"Everything okay Bill, you all right?"

"Yah, I'm fine. It's just time for my annual physical. See you Monday!"

I decided to make some notes regarding the week's events, when suddenly my breath was taken away by the realization that Richard Markett was standing in front of my desk. "Man for such a big guy, you sure walk softly! I didn't hear you come in."

"Sorry about that! I waited until your friend left, so I could talk to you privately. I hope you don't mind."

"No! No, I'm glad to see you again, you just caught me by surprise. Pull up a chair. How are you, and the family?"

"We're good, thank you for asking. The reason I stopped by was to let you know that my wife and I are flying back to New York tomorrow afternoon. My assignment here in Denver is done. We've closed the house down and are all ready to go. But, I wanted to stop by and say goodbye before I left. I've really enjoyed our friendship. You've been one of my nicest assignments and I'm truly glad I got an opportunity to meet you."

Taken aback by the surprising news, I responded, "Man, Richard, I thought you would be out here until after the Pope's visit. This is a surprise. Because I, too, have enjoyed our friendship very much, it was such good fun. I really appreciated the time we spent together. So I guess I'll just have to fly out to New York next time I want a real Cuban cigar, right?"

Smiling broadly, Richard replied, "Absolutely! I'll always keep one on hand for you. Just give me a call, anytime."

His smile dissipated as he looked down, and then as he looked back up with an expression of seriousness on his face, he said, "JD, I want to say one last thing, personally, not officially. You can't meet with the AP. You have to cancel your meeting. If the story breaks before the investigation is completed, the probability of success will more than likely become zero. Thousands and thousands of man-hours will be lost, the bad guys will get away, and the opportunity to remove the chairman will be lost. Trust me, take my advice, please. Don't go to that meeting. I say this from the bottom of my heart. Will you do this one thing for me?"

"Jesus, Richard, of all the things. I can't even believe you know about the meeting."

"Of course I know! You're the center pin of a huge criminal investigation. Part of what's been going on is to make sure no harm comes to you or your family until this is over. But it takes time, and you have to wait until the chairman's gone before you say anything publicly. If you don't, the government's retribution will be more than you ever imagined."

"Come on, Richard, I've been shot at with real bullets. Do you think I'm gonna be afraid of paper ones."

Richard interrupted, and said, "It has nothing to do with fear. It has to do with consequences, and who is impacted by those consequences. Keep that in the forefront of your mind when you decide what you're going to do. You are my friend, and I've given you the best advice I can. Do with it as you see fit."

He rose and extended his hand across the desk, and as I grabbed his hand, he added, "Regardless of what may happen, I wish you and your family every happiness."

I responded, "Richard, I thank you. I will give your advice very serious consideration. I'm taking it to heart, and I trust you. It has been such a personal pleasure to know you, and I wish you and your family every happiness as well."

The next day was a beautiful Tuesday morning as I walked in the office and said, "Good morning, Bill!"

"Good morning. A guy named Charlie has called for you three times. He sounded really weird, and asked me to tell you to please wait for him to call back again. He wouldn't leave a number. In fact, he said, don't try to call him."

"That's strange! I think I know who it is, but I don't get the part about not calling him back."

Bill answered the phone and I heard him say, "Yah, he's here now. He just walked in. Hold on a minute and he'll take your call. It's him. It's Charlie."

The first thing I gotta do is warn him, "Charlie, be careful what you say, my phones are tapped. How are you and what's going on?"

"JD, in case I have to hang up, answer me this one question. Does anybody know that I worked with you on Archibald? I mean, did you ever tell anyone about my involvement?"

"No, Charlie, I've never disclosed your identity to anyone. Why do you ask?"

"Well, you wouldn't believe what's going on right now. You know how I always come to work early. Well this morning the main doors were unlocked when I walked in, and as I walked past the reception area I saw a small army of people, everywhere. I had no idea what was going on. So I just headed towards my cubicle, and as I stepped inside, this guy walks up to me and flashes his GAO ID badge and tells me that I can't stay in my cubicle. He then escorts me to the lunch room and tells me that I have to stay here. When I asked him what was going on, he told me that I would be informed later, and to just remain here in the lunch room. Fortunately, there's a phone in here, so I've been

* * *

calling you every time I get a chance. A lot of other people have showed up for work, and we're all just milling around waiting to find out what's going on. I just had to know if they're gonna be looking for me?"

"Wow, Charlie, rest assured, nobody but me knows your identity or involvement. Your secret is safe. You don't have to tell anyone about your involvement with Archibald. If they ask you directly, just play dumb. Listen very carefully to any questions they ask you, and only answer the question. Do not volunteer or provide any additional information. If the question is incriminating, use your best judgment and try to avoid answering."

"JD, I gotta hang up."

"Call me, Charlie, call me back." As I listened to the dialtone, I realized the investigation was in full swing.

Later, as I sat at my desk eating lunch, I answered the phone on the first ring, and waited for the response, to determine if it was Charlie. It was, thankfully, and the apprehension started to dissipate.

"JD, they let us go to lunch, so I'm at a pay phone in the lobby of the building across the street. So I can talk now."

"Good, Charlie, good! How's it going?"

"It's incredible! We got blindsided! There was no warning. There has to be at least a hundred people from Washington in the office. They came in around 10 o'clock and explained they were here for a complete examination of the Denver office. Apparently they're doing the same thing at the regional office in California. We were instructed to stay in the lunch room until our names were called and then we would go with that person to our workstation.

"I got called about an hour ago, and it looks like I'm going to be spending the rest of the day working with this guy, and possibly tomorrow as well. They are going through everything. They started out by making a complete copy of all the data files on my computer. Then we started going through each and every asset package I was working on. When they let me go for lunch, they said we would need to do this on every asset sale for the last 24 months.

"JD, they have a two page checklist for each and every asset package. They're looking at everything. And riding down the elevator, and then in the lobby, I'm listening to other people talking and it's unbelievable. They're inventorying everything, including the number of boxes of paper clips. I've never seen anything like it. I guess Archibald did his job!"

"I'm glad you called, Charlie, but the question is have they asked you about Archibald?"

"No. No, they haven't, but I'm scared to death that they will. I swear I'm about to have a heart attack."

"Charlie, Charlie, listen to me, take a deep breath and relax. You're gonna be just fine. Nobody knows your identity or your involvement. You've done nothing wrong, so don't sweat it. You just have to act natural. People can sense fear, so don't act like a nervous Nelly. Just be yourself.

"Now listen carefully. Go have lunch and relax, then go back to the office like any other day. When you get off duty, go to another payphone somewhere in a different building and call me. And Charlie, you and I know that I've called you Charlie, after the Charlie Brown character since shortly after we first met, as a joke. Whatever you do, don't ever use your real name when you're on the phone with me – Ok? Will you do that? We can talk more then – Ok?"

"Yah, okay, I'll call you after work."

It was so quiet Bill had decided to go home for a late lunch. I sat at my desk, looking out the window in silence, still haunted by Richard Markett's last words to me. I felt 95% certain I was making the right decision to proceed with the meeting with the AP tomorrow night. But, yet, there was this nagging feeling I just couldn't put my finger on, telling me to beware. No matter how hard I tried to figure it out, I just couldn't nail down the trepidation I still felt. The afternoon seemed to drag on endlessly as I waited in anticipation for Charlie's call.

Five o'clock came and went with no phone call. By six o'clock, I was beginning to worry about Charlie. Finally 10 minutes later, the phone rang and I said, "Charlie, you okay? You're late."

"Yah, I'm okay, they kept everyone late, and didn't shut down until 6 o'clock. It's been a long, tough day. I'm totally exhausted, but let me tell you what happened. Around 3 o'clock, a bunch of uniformed US marshals came into the office and about an hour later, they left with four people in handcuffs. Apparently they were arrested. You remember Mike Donnley, the department head for supply and logistics. He was one of them. I didn't know the others."

"Boy, I didn't see that coming, how about the boss lady and any of her minions?"

"No, in fact I didn't see her or any of the other department heads all day. I don't know where they were or what was happening with them."

"Well, it seems like all our hard work is finally coming to fruition."

"Well, they sure took their sweet time. It's been over a year. Did you know this was going to happen?"

"No Charlie, I had no clue. You know I've worked with the GAO trying to sort through all the stuff we gave them. They never gave any indication of how they would proceed. Say listen, while I've got you, I'd like your opinion on something. Have you got an extra minute or two to talk?"

"Yah, go ahead."

After giving him the details regarding my upcoming meeting with the AP newswire, I asked, "Since you're involved Charlie, I'd like your opinion. What do you think I should do?"

"I don't like it JD. I don't trust the press. They're never interested in the truth, they're after the headlines. Their only objective is to sell papers, no matter how much they have to distort the story. And, so far, you've done everything right and things are starting to happen. Why risk the possibility of destroying all the work we've done. I think you should wait until the GAO finishes what they started."

"Well, that's a good and valid recommendation and I thank you for that. I will think very seriously about what you said. Now back to your situation. Charlie, I know my phones are tapped, or whatever legal term they want to use - the government's listening to my phone calls. In order to protect your identity, we can't talk again until after the Pope leaves Denver. There's too great a risk of them figuring out your real name. I don't think they have yet, since you haven't been singled out, and are just being treated like everyone else. So let's keep it that way. Unless it's an emergency, don't call me again until after the Pope's gone. In the meantime, just relax and take one day at a time. The GAO will eventually finish up and be gone. Concentrate on taking good care of your family and just keep on truckin'. Stay safe, my friend."

"I understand. You know you're more than just a friend to me. I trust you and I trust you'll make the right decision regarding the AP. Give my regards to your wife and take care of yourself. Good luck with the concert. I'll call you after it's over."

 T-8 Days and Counting ...

"Good morning General, how we doin'?" I asked anxiously as I picked up the phone.

"You're going to be doing great! Xe just called, you need to call him right away. He just got off the phone with Vietnam, and he got you your audience with the Pope for Michael Jackson and his guests. Call him right away. Then call me back and let me know what's going on. Bye!"

"Xe, it's JD. The general told me to give you a call."

"I have very good news for you. My friend, the Archbishop, has completed the necessary arrangements for Michael Jackson and his guests to have a private audience and meet the Pope, Saturday, August 14, at 4 PM. I will be in charge of helping and assisting you with the necessary arrangements. I hope this news pleases you."

"Oh my God! Xe, you are just incredible, I can't believe you did it. Do we have some kind of documentation?"

"No, not yet. The letter of confirmation is being prepared and will be sent from Vietnam."

Excitedly, I interrupted and said, "Xe, is there any way to get a fax copy of the letter today?"

"No, that can't happen. Fax machines are still a very rare thing in Vietnam, but I'll see if I can make arrangements to get a fax copy once the Archbishop has signed it. Otherwise we will have to wait for the letter to arrive in the mail. It is being sent to me and normally it takes about a week to get here. I'll call you as soon as it arrives by fax or mail."

"Okay, I guess we'll just have to wait. Xe, I can't even begin to tell you how much I appreciate all your efforts in getting this done for me. I sincerely thank you so very much, but if there is any way for you to expedite this process, it would certainly be appreciated."

"It was my pleasure. I'm glad I was able to assist you, just be sure and thank the general."

"Hey Bill, come into my office, I want you to hear this next phone call!" I bellowed. "We did it, buddy! We got it done! Pull up a chair. I want you to listen in on this call to Tommy.

"Tommy, I've got you on the speakerphone with Bill. It's done. We did it. I just got the call, Michael Jackson and his guests have a private audience with the Pope on August 14 at 4 PM. Is that incredible news or what?"

"That's terrific news JD. Can you fax me a copy of the document?"

"No, I can't, not yet. It's being prepared for the Archbishop's signature. Apparently they don't have easy access to a fax machine over there, but they will try to get us a fax, if possible. They think it will be here within a week."

"Shit, JD, that's really pushin' it close to the deadline. I can call everybody and let them know, but I believe nothing is going to happen until we have an official document. Jackson's agent simply won't budge on the basis of a phone call. He's not going to proceed without documentation. We still can't move forward until we have that document. Please, call me if anything changes. And, JD, congratulations on a job very well done. Let's just hope we get written confirmation in time. Talk to you later – bye."

Excitedly, I said, "Well, Bill, what do you think of them apples?"

With extreme reservation dripping off his words, he replied, "It is incredible news. I almost can't believe it, but I feel even less certain about it arriving in time. It's taken so long. And now it's going to take even longer, while the document is prepared for signature. I don't understand why they can't just sit down on the computer and crank it out?"

"Come on Bill, quit being so negative. We did it, we're the men. We did the impossible."

"We'll see - it ain't over 'til the fat lady sings, and I don't recall Michael Jackson being very fat. I'll believe it when I see it.

• • •

I just think we need to wait until Jackson actually signs the contract before we start celebrating."

"I agree! And I know the last couple a three weeks have been pure hell, just sittin' here waiting. But, we did it. We completed each and every step necessary for this concert to happen. Now it's out of our hands. We just need Michael Jackson to sign his name and the concerts on."

It's after six and time to go, and my elation over the news of the day is overtaken, by the dread I feel about my upcoming meeting with the AP newswire. I still feel reticent about the whole thing. But, Ron did fly from Washington to see me, so I guess I owe him the courtesy of at least meeting with him. As I headed down Parker Road, I noticed I was just about out of gas. The south side of the intersection at Havana Street, where I needed to turn had a service station, so I pulled in alongside the far pump. As I stuck the nozzle into the fuel tank, I looked up and noticed two black SUVs pulling into the driveway. The first one continued on past behind me, as the second pulled in behind me and stopped. As I looked away, I noticed the other SUV pulling up right in front of my car. The passenger door opened and out stepped a huge man, meticulously dressed in a suit and tie. I thought as big as he was, he could play football and not even need the uniform. But then, when he started walking towards me, instead of towards the building, my early warning system activated, and it was fight or flight time, thinking, what the hell does this guy want? As he continued towards me, he removed from his inside jacket pocket, a black case. I recognized, having carried one, he was about to flash me his government ID. I continued to hold onto the gas pump handle and look nonchalant at the same time. He stopped less than a couple of feet from me, momentarily flashing his ID, allowing me to make out the three big letters in the center, NSA.

"Excuse me sir," he said, "I'm with the NSA and I've been ordered to give you a message from Washington. You must not meet with the AP tonight. Your meeting could jeopardize a major government investigation. If you do, there will be serious repercussions that will affect not just you, but your entire family, including your parents and your brothers and sister. The full force and effect of the government will be directed at you with extreme prejudice.

"I could go on, but from the look on your face, I think you already have received the message. Have I made myself clear?"

"Yah! And I'm really pissed. I can't believe you guys are stooping so low, after all I've done, and after all I've been through, I just can't believe you're doing this."

"Believe it, sir. That's just the way it's going to be. Have a good evening."

I stood there, just fuming, as I watched him get back in the car and both SUVs back up and pull away. A thousand thoughts flew through my mind as I watched them pull away. On the one hand, I just wanted to show them, and proceed to the meeting anyway. Then I finally got my stubborn streak under control and took a look at the broader picture. Now was not the time to take on the whole United States government, and I realized from my own experience inside the agency that they were capable of doing everything they said.

So I walked over to the payphone, dialed 113, and asked for the number to the Marriott Hotel.

"Ron, it's JD, and something has happened. Can you guarantee me, in writing, that you won't publish the story until after the GAO investigation is completed?"
"No JD, that's not how it works. The story goes whenever my bosses decide it goes. There's no way I can make that guarantee, and knowing my boss there's no way he'll do that."
"Then I'm sorry, but I have to cancel our meeting."

"Why? I flew all the way out here just for this meeting with you."

"Because of what just happened, I was blindsided. Let me tell you..."

T-0 The Day Has Arrived

"**T**ommy, glad I reached you. I just got off the phone with Xe. He spoke with the Archbishop personally and confirmed he will arrange to have a document prepared in the US since they can't find a way to fax it from 'Nam. Can you get us a one-day extension?"

"I really don't know, JD, I'll make the call, but I don't think it will happen. We have 'til the close of business today to perform, or were just dead ducks. I'll call you back as soon as I get off the phone."

As I hung up the phone, Bill inquired, "What did he say?"

"He doesn't think our chances are very good. I don't know what else to do. So I guess we just have to wait."

It seemed like hours had passed, but not even five minutes passed before the phone rang, and Tommy said, "It took a bit of fast talking, but I got you an extension. We have until noon, LA time tomorrow to deliver the goods. This is it because apparently there's quite a bit that has to happen in their New York office for them to be able to pull the trigger on this deal. I am amazed at how much effort IBC's putting into this. They really want to see it happen. Anyway, call me as soon as you know something."

"I will Tommy, I can't thank you enough for making this happen. I'll do everything in my power to make sure I don't disappoint you."

Line 2 was ringing. I answered, "This is JD, can I help you?"

"JD, it's Xe. I'm traveling right now, so it has not been convenient for me to reach you. However, I wanted to call and let you know, I spoke with the Archbishop and asked him to get us the documentation immediately. He has made arrangements to have the head of the Vietnamese operations for the US World Youth Day VIII activities, to formalize the invitation and fax me the documentation. I have spoken with them, and I will have it first thing tomorrow morning. I just wanted to let you know. I will be in the office tomorrow morning when it arrives, I'll call you then."

"Thank you Xe, for the extra effort - talk to you tomorrow morning."

"Well, Bill, we live for another day. Let's just pray it all comes together tomorrow morning. I'd really like to take the rest of the day off. Can you stick around and cover the phones just in case something happens this afternoon. I'll be at home, you can call me if you need me."

"Yah sure, I'll call you if I need to, see you tomorrow."

 # The Day Has Arrived -- *again!*
T+1

"**Y**ou're in early, JD, any news yet?" Bill inquired.

"No, not yet, but Xe's office doesn't open until eight. So I'm going to wait until 10 after before I call him."

"So we have 20 minutes to go, huh!"

"Yep, that's about right."

Bill and I sat there together in my office waiting for the phone to ring recalling the past year's events. It seemed like forever, as we constantly looked to the phone as if to make sure it was still functioning, when it happened. Then a fax line rang, and Bill jumped on it

Seconds later the phone rang. I hit the speaker button to answer, it was Xe.

"Xe, how we doin'?"

"Fine JD, did you get it?

"Yes thank God, it just came in, I've got it. You're incredible Xe, but I need you to fax it again to my landlord's office upstairs. I only have thermal paper fax machines and he has a paper fax, here's the number... I'll call you back, as soon as I read it. Thank you."

Bill interjected, "I'll go upstairs and get it."

As he handed me the fax and headed out the door, I said, "Thanks Bill."

In the quiet of the moment my heart raced from the thrill of holding the final piece of the puzzle, the key to unlock the treasure chest I had dreamed about every night for so long. Savoring each word deliciously as I read, my soul was singing, Hallelujah!

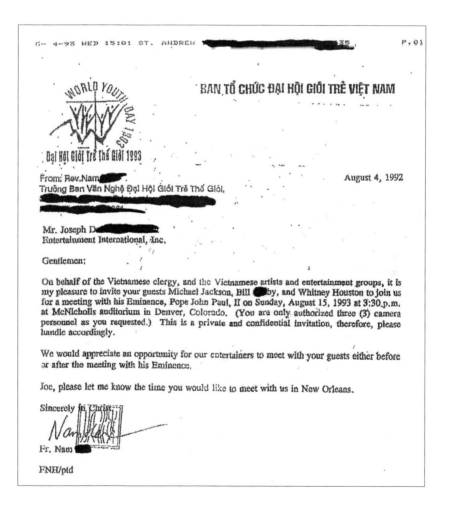

Suddenly, my heart stopped. All the wind in my sails disappeared, and my stomach turned upside down. I realized they had left out Sinatra's name and typed the wrong date on the letter. My God, how could this be. It needed to be perfect. But, it wasn't, it was flawed. My thoughts exploded as my mind crashed into a wall at full speed.

I began to try and reassemble my thoughts, thinking, *can this be overcome, can I salvage the deal with a flawed document? Can I get Xe to have them send another corrected one?*

As Bill walked in with the paper copy I decided the only thing to do was call Xe and see what options we might have.

As Xe answered I blurted out, "Xe, we have a huge typo that may affect the credibility of the document."

"Where is it JD, I don't see it."

"It's the date and they didn't include Sinatra and his family. Xe, can we get them to correct it and retransmit the document?"

"I'm sorry, JD, there's no way. This was typed on a manual typewriter and there's no way to get it redone in time. Please explain to your recipient, it is just a typographical error and there will be no problem with Frank Sinatra's family being there and meeting the Pope personally, I absolutely guarantee it. I'm sure they will understand. I just can't get it re-typed and faxed back here by noon, it's not possible."

"Okay, Xe, we'll just have to go with it. I just can't believe they typed in 1992, instead of 1993, it baffles me."

"I'm terribly sorry JD."
"Don't worry about it, Xe. We have no time. We will just have to proceed with it. And again, my thanks; I'll let you know how it turns out."

● ● ●

Bill headed to the fax machine as I began dialing Tommy, "Tommy, I hope you're near your fax machine. Bill's faxing over the document to you now. I just want to make sure it comes through okay to you."

"My fax machine's going off right now, JD. Hold on a second and let's see what came through.
"Got it! Incredible!

"Tommy, there is a problem …"

Having explained the problems with the document, Tommy responded, "JD, I don't see it as a problem. Frank will understand and if necessary we'll take care of it later. As for Michael and his agent, I'm sure they will overlook the date issue. This is exactly what they asked for and you got it. Don't worry about it, I'll take it from here.
"I have a lot to do now. I'll call you back as soon as I know something. Talk to you later."
"You go, buddy, you go," giving him my relieved, and best exited cheer as I hung up.

"That's it, Bill, everything's done. Now we just have to wait for the phone call telling us Michael Jackson has finally signed the deal. Let's go out and sit in the sunshine for a while and take a break."

Minutes turned into hours and hours turned into even more hours. Lunch was long since over, and it seemed like the phone was never going to ring. Bill and I sat there, back in the office, with the silence only being broken from time to time by a random thought being voiced and passing through the room unnoticed and unworthy of any response.

Finally, at 3:30, the call arrived.

Tommy's voice echoed over the speakerphone as he said softly, "JD, I'm so sorry. The deal is dead."

I could've sworn I heard tears in his voice as he continued, "Michael Jackson's agent faxed me and IBC the final refusal letter, moments ago. There was no reason given.

"It simply states that Mister Jackson respectfully declines our offer for him to perform at the concert.

"That's it. It's only two sentences long.

"I tried to call his agent and was told he was in an extended meeting and unavailable. I talked to IBC and they were as surprised as I was. They have no idea, either, as to why Jackson reneged on the deal. I don't know what to say JD."

I instantly felt like I was experiencing the impact of a head-on collision at 100 mph. The reverberations shaking up every cell in my body told me I was experiencing complete and total devastation. I had never before experienced what seemed like a complete implosion of my entire being. It felt as if a thousand elephants had sat on me at the same time. It was as if time stopped, and I couldn't move or react. I could see out of the corner of my eye, Bill sitting with his head in his hands, bent over as his elbows rested on his knees. I started to reassemble my thoughts as I realized my brain was once again functioning, but my body remained locked in place.

I had no sense of how much time had passed, probably not much, as I was finally able to move and began to formulate my response to Tommy.

"Tommy, I don't know what to say either. I'm crushed by the news and left nearly speechless. I just cannot understand why he backed out this late in the game. It makes no sense at all. What a waste of time, energy, and money.

"Can I ask a favor, would you be kind enough to call the Dawsons and let them know? I'll take care of everybody else that needs to know.

"And, you know, there was one good thing that came out of all this Tommy, and that's our friendship, and the good times we had working together. Let's talk again soon, okay?"

"I agree. You're right, JD, it truly was a delight to work with you. I'll take care of the Dawsons and may God bless you and yours always."

"And may God bless you and yours as well Tommy, let's talk again real soon, goodbye my friend."

And then we all cried:

The Day The Music Really Died!
August 5, 1993

The End of Part I

Drafted To Serve

POPE JOHN PAUL II
A SAINT

Making Miracles Happen

PART II

THE POPE HAS ARRIVED!

DENVER COLORADO

AUGUST 10, 1993

CHAPTER 13

Place Your Trust In God

... "TP, you still interested in trying to make a few bucks on the Pope's visit? I have an idea!"

Walking out of the landlord's office, August 10th Tuesday afternoon, I noticed TP sitting in the reception area. I walked down the stairs and through the lobby to the front doors, blocked open to let in the fresh air of a late summer afternoon. I sat down on the front steps to just think and contemplate my situation.

The last several days had been just miserable. The news of the Pope's arrival today was everywhere, and overwhelming, as a constant reminder of what could have been, continuing relentlessly to deepen and expand the depression and burning rage, I felt about what had happened.

Today was my first day out of the house since I went home the night the music died. Until my scheduled meeting with the landlord today, I hadn't spoken to anyone other than my family. The memories of those conversations will haunt me for a very long time, and still fill our house with great sadness.

How do you overcome complete failure? And climb out of the depression pit that always accompanies failure? The pit seems so deep and vast with walls made of vertical glass covered in oil, dashing any hope of climbing out. And the absence of light makes the darkness feel like it's consuming and suffocating you. *Is there no hope of escape* I thought, or shall I have to wait for *time* to heal these wounds in my mind, as I continue to do nearly daily with the PTSD I brought home from Vietnam?

And what have I learned? The higher you climb the further you will fall. And if you fall, there is only one thing you can do: *Place Your Trust In God.*

That being said, I better make the call for help before I hit bottom. My Lord God, Jesus Christ, please hear my prayer for help. I do not understand nor can I explain how I got to this point in my life. I do not know why I find myself here at this moment, filled with rage and hate for a person I've never met. Help me forgive Michael Jackson and forget the animosity I feel towards him. For it may have not been his fault, but your will. I must put this all behind me and go on. Forgive me, and help me find the way, so your will may be done. And restore the light of hope in my heart, Amen.

The sun was bright and the mid-morning was heating up. It started to feel good again to be alive. After a while I heard footsteps come down the stairs.

Turning, I saw TP coming through the doorway. As he sat down and leaned back against the opposite railing he pulled out a cigarette and lit it up. I turned slightly to lean against the railing on my side of the steps and facing him inquired, "I saw you in the reception room, how did it go?"

Exhaling a deep drag on his cigarette he responded, "Not well, I have to be out by the 26th, and I have no idea where I'm going now. How about you, how did you do?"
"Not any better, I have to be out by the end of the month. But, you know, for an upset landlord, he was very nice about the whole situation. I told him I was going to leave all the office equipment for him."

After a few minutes of silence, I lit up a cigarette and asked, "So what are you gonna do now?"
After a few moments he answered, "I don't have any plans. I have about 350 acres of rangeland down in Castillo County and one of my neighbors called and told me there were some range rustlers running cattle on my land. So I've been thinking I need to go down there and deal with the situation."

"What in the hell are range rustlers?" I inquired.

Smiling as he looked over at me, he explained, "Range rustlers are livestock owners who truck their livestock onto someone else's property and leave them there for a while to graze and eat all your grass without paying for it, to fatten them up for free."

"Oh, really!" Still curious – I added, "So what can you do about it?"

"Well I've been talking to the U.S. Range Warden. He told me I can legally go down there, round up the cattle, remove them from my property, and then take 'em to market. He would have to be there to write up a seizure order to transfer ownership to me to be able to sell the cattle."

"So is that what you are going to do?"

Thoughtfully, he looked over, answering, "I don't know. My neighbor thinks there are at least 400 maybe 500 head of cattle on the property now. It's a big job to round 'em all up, re-brand 'em, and then get them loaded up into trucks and taken to market. What about you, what are you gonna do?"

Thinking, boy, we're both rowing the same broken down rowboat, I replied, "I don't know, it's so depressing. So much time, money and effort was spent trying to produce the concert. Before I made the concert decision, I sent out over 40 resumes without a single response, and the job market ain't any better today."

Suddenly, in midsentence an idea started forming in my mind and the questions were; *was the idea worth a shit and would TP partner up with me?* So I blurted out, "TP, you still interested in trying to make a few bucks on the Pope's visit? I have an idea!"

In a somewhat dejected voice, he responded, "Well, being flat broke at the moment, my answer would have to be yes. What have you got in mind?"

Lighting up a cigarette to buy some time to formulate my opening question, thinking, *this is insane, I can't believe I'm even thinking about this??*

"TP, did you ever set up a lemonade stand when you were a kid?" Not waiting for his answer, I continued, "Here's what I'm thinking. The last day of the Pope's visit is Sunday, when he's going to serve Mass and give his final message to the kids during his sermon at Cherry Creek Park out by the dam, not downtown. Now the problem is how do you get 30,000 people from downtown out to Cherry Creek Park?

"I don't know, and apparently neither did the brains behind this deal. So finally, they decided to have a forced march and simply have everyone hike out to the park. Last night on the TV News, they said event officials had examined every possible mode of transport to get all the people from the stadium to the park and couldn't find a better solution. There's an estimated minimum of 20,000 people showing up at Bear's Stadium Saturday morning. And now they'll have to march all the way to Cherry Creek Park, hopefully before nightfall, to celebrate Mass Sunday morning and hear the Pope's final sermon.

"They're gonna have to march from the stadium to the park utilizing the Cherry Creek bicycle path. That's like 20 plus miles on a hot August afternoon. They're forecasting midday temperatures over 100°.

"Being an ex-marine, I'm sure you'll agree with me, this is going to be an ordeal for all these people who have probably never walked or marched five continuous miles, let alone 20 miles. They've had no training for this, and in the heat they're gonna get dehydrated and won't be able to carry enough water.

"Anyway," the old brain was cooking as my words rolled out one after another, "my idea is to find a spot on the bicycle path half way between the stadium and the park, and set up a refreshment stand, a lemonade stand, like when we were kids, and sell bottles of water and soft drinks.

"I'm thinking, if only 10% of 'em stopped and bought a drink for a dollar or two we could gross maybe $3000 or $4000 above our cost and, if more than 10% purchased drinks, we could make some real money! What do you think?"

For the next couple of hours we sat there and discussed the concept in its entirety. After answering what seemed like a thousand "what if" questions the plan came to life. The high per unit wholesale cost of bottled water left us with a single product line, canned soft drinks. Besides the product, we would need ice, some 30 gallon plastic trash cans, two or three folding tables, a couple of chairs and, most importantly, the location. TP reminded me he had the old school bus which had all the seats removed and we could use it for transporting everything to and from the site. This was doable!

"TP," I queried, "we only got three days, three full working days to pull this off. Do you think we can do this in time?

Somewhat pensively, he responded, "Yah, I think so - what the hell, let's give it a try – mount up – let's go find a location."

In my mind there were still some serious questions remaining. Since we were both broke, how do we come up with the cash to purchase 2,000 or more cans of soda, and what would we do with them if we couldn't sell them. While these questions and others continued to bang around in the back of my mind, we jumped in my car and headed for the park while continuing our discussions of the project.

It was only about a 15 minute drive to the park. We figured the best way to find the location we needed was to start at the destination, the park, and follow the bicycle path towards the origin. Our location had to be accessible by car in order to get our product to the location. It had to be far enough from the point of origin to ensure our potential customers would definitely be in the market for something cool and refreshing to drink. So the first 6 or 7 miles of the route were ruled out, too close to the destination. It became evident we needed to follow the bicycle path which ran alongside the creek through the residential areas where road access was viable. Needless to say the creek meandered and the streets went straight requiring a never ending series of turns up and down different streets to try and follow the creek. As night fell, we could no longer evaluate the terrain alongside the creek. Having examined only about 3 miles of the bike path we decided to give up for the night and come back tomorrow to continue our search. After dropping TP off at the office, as I headed home I realized the

• • •
177

biggest problem of all was how to explain all this to my Lover Snugger.

Wednesday morning I pulled up to the office and TP jumped in the car. As we pulled out of the parking lot headed back to the bike path he said, "I thought about this deal a lot last night and I think if we can find the right location this is a good idea. But how are we gonna buy all the soda? Right now, I don't have any money to throw into the pot. Can you put up the money?"

I didn't want to put a damper on the energy and excitement we were developing, so I took a deep breath, and began to carefully articulate my response, "Right now the answer is no. I told my wife about the idea last night and she thinks I'm crazy as a loon, so taking what little money we have available in the household budget ain't gonna happen. I'm on my own on this one. She's still depressed and disappointed over the canceling of the concert.

"I do have one idea to pay for the sodas, but I want to see if we can find the right location before I go into that. Can you take care of the folding tables, chairs and at least half a dozen trash cans we need?"

Nodding affirmatively, he replied, "Yes, I can handle that part plus I'll have the bus ready to go, so we can get everything to the site."

Inquisitively, with a touch of doubt in my voice, I asked, "How are you gonna get a half-dozen plastic trash cans, if you ain't got no money?"

Chuckling, he replied, "I'll go over to the store tomorrow and use my store credit card to buy them, and then on Sunday, I'll take them back for a full refund. The only thing they're going to have in them is ice chilling cans of soda, anyway, so they'll be as good as new!"

"Terrific," I exclaimed. "Let's go down to Colorado Boulevard and follow the bike path back eastward toward the park this morning rather than trying to find out where we left off last night."

"OK!" was his upbeat reply.

As we drove through the neighborhoods alongside the creek, wherever possible we would get out of the car and walk up and down the bike path looking for a large enough space in the foliage next to the path to set up and operate our lemonade stand. Three hours later, our excitement waned and pure frustration began to overwhelm us in the heat of the midday sun. Man was it hot!

We decided to take a break and go to the burger barn and get some lunch. As we pulled away from the drive-up window with our lunch, we decided to keep driving around while we ate. We were traveling north on Yosemite Street, and as we came around the curve to head west, I grabbed the first right turn into a residential area. We started meandering through the neighborhood trying to reach the creek and finally made a right turn, which curved around back towards the east. As we headed to the end of a cul-de-sac there was a large break between the houses in the middle of the block with a partial paved roadway to the north on the left. As we slowly rolled up to the corner of the fence of the last house, before the break between the houses, we could see where the roadway had been extended about 100 feet into a small grove of trees, probably to make maintaining the roadway easier. And it was evident cars had been driven up in between the trees, so we pulled in between the houses and drove into the grove of trees and BINGO! We rolled past the trees on either side and stopped. Nothing had to be said. We looked at each other, grinning like 7-year-old kids who found the cookie jar. We found the site, the perfect site, to set up our lemonade stand.

How to describe the site? I'd stopped the car facing due north. The trees and foliage on both sides of the car curved around up to the bike path. Traffic from cars coming in and stopping eliminated any foliage growth on the dirt between the car and the bike path which was a distance of about 200 feet. The bike path tarmac stretched straight across the opening from the west to the east with a width of about 8 foot.

On the north side of the bike path, wild grasses and other low lying foliage extended about 15 feet to an apparent drop off with the creek hidden below. About 30 yards east of center, there was a small white bridge for pedestrians to cross over the creek to the north side. On the north side of the creek there was what appeared to be about a 500 yard open area before you could see where the housing development started and continued as far as you could see to the north and east.

We got out of the car and TP headed off to the east walking along the bike path, while I headed to the west. The marchers would be coming from the west headed eastward toward the park. Stopping in the shade of the overhanging branches of a really big tree, I could see there was a noticeable uphill grade for what appeared to be about a half mile stretch of the bike path westward from this point, until the path turned northward. It was now about three in the afternoon and the trees were providing about 10 yards of shade on the path. I turned around, standing in the middle of the bike path looking east. The bike path appeared to be a straight shot of at least 150 yards of tarmac creating the northern edge of our half circle of dirt before the bike path was closed in by the foliage once again.

Still standing in the middle of the bike path at the west end point where the shade ended, I began to envision in my mind what the children marching up the path would see and think, at the exact moment they reached this point. Trying to figure out the best possible layout for our lemonade stand, where should we put the tables? What kind of angle should they be at to catch the kids' attention? Thinking – *Hmm, why not set up two tables perpendicular to the path and right on the path, like a barricade, so everyone has to either stop or go around us, Hmmm, maybe that's not such a good idea.*

Where and how should we arrange our chairs so there would be some seating available? More importantly, how do we set up the tables and seating arrangements to accommodate moving traffic, while also serving others who stop to get refreshments? Again, my mind was racing to try and figure out the answers and the correct solutions. I looked up the path again to the east and saw TP coming around the curve headed back to the lemonade stand. As he approached, I shouted, "How's it look up your way?"

Smiling, lifting up and waving both hands above his head, he hollered back, "Boy, this is the last flat spot for quite a ways. The path drops down a pretty good grade, goes around a curve and then goes back up an even steeper grade from there."

I yelled back, "Yah, and they'll be coming up a grade to get here from the west and there ain't no shade between here and as far as you can see back to the west. Without a doubt, this is our spot." Closing in on each other, in a normal voice, I said, "Man this is THE lemonade stand. I feel like we should put up a flag and claim this spot for God and King."

Jokingly, TP countered, "Yep, there you go! We can sit down and make up a coat of arms and have it printed on some flags and mark this as our spot, just like Columbus probably did!" Laughing together we walked over to the west end and sat down leaning against the trunk of the big tree. "Well, TP, what do you think?" I inquired.

We sat there together until we noticed it was almost 5 o'clock and decided we didn't want to get into rush-hour traffic. So we stayed and continued our conversation, trying to formulate the best layout for the lemonade stand. We went over the logistics and steps to be taken for the entire plan. The only issue we never brought up to discuss again was how in the world we were going to pay for the product we wanted to sell.

I felt TP, being a premier con man, realized I still didn't have the answer to this question. It was evident he was just waiting in the tall grass, for me to come up with the answer, and present it to him. This was the 'Achilles Heel' of the plan haunting me, as I tried to push it even further back in my mind, because I still didn't have a clue as to how I was going to resolve it. Where in God's name, am I gonna get the money to buy the product? The killer question!

As I pulled into the driveway at home after dropping TP off, my thoughts now centered on how I was going to give my wife an update without an answer to the $64,000 question of how I was going to pay for the product to resell. I went up the stairs and could smell the sweet aroma of dinner being prepared when Chris came running around the corner and jumped up on me and with a hug said, "Daddy I love you!" Wow, after a long hard day, it became apparent this is what life is all about, as all the trepidation, worry and fear of success or failure dissipated from my body. I suddenly felt warmth and happiness. It was so good to be home! After some more hugs and a little horseplay with Chris I walked into the kitchen and announced, "Hi Sweetheart, I'm home and I have some good news."

She walked over with a touch of a smile on her face and gave me a hug and a kiss and replied with an element of inquisitive interest in her voice, "Oh good, you got a job? I've got about 10 minutes before I'm ready to serve dinner, so tell me your good news."

Oh Boy, she's thinking job and I'm thinking deal, new adventure. Oh well, here goes. Smiling I responded, "Yah-Ok, that'll work," sitting down at the kitchen table. I then began a litany of the day's events, trying to share the excitement of a plan coming together, to lift her spirits and mine as well, I guess. "So what do you think," I finally probed, as I concluded the story.

She turned, as she set the ladle down again, and somewhat distressed, begrudgingly remarked, "Where are you going to get the lemonade to sell to all those kids?"

Stammering a bit, trying to inject a bit of humor, I responded, smiling, "Well, TP is going to get half a dozen plastic trash cans, then we'll get a few cases of lemons, a bucket of sugar, add water and serve the lemonade right out of the trash cans!"

"Yah - right! Seriously, Joe we don't have the money for this. I thought you had decided to sell cans of soda?" She queried with a stern and serious expression on her face. There was just enough disdain in her voice to know she didn't find my response humorous, and was still very concerned about how the plan was going to play out.

"Don't worry Lover, I'll figure something out and let you know," I replied, somewhat distraught over her obvious disappointment with the whole plan.

She then said, "Get the kids for dinner and help me set the table, please."

As we sat around the dinner table listening to the light hearted banter from the kids, Steve suddenly blurted out, "Mom and I are going to the Pope's mass Sunday!"

"Really, that's cool!" I answered, as I looked over inquisitively at Snugger.

"Yes," she interjected, "I really want to go and see the Pope and I'm going to take Steve with me. The mass is at 11 AM so we're planning to leave at 4 AM to hopefully get good seats. I'm hoping you'll take care of Chris because I don't think he would be too happy waiting six or seven hours for the mass to start. Then waiting a couple of hours to leave as I'm sure it's going to be very crowded, -- unless you want to go with us?"

Looking over at Chris, I replied, "No, after spending the day at the lemonade stand, I don't think I would be up for another 12 hour event the next day. Chris and I will go find something fun to do and just have a good time together. Right, Chris?"

Suddenly, Chris, beaming with happiness said, "Right Dad, you and me can go have some fun together!"

Man life is good! I thought.

CHAPTER 14

The Fools Mission

TP, you pony up to the bar, and tell him what great guys we are and we'll see what happens.

Thursday, 2 days left. "TP, its JD," I said as he answered the phone. "It's time to go find the product. How about I pick you up at the office?" "What's the plan, exactly?" he queried.

Not wanting to answer the question on the phone, I artfully dodged the question by replying, "I'll go over everything with you in the car. See you at 2." I did not want to admit to him, I had no plan.

Driving over to the office, I could not understand why I was even proceeding with the plan. As I trudged through all the thoughts going through my mind nothing made any sense. My wife, God bless her, I could tell by the tone in her voice, didn't think this idea had any merit. Probably the only reason she didn't put up more of an argument against it was because she didn't think it could be pulled off in two days anyway. There was never any doubt I married a very smart lady, so why am I going through the motions to pull this off. I've lost every dime I had, chasing the concert. The checkbooks are empty. I've got about $30 and a handful of change in my pocket and my one remaining credit card is probably close to maxed out. What in the world am I doing? I have no idea how to pull this off! Well, if nothing else, if I've lost my mind, then hopefully I'll find it on the way to wherever the hell I'm going.

As TP closed the car door, he inquired, "So where are we going?"

Thoughtfully, I replied, "I don't know yet. What I've learned over the years is - when all you have is an idea to sell, you have to practice your pitch on your secondary targets, to get the necessary feedback to formulate a viable presentation for your primary target."

I turned off Mississippi on to Havana; the King Soopers grocery store sign caught my eye, and for some unknown reason, it seemed like the perfect place to start. So I pulled into the parking lot, continuing on with the conversation, saying, "Let's start here. I have no idea what I'm going to say, TP. There is no script. We buy groceries here and a few months ago I met the manager who was a very nice guy. Maybe he'll remember me. TP, I need you to go in with me, follow along with me, and from time to time nod positively. If he looks to you for reassurances, TP, you pony up to the bar, and tell him what great guys we are and we'll see what happens."

Being midafternoon on a Thursday, the store was nearly empty. There was a clerk stocking shelves in the main aisle as we walked in the store. I came up to her and asked where I might find the store manager. She pointed out a gentleman with sandy brown hair behind the Customer Service desk. TP and I headed over there, and as we got closer I was sure I'd never seen him before. Once he introduced himself as James, I asked if he was the manager and he informed me he was actually the assistant manager. He was the acting store manager until the real manager returned from vacation next week.

The question at the forefront of my mind was *do I take the time to make a pitch? Did James have authority to do anything with us?* James was such a young fella, all of about 24 or 25, maybe? *Oh, what the hell, we're here to practice anyway, let's give it a whirl*, I thought to myself, as I fired the opening salvo, "James, TP and I are with the Children of the World organization trying to help out with the Pope's World Youth Day rally. I don't know if you've heard, but all the children are going to have to march from Bear's Stadium out to Cherry Creek park Saturday."

James responded, "Ya, I saw the story on TV last night. Looks like it's going to be quite a hike."

Ahh, the perfect response! I answered quickly, "Yes, it sure is! Everyone is very concerned about the kids making that hike, especially with afternoon temperatures forecasted at over 100°. So we've been asked to see if we could set up some kind of refreshment stand midway along the route. And because you're nearby, we thought we would stop and see if maybe you could help us out! It's the kids you know, we're concerned they may get very dehydrated and exhausted on the march! It's such a really long hike, you know what I mean. A lot of those kids have never been at our altitude and everything." Both TP and I nodding thoughtfully, as we waited patiently for James to start nodding along with us, then it happened.

As James started to nod, he said, "How can we help you?"

Wow, we got a nibble on the line. The 'trick' now was to get James involved in the idea and lead him to suggesting solutions so they appear to be his idea. So I asked, "Do you have any suggestions?"

"Well yes," he replied, "Let's go over to the beverage aisle and see what we can do. What exactly are you guys thinking of doing?"

I explained to James, we wanted to set up a refreshment station and told him about our location and what we thought would be happening, in such a way as to induce him into making some more suggestions.

As we walked down the beverage aisle James brought up the suggestion of bottled water. This was my opportunity to test the financial issues plaguing us. So I answered by saying, "Well, James, our organization doesn't have a lot of money and so we'll be asking the kids to make a contribution when they get a refreshment, to help cover the cost. We're afraid they don't have a lot of money. So, at 60 cents or more per bottle, I think we have to rule out bottled water. How much are Coke and Pepsi?"

"We could let you have those for about 28 cents a can." he replied.

"Much better," I said, "Do you have anything less expensive?"

As James and I started down the aisle with TP in tow, James responded saying, "I have just the thing. I think this might work for you. Why not use our private label brand..."

I interrupted him jokingly, in midsentence, "Oh, you mean brand X?"

James turned and smiled, and said, "Well yes, we don't call it brand X. But, it is our own private label soft drinks. They come in numerous flavors and it's good stuff. They come in the same size as Coke and Pepsi. But, the part you'll like the best about brand X," with a sly grin all over his face, "is the price. I can give you these drinks for about 65% less per can, if you buy them by the pallet. Now, *how does that sound to you*?"

I glanced at TP, who was now standing behind James, and had raised his right hand in a clenched fist above his head, bringing it downward and mouthing the words, "Oh yeah!"

Time to reel James in, but I have to make it appear he's closing the deal. I put on my best facial expression of disbelief and said, "James, are you sure on the discount percentage?"

"Yes, as long as you're buying them by the pallet, I can make the discount percentage work." He answered.

Not wanting to seem desperate or especially over anxious, looking down at the floor, I said, somewhat softly, "Well, this is really worthwhile when looking at the alternatives. How many different flavors are there?"

Seeming a bit more excited, James replied, "Oh, there are several. We have root beer, cola, lemonade, black cherry, and orange."

I thought quickly, trying to figure out how to structure these negotiations. To see if I could solve all the problems we were faced with at the same time, and see if I could make this work, I said, "But we would have to take a minimum of one full pallet of a particular flavor, for the pricing to work with your discount, correct?"

James responded somewhat kind-heartedly, "Well yes, it just wouldn't be worthwhile to try to mix up the pallets with various flavors."

Did he just put an "S" on the word pallet? My mind, made a mental note; we were now progressing to more than 1 pallet. Recognizing the progression of the 'deal', I continued on. "Well, how could we work this out, if they drink the entire black cherry pallet, and only half of the cola pallet, for example? I don't know what we would do with a half a pallet of soda left over after the event has concluded."

Thinking fast, I added, "Could we return, uhmm -- would you give us credit for - the unused drinks?"

I could see the wheels turning in James' mind, when after a somewhat pregnant pause, he finally responded, "Ok, we can do that, but it would have to be by the case. We couldn't take back a partial case at that price. *Does that help you out?*"

Lookie there, young James had just executed his second trial close, to see if he had sold us the pop yet. Interesting, I thought. Not wanting to respond too quickly, I turned and looked towards TP and said, "Well, TP, what do you think? Can this work for us? You think the big boss and his assistant will approve?"

It was evident TP had picked up on the strategy being employed at the moment. After a few seconds of rubbing his hand on his chin and looking down at the floor and then back to me, he said thoughtfully, "You know, I think as long as we can return all the unused cases, I don't think there's any problem in your getting approval to do this. But it's up to you, you're the team leader."

Control of the conversation and the negotiations was now back in my hands. So now it was time to figure out how to get the sodas out of the store without having to pay for them up front and close the deal, I mean let James close the deal. I couldn't afford to buy several pallets of soda, even if I could get the money back for the unused soda. I simply didn't have any money available to buy even one pallet of soda.

I tried to think of how to formulate the words precisely, to see if there was some way to do something like a consignment deal, without using the word consignment. I felt such complexities, even if acceptable to Mister James, might take the deal out of his hands and authority. I did not want to create a situation where he had to get approval of management outside the store, under any circumstances. So as I stalled for a few moments and said a silent prayer, *"Lord – John Paul, if this is supposed to happen, if you Guys want this to happen, you have to help me out here and guide me through the rest of this conversation."*

Walking around in a circle, I finally turned to James and said, "James, I'd really like to do this deal with you, and what I'm thinking is - what if we could take one pallet of each flavor and hopefully come back with less than one complete pallet of returns. And if we did, and could return a partial pallet, of let's say, two different flavors of soda, and you gave us credit for those cases we return. Then the only question remaining is how we would pay you. As you can imagine, we're not the United Way or a large charitable organization with an unlimited amount of cash on hand. Our plan is to ask for contributions from each person taking a drink out of the ice chests. In such a fashion we'll be able to raise some money to pay for the drinks. I mean, everyone will be able to afford to throw in a quarter, or maybe a little more. We are not worried about ultimately raising enough money to pay for the drinks, especially at this price. The problem is we don't have the budget to pay for five pallets in advance. Could I leave my driver's license with you or something, and we settle up when we return, after the event Saturday night?"

Hearing my own words while watching James' facial expressions intently, I couldn't understand or believe where the words were coming from. They were so simple, and lacked the razzle-dazzle I would have normally included. I was astounded and amazed. On the one hand, I wanted to continue on. I was on a roll and the adrenalin was pumping, but a command from way deep down inside my mind screamed out, Stop Here!   Say no more!

James, moving a bit closer, looked me directly in the eye with as much intensity as he could muster -- needing to decide whether or not we were trustworthy -- asked, "This is for the Pope's March, correct?"

I recognized his question was a request for us to reaffirm this important fact, so in his mind, he could rely on it.   Without even blinking, I replied instantly, "Yes, of course!"

Apparently needing a bit more justification, he responded with, "It is happening in our neighborhood right?"

Suddenly, in my mind, I was seeing the store's community support policy flashing before my eyes.   I just couldn't make out the words.   So I immediately replied again, "Oh yes, we will be no more than a mile and a half from here.   That's why we're here in your store, in King Soopers, because you were the first closest store to where our event is going to be held.   And everyone is going to recognize the drinks, because of the private label name.   They'll know they came from King Soopers.   There will be no doubt where the sodas came from."

James glanced down for a moment and took a deep breath. Then smiling, he looked up and said, "You won't have to pay for the drinks when you pick them up.   What we'll do is load them up in your truck and you'll sign for them.   And then when you return Saturday night we'll tally up what was consumed, and you can pay for what you used then.   *How does that sound?"*

WOW! James just closed the deal for me!   Yahoo!   To say there was a small explosion going off in my mind would be an understatement.   Between all the stars and the bombs bursting in air, I tried to contain myself and maintain my posture and respond as unemotionally as I possibly could.   "You know, James, - that makes it work, and I sincerely thank you.   We have an old school bus without any seats in it.   Could we bring it over to your dock midafternoon tomorrow and pick up the sodas so we can get set up early Saturday morning?   We have to be at our site on the Pope's path by about 6AM to get set up.   Then after the event has concluded, we will be returning here, probably sometime around 7 or 8PM, maybe a little bit later, to settle up with you."

James reached out and extended his hand. As we shook hands, we started walking towards the front of the store, and he replied, "Yep, that's no problem. That'll work out perfectly. How many pallets of which flavors do you want to take Friday afternoon? I'll have them ready at the dock for you."

I turned to TP and said, "What do you think, TP, one pallet of each of the five flavors? Do you think five pallets will be enough for us, or do you think we should get a second pallet of one of the fruit flavored drinks like lemonade, orange or black cherry?"

TP responded, "Well it might be a good idea getting a second pallet of maybe orange or lemonade, because the fruit flavored drinks will be very popular, especially if the temperature goes over 100° as suggested on TV today."

We walked up to the Customer Service booth. James stepped inside and came to the counter with pencil and paper in hand. I said, "Yah, I think TP may be right. If we do one of each flavor except for the lemonade, and we get an extra pallet of lemonade, we may be better off. Will that work for you James?"

"Yep, that's fine. We'll do it that way. I'll have the pallets lined up at our dock tomorrow. You'll see them there. There are two different types of dock doors. You can use whichever door you wish, the sodas will be palletized nearby for you."

I extended my hand to shake once again and exclaimed, "James, we can't thank you enough for your help with this! We were so concerned we wouldn't be able to find a solution to meet our needs. You and King Soopers provided the solution we so desperately needed and as far as I'm concerned, it's a miracle. And I thank you and King Soopers, so very much."

James smiled, and replied, "Well I don't know about a miracle, we like to help our community and participate with and in our community. So it's my pleasure to have been able to help you solve the problems you were faced with. I hope your event is a real success. Thank you for coming to King Soopers." TP and I then turned and proceeded to the front door of the store.

TP started to say something, and I cut him off, saying, "Don't say anything until we get to the car and we actually get off the parking lot."

I was pumped, ecstatic and now extremely excited. I could tell TP was pumped as well. As I pulled up to the driveway to exit the parking lot, I said to TP, "Wait 'till we get down to the service station where we can get a cup of coffee and then we can talk."

Coffee cup in hand, I turned in the seat and said to TP, with excited emphasis, "Well, what did you think of **that**?"

TP threw his head back and with a giant smile on his face started to laugh as he said, "You are one silver tongued son of a bitch! I can't believe what I saw, it was incredible. I can't believe it - you did it without a script or without even practicing before we went in. I would've had to memorize a pitch, if it was me, but I would've never thought of doing it the way you did, it was stupendous!"

I recognized the sour taste of adrenalin in the back of my mouth and could only reply excitedly, "I can't believe we did it either. I appreciate your compliments and kind words but, I have to admit, it wasn't me." The words flowing faster, "Right in the middle of the conversation with James, in the middle of the pop aisle, I swear my guardian angel stepped in and took over. There's no question in my mind he guided us the whole way. I never dreamed we'd pull this off on our first stop. I figured we'd be spending the entire afternoon and most of the evening, going from one store to another, trying to hone our skills, trying to figure out how we were going to talk somebody out of the product we needed to sell. And then be able to pay for it after we sold it. It's beyond belief! James was such a nice guy and I can't believe he would go out on a limb like that for us. What an incredible afternoon!

"So, let's put our plan together on the way back to the office. I can drop you off and go home and tell Mama the good news, if she'll even believe this story." We agreed upon the plan. TP would get the bus ready, get the folding tables and the 30 gallon plastic trash buckets to hold the ice and drinks. I had the folding chairs. So it was decided, Friday afternoon 3 PM, we would take the bus over to King Soopers and pick up the sodas. Then turn in early for a 3 AM rendezvous at my house to pick up the chairs. Then depart to our secret lemonade stand to get set up for the march before dawn and before traffic started to build up in the area.

 Friday Afternoon

I sat at my desk, in my office at the house, trying to clean up a few remaining loose ends left over from the concert. Steve came running up and sat down in the side chair next to my desk and said, "Hi dad, so what yah' doin'? Anthony had to go somewhere with his grandpa, so you want to go hit some golf balls and have some fun?"

Looking at my watch, I knew I had to leave in about 10 minutes to meet up with TP. I answered, "Gee, Steve, it sure sounds like fun and I'd really like to go, but I have to meet TP at King Soopers and pick up the sodas to sell at the lemonade stand. Steve's expression was reflecting great disappointment, so I said, thinking quickly, "How about you go with me. We'll get the sodas loaded up, and then you and I'll go over to the golf course and knock out a couple of baskets of balls. What do you think of that idea?"

His face lighting up, happily queried, "When do we leave?"
"In about 10 minutes." I answered.

At 3 PM, we pulled up at the back of the store, backed the bus up to the loading dock, climbed up the ladder, and stepped inside the store. Right there by the door stood six pallets of sodas as promised. I told TP and Steve to wait here, and I would go to the front of the store and find James. Upon arriving at the customer service booth James came up from behind me and said, "I saw you coming. I have the paperwork ready, so we can get you loaded up and out of here as quickly as possible."

I responded, "Thank you, I saw the sodas stacked out there by the door, exactly as you promised and I sure appreciate it, and what you've done for us."

James answered, "No problem, glad to do it. Glad we could help you guys out, hope it goes well for you." As we walked into the back room James called a couple of store employees over to help us load the bus.

I stood on the edge of the dock as one of the employees handed me two cases at a time. I turned and set them down on the edge of the dock so Steve, standing in the rear doorway of the bus, could reach up, grab the cases of sodas and hand them to TP. TP would then move the cases towards the front of the bus, stack them, and return for the next ones.

Each case consisted of a cardboard box, the walls of which went halfway up the side of the cans of soda. The packing was tight, but the cans were individually loose, requiring a little care and support as each case was moved. Once we got a rhythm going, after a couple of dozen cases had passed by, the cases started moving into the bus at a pretty good clip. The paperwork James gave me simply stated, '6 pallets' for the quantity of sodas, and I still had forgotten to ask him how many cases were on a pallet. Midway through the first pallet I got distracted for a moment, and lost count of the cases already in the bus. Rather than interrupt the momentum of the movement of the pop, I chose to quit trying to count the number of cases, as we could count them when we were taking them out of the bus. So in fervor, we continued, case after case, emptying pallet after pallet. About 45 minutes later, the sixth and last empty pallet was being picked up by one of the employees and leaned up against the wall. The other employee called on the PA for James to come and we waited for his arrival.

Smiling as he walked up to the edge of the dock and looked inside the bus, he happily proclaimed, "Looks like you guys got it all in there. I'm surprised! But, it looks like you've got some room left. Do you want to take a couple more pallets?"

Thoughtfully, I responded, "Gee, James that would be terrific! Let's do it!" James left to get the paperwork from the front of the store and make the necessary changes, while one of the other store employees got the forklift and placed another pallet of black cherry sodas on the dock and once again, the transloading process began. Case after case disappeared into the bus until another pallet was empty. Since I could no longer see Stephen or TP I hollered into the bus, "Hey, you guys, can we get another pallet in there?"

Steve responded, "I don't think so, dad."

TP, having to exit from the front door of the bus, came around to the dock and leaned in motioning me to bend down, and whispered, "JD, that's it, there ain't no more room. I don't think we can get another case in here!"

Laughing, I exclaimed, "Wow! That's just great! Let's call it a done deal." Hollering out, "Thanks everyone – That's it, the bus is full!"

The store employees put away the last empty pallet and the forklift. James walked up to me with some new paperwork and wrote in '*7 Pallets*', which I signed, and again thanked him as we said goodbye. I climbed down the dock ladder into the parking lot. Hearing the warehouse door closing, I knew it would be okay to speak freely to TP and Steve. I was excited. We had enough soda, seven pallets. If we only made a dollar a can, we would do really well.

I stepped into the bus and Steve, with a giant grin, said, "Wow, dad, you sure got a lot of soda pop here."
TP interjected, "Come over here and look at this," pointing around the bus. "There's barely room to move. This bus is absolutely filled to the gunnels. There simply isn't enough room to put another case in here. I am absolutely amazed. I don't know how you did it JD, but it's impressive."
"Thanks!" I replied. Adding, "What about the tables, chairs, and trash cans?"

"The tables and chairs fold up, they'll slide in right on top. They'll be fine. The trash cans will fit right inside the step well, not to worry!"

"So we're on for 3AM at my house in the morning? Right TP?"

"You got it. I'll be there at 3AM for sure! By the way, how many cases do we have here?"

Sheepishly, I answered, "I don't know, I lost count during the first pallet. I guess we'll have to count them as we take them out. It really doesn't matter right now, anyway. We certainly have more than enough to make some good money tomorrow." Then turning to exit the bus I said, "Steve and I are going over to the golf course and knock some balls around. So I'll see you in the morning, TP, adios."

Stephen and I stepped out of the bus and headed to the car. Finally, I was going to have a little stress free, quality time, with my oldest son. I was feeling both relieved and pleased with what we had accomplished so far, and was anticipating the opportunity to really succeed tomorrow!

CHAPTER 15

The Day of Miracles Begins

... with Police HQ set up right in the center of the lemonade stand.

As I set my coffee cup down and put out my cigarette, I looked over at the clock. It was 3:33 Saturday morning, the Pope's big march day.

I heard TP's bus pull up in front of the house and met him at the door. We went to the garage to get the folding chairs we would need along with a small toolkit, and a partial role of white butcher paper we thought we might use for signage, and loaded everything into the bus. As we prepared to leave, I said, "TP, follow me over to 7-Eleven so I can load up the station wagon with ice, and then we'll go together from there over to the lemonade stand."

"Okay!" he replied.

At the first 7-Eleven we found they only had one bag of crushed ice, and four big blocks of ice, so we purchased those five bags. Since I would need to stop at another store to get ice, we decided that TP should go ahead to the lemonade stand and start setting up. We split up and went our separate ways. At the second 7-Eleven store I walked up to the ice box and opened it. Fortunately the crushed ice section was completely full. I loaded bag after bag of crushed ice into the car and a couple of more bags of blocked ice and went inside to pay for the ice. The station wagon was full and the bill came to $77, so I gave the clerk my credit card and waited to sign the ticket.

Then the clerk said, "Your card was declined Sir."

As he started to hand me back my credit card, I quickly realized I had maxed out my card. I reached in my pocket and pulled out my cash, all of $27. I then said to the clerk, before taking my credit card back, "Can you deduct $25 off the total and rerun my card?"

"Sure, let's try it," he said. Moments later, he replied, "Nope, it still won't take it!"

"Okay, let's try one more time, but this time, take the four blocks of ice off the tab as well, and try one more time, would you please?" I asked, as two people walked up to pay for their purchases.

Beginning to look a bit disgruntled now, the clerk in an exasperated tone, said, "Okay!"

Thoughts of complete failure suddenly filled my mind. If I couldn't afford to buy ice to cool the sodas, nobody would buy sodas, especially sodas sitting in the hot sun all day. I was beginning to feel an emotional crash.

As I waited for the credit card machine to finally decide whether or not it would accept my purchase, fears of failure began exploding in my mind. Suddenly the blessed sound of the little printer on the credit card machine sounded off as the paper started coming out of it which would require my signature. A giant feeling of relief poured through me as I scribbled my initials on the ticket and thanked the clerk. I went out, returned the four blocks of ice, and got in the car ready to head for the lemonade stand.

I shifted the car out of park into reverse and my second nightmare exploded in front of me. The gas gauge, the damn gas gauge was barely above the big E for empty. Oh crap! I thought, what the hell am I gonna do now? How could I have overlooked this? There wasn't enough gas in the tank to make it all the way back home to get some money from mama and I was running late to meet up with TP.

After finding 85 cents under the seat of the car, I went back inside the store and gave the clerk $1.85 for gas, leaving me with one US dollar in my pocket. To this day I don't know why I saved the one dollar. After putting gas in the car, I pulled out of the parking lot, noting the gas I had purchased just barely moved the gauge. This left me with a very sick feeling in the pit of my stomach, as I once again acknowledged to myself how flat broke I actually was. Knowing I had at least enough gas to get to the lemonade stand, I proceeded forward as dawn's early light was beginning to break the horizon.

Rounding the curve at the lemonade stand site, my view between the trees became clear and I realized I didn't see the bus. I was looking at a half-dozen police cars in our spot. So I literally let the car crawl into the clearing until I saw the bus off to the left and pulled up alongside it between the bus and the creek. TP immediately came out of the bus and walked up to me and said, "Don't say anything, just park your car directly behind the bus."

Recognizing an element of danger or warning in his voice, I didn't say anything. I parked behind the bus, got out of the car, and said to TP, "Why did you want me to park here?"

Moving so his back was to the gaggle of policemen, who were setting up their tables and chairs in front of their cars, TP leaned close to my ear and said, "I had you park here, this way, so they can't walk close to the back of the bus and see the piece of cardboard I put on the bumper to cover up the empty license plate holder. I don't have any license plates on the bus. I don't even have an inspection sticker or insurance. So I want to make sure they don't get close enough to the bus to come and ask me about it."

I then turned so I was looking directly at him and could watch the policemen doing whatever it was they were doing and said to TP, "What the hell is going on here? Why are there police cars here? Have you talked to them or have they talked to you yet?"

He replied quietly "Yes and no, let's go inside the bus so we can talk. That way they can't hear us. You are NOT going to believe this!" he added with a lot of emotion and urgency in his voice, as we pushed open the door to the bus and climbed up inside.

Once the door closed, TP started shaking his head and said, "Be quiet for a minute and let me tell you what's going on. When I got here, nobody was here. I set up the two tables out front, and was getting ready to set up the chairs, when the first three police cars pulled in. Boom, boom, boom they got out of their cars and started walking around, and then came over to me. They asked me what I was doing here, and I had no clue as to what to say or how to respond. Then it just came to me, and I said, - we're the **First-Aid Station** for the march!

"So I've been in here making up Red Cross signs with these felt pens on some of the butcher paper. I got them ready to tape onto the side of the bus. But, the first thing I had to do was hide the empty license plate holder on the back of the bus. So whatever you do, always make sure we have kind of a barricade there so the cops won't go nosing around and notice there ain't no license plate."

My head was spinning like a top at high speed. I thought: *What the fark was TP trying to tell me? Was our goose cooked, - the show over? What the hell are we gonna do with the seven pallets of soda pop sitting next to us? I'm outa money, outa gas, then ice delays, and now this, the FRICKEN police. I couldn't find a job! I couldn't pull off a concert! And now I can't pull off setting up a simple lemonade stand for 20,000 hot and thirsty kids! My life is getting just ridiculous! I should go out and jump in front of a bus and end all of this crap! My Lord God Almighty, what in the hell am I doing here?*

Finally, with a deep breath, I looked over at TP and said, "Did they buy your story?"

With a twinkle in his eye he said, with a chuckle, **"Yes, can you believe it?** I couldn't believe it when **they said okay!** It was unbelievable! I told them we'd stay out of their way," and one of them said, "No problem. We're here to set up the command center for the march, so there will be a lot of police vehicles around here, but you'll be fine over in this corner."

Breathlessly, TP continued, "JD, can you believe this shit? We picked the *Denver Police Command Center* location to set up our little lemonade stand. I just can't believe this - two great conmen like us, with no vendor's license, just out trying to scrounge up a few bucks, by selling overpriced soda pop to 20,000 kids, and the site we pick to do this, **just happens to be**, police command headquarters. This is just unbelievable! If we had a movie camera it would be a number one hit comedy for sure."

With extreme disbelief, while trying to break a smile, I replied, "Yah, you're right, and I guess since we're here, -- we should, -- we need . . . to go ahead and proceed, I guess. What the fark else can we do and what the fark else can go wrong? ...WOW! Look out the back window.

"Look at all the police cars now, their big trucks and look! It's a huge communication van. There must be 50 or 60 cops out there. But, they seem to be coming and going. Oh boy, this is **gonna be something**! TP, let's have a board meeting and put a plan, and a script, together so we're in perfect sync, and let's get out there and try and do this, maybe we can still make a success of it."

Minutes of the meeting, as was recorded in the sand:
TP: OK, our story has to center around the fact that we're a first aid station.
JD: You're right; do we have any first aid supplies or anything else in the bus to use as props?
TP: (smiling):   Yah, I've got this first aid kit.

He reached around behind the seat to open what looked like a little trap door and pulled out a small light gauge steel box about 8 inches wide by 6 inches long by 3 inches tall with a big Red Cross painted right on the top of it. It looked like it was a World War II first aid kit of some type, and probably hadn't been opened since the end of that war. He pulled down the two latches holding it closed and lifted the top. I couldn't believe it was actually a first aid kit with real first aid materials in it, including a box of bandages, an ace bandage, iodine and some other little odds and ends plus a little pair of scissors. It was kind of a small jim-dandy first aid kit.

JD: Now all we have to do is try to figure out how to make it look five times bigger than it is. Maybe if we set the box out there and take out all of the items and set them out near the box, we can make it look like there's more here than what is. What do you think?

TP: (thoughtfully): Yah, that'll help. And after we get a few cans of soda chilled down we can set them out there as well. But, if anybody asks what we're doing what are we gonna say?

JD: after pausing, (excitedly):   I think I got it. How's this for a story?
     'We are the first aid station assigned to this location. We are not anticipating any kind of serious injuries. We do have some supplies for small cuts, abrasions or blisters, the marchers may have encountered on the march so far. We're more concerned about dehydration and the effects of dehydration, which is why we've brought these lawn chairs and folding chairs for people to sit on, so they can rest. We want to get them in the shade, under the trees so they have a chance to get out of the sun, catch their breath, and get some refreshments. And most importantly, get rehydrated.'
     What do ya' think? How does that sound?

TP: (raising his right hand in a clenched fist salute): Perfect! That's it! That's our script! (Together, laughing): **That's our story and we're stick'n to it!**

JD: OK! Let's get out there and start setting up for this. Let's go sell some sodas!

TP: Right ON! Meeting Adjourned!

     We stood up grinning, and shook hands. We hugged each other, and patted one another on the back, pleased we had resolved this crisis so quickly.
     TP then said, "JD, go out and do a reconnaissance mission, and reconnoiter the area, see what it might look like once this parade gets going. I'll finish setting up."

"Yes Sir, Major," I responded, with a faux salute, and big grin, as I headed out the door.

The first thing I needed to do was create a map in my mind of what the area now looked like, with Police HQ set up right in the center of the lemonade stand. The bus and car were parked where the noses were pointed west and the tails pointed east as close to the trees as we could get them. There was a slight incline to the ground where we were parked, but for the most part it wasn't noticeable. Our tables and chairs were on flat ground and were about 80 feet from the north side of the bus and the south side edge of the pavement, where the kids would be marching. As I stood with bus behind me and the tables in front of me, I looked to the west, where the trees came up to the edge of the path and would be creating some shade for the marchers later on.

I walked over to the path by the tree, to imagine the marchers' initial view and reaction to the open area where the lemonade stand was located. As I turned to look to the east, it was glaringly evident the police command center and vehicles were the overpowering impression any individual would have as they came to this spot. Would the marchers even notice our little lemonade stand?

As I contemplated the situation, I finally surrendered to the fact that police HQ was going to overwhelm the site and minimize the value of any kind of signage we could create to attract the attention of the marchers. The best we were going to be able to do was to position our tables at an angle to the path in such a way as to try to attract the marchers' attention. This meant we would not be able to just sit behind the tables with our bright shining faces, and big smiles, collecting money from the marchers. We would have to use the tables as props, stand out in front of them, and literally hawk our products, like a beer salesman at a football game. It seemed the Good Lord was not going to make it easy for us to make a few bucks on this deal.

Whenever I attempt to take an idea and turn it into a reality, I try to create in my mind a complete video production of every possible aspect of what exactly needs to be done and how it will be done. So as I leaned against the tree, I began creating a new video in my mind, watching the marchers going by, one by one, larger groups and even throngs. Seeing TP and myself, with a cold soda in each hand, trying to make change for a $20 bill. The more I tried to edit the footage and restart the production, the worse the ending became. I felt like I was creating a horror film. There seemed to be way too many problems to overcome to have a happy ending.

The sun finally began to break the horizon. I decided to stop trying to choreograph the event. We will have to ad-lib the whole thing without a script or dance plan.

I decided, in desperation, it was time for prayer, which has bailed me out a number of times in the past, and said, *"Heavenly Father, listen up, if you have a moment, please. I'm in some really deep shit here! And, would You please let Pope John Paul know, I could sure use his help out here today as well. I don't know how I got here, and I can't seem to figure out how to resolve all the problems I can foresee. I can't seem to figure out a plan to take care of business. I don't even know how to verbalize any specifics to request of You. And, Pope John Paul, even though my intention or our intention was to make a few bucks on your rally, under the circumstances, I'm not sure our efforts will be successful. We will do our best to provide the marchers with some refreshment to help them out on this long, hot march. But if you could put in a good word for us we would appreciate any help we can get, and thank you Lord for listening, Amen.*

"It wasn't the Lord's prayer, but maybe He listened anyway," I thought, as I headed off to find TP.

CHAPTER 16

The Ice!!

...smack dab in the middle of police command headquarters,
and still not in handcuffs.

W hen I returned to the bus, it was obvious TP hadn't unloaded anything else. He must still be inside. I grabbed each of the 8 foot long folding tables and set them up at a new angle close to the path, so they could be readily seen by the kids. Then I stepped into the bus and saw TP on his knees, on the floor, crouched over a sheet of unrolled butcher paper with felt pen in hand and said, "What'cha doing guy?"

Looking up from his work at hand, smiling, he replied, "I think I've got the signage all done! Check this out. He unrolled a length of paper onto the floor. How's this?"

After examining his sign for moment, I had to chuckle and said with a smile, "Looks somewhat crude and kind of infantile, but at least you spelt all the words right, 'First-Aid Station', and those red crosses on either side, they look a bit washed out."

Defensively, he replied, "Well, the damn marker pens are running out of ink. I've only got three of them, a red, a black and a blue, what more do you want?"

I retorted, "Yah, knowing you, you probably took them home when you retired from the Marines. Let's see the other signs."

We took the signs outside and started duct taping them to the side of the bus. TP had also made one for each table. If the wind came up, they wouldn't survive, but we taped them to the tables anyway. The signage was all in place now. We stepped back to the path to check out our handiwork. Pleased with what we saw, and what we had gotten done, we decided it was time to get the chairs out, and the sodas chilled and ready.

After we got the trash cans and the first six chairs out, it was time for a smoke break. As we sat at one of the tables, a police officer walked up. Thinking to myself, *oh hell, what now?* The policeman stopped and said, "Sorry to bother you, but we wanted to let you know the ice in the back of your wagon is melting, big time. A big lake is forming underneath the back of your car." TP and I looked at each other and jumped to our feet, stomping out our cigarettes. Simultaneously, we began thanking the police officer profusely for letting us know. We raced over to the car to save the ice, which we both had forgotten about.

As I opened the tailgate my feet squished in the mud. I turned to TP and said, "How are we going to protect this ice? It's only 8 AM and it's melting like crazy. This is all we're gonna have since I'm completely out of money and can't buy more!"

TP, looking around, said, "Okay, here's what we do. Let's put two or three cases of soda in the bottom of each of eight trash cans, which leaves us with four trash cans for empty soda cans. Then we can put a couple of bags of ice on top of the sodas in each trash can." He headed over to the bus and got down on his hands and knees and looked under the bus. As he rose, he turned to me and said, "The bus is sitting over a small berm which will act as a windbreak to help keep the ice cool. So, let's store the rest of the ice underneath the bus."

We started pulling ice out of the station wagon stacking it up by the bus. Once the car was empty, TP crawled under the bus just forward of the rear axle. I started shoving one bag of ice at a time. Underneath the bus TP tore open each bag and threw the empty bag out, which I piled nearby. We then put three cases of soda into each trash can. After the first trash can, we figured out it would be a lot easier to put the trash cans in their final resting spot and then fill them with the sodas, Duh!

We both started grabbing the last bags of ice two at a time to pour over the sodas in each trash can. We got an empty trash bag and went around collecting all the empty ice bags and policed the area. Upon putting the trash bag in the bus, "The Lemonade Stand" was now complete, almost.

As we stood on the path and looked out over our handiwork, it suddenly dawned on me, "TP, how is anybody going to know what's in the trash cans? I mean, they look like trash cans. What's going to keep people from throwing trash in them?"

As I turned to look at TP, he grabbed the bill of his baseball cap, lifted it up a bit and began to scratch the top of his head. Chuckling he said, "Good point! You are absolutely right! They do look like trash cans for sure." Now laughing heartily, he continued, "Maybe we should put some signs on them? DUH!"

After a momentary pause, trying to stop laughing and envision a sign on a trash can, I replied, "Yep, I think you're right! We've got to put signs on the trash cans. What do you think the signs need to say?"

"Well Gee Whiz, I'm ...," stopping suddenly in mid-comeback as his laughter ceased, he continued seriously, "We gotta be careful, we don't want people to think they're free and we don't want to put a price on them, because we don't want the cops to come over again and ask us what we're doing. We gotta figure out a way to do it and protect our cover!"

Acknowledging his thoughts were dead on, I replied, "Right! Let's go in the bus and try to figure this out. Then we can start making signs."

After bantering back and forth about the signs for 5 minutes or so, we finally agreed on a solution. The signs would simply read, 'SODAS, Take One', thinking we could then just remind people to make a contribution. It seemed to be the best solution, considering all the circumstances involved.

There simply wasn't enough room in the bus for us both to try and write on the floor, so we went out and sat at one of the tables to craft the first sign. The red marking pen had officially died so we decided to make the word, 'SODAS', in blue and the words, 'Take One', in black, so we could both work on them at the same time, each with a different colored pen. After completing the first sign we decided to tape it to one of the trash cans to see how it worked out. It looked good, but we were still concerned people might interpret the sign to mean the sodas were free, something we did not want to happen. But there didn't seem to be a better alternative. We had to protect *our cover* as a first-aid station.

Suddenly TP said, "I got an idea! I gotta run back to the bus. Be right back." And off he went.

Upon his return, carrying two empty coffee cans, he beamed and said, "Look at what I found behind the seat in the bus. I dumped out the nuts and bolts, and like magic, presto, money cans! We put a sign on 'em , saying: *Contribution.* We could even put a dollar amount on there. What do you think?"

Thrilled with the idea, I exclaimed happily, "Perfecto! What a great idea, TP! We can set them at either end of the tables and if necessary, carry them around with us. Let's do it!

We sat there creating signs, including new ones for the coffee cans. About 20 minutes later, three cops came walking down the path, going past us and down past the tree, talking among themselves. We noticed, but continued to finish up the last sign. The cops, continuing to chat, turned and came back down the path in our direction. When they neared the table they stopped for a moment, checking out our display, and then came over to our table, and one of them said, "How are you guys doing? A first-aid station, what a good idea. We may need one, and cold sodas! Can we have one?"

I replied, "Sure! We have different flavors in each bin, lemonade over there, black cherry in this one here, whatever you'd like." As they started digging through the trash cans, I picked up the can for contributions, and moved it over in front of the bin two of the officers were searching in. Just as a friendly reminder. They each picked out a soda, opened them up and the one who had spoken previously, nodding his head in a positive manner, said, "Thanks a lot, we really appreciate it."

The officer standing next to him, pointing towards the bus, said, "Are you planning to use all those cases of sodas in the windows of your bus? It seems like an awful lot of soda."

There was something in his tone of voice, and I was trying to determine if there was something hidden and sinister in his query, while formulating a response. But TP beat me to the punch and responded, "No, we actually have another event tomorrow over at the church, after the mass, and we'll need them there. We didn't have any place else to store them in the meantime, so we brought them with us. It saves us another trip."

The officer simply nodded and replied, "Oh!   Ok," appearing to be caught off guard by TP's response.

As they walked off I noted, "Good job, nicely done! Good thing you brought your dancing shoes today!"

TP smiled and nodded as I went over to check the contribution can. Its emptiness reflected their election to ignore the contribution can entirely. Totally exasperated, I turned to TP and said, "I certainly hope this ain't an indication of what's going to be happening the rest of the day." TP looked over and decided to not even respond, as we went back to finishing the last sign.

Having finished all the signs, finally, we taped them onto the trash cans. Then walked all the way around the lemonade stand area to make sure everything was finished, perfect and ready for the kids to come. We were ready! Maybe? Lifting his hat and wiping his brow TP exclaimed, "Boy, it sure is starting to heat up! Let's go over and sit in the shade under the tree and take a break!"

I replied, thankfully, "Sounds good to me, let's do it!"

We were sitting next to each other leaning up against the big tree. To the west the magnificent beauty and splendor of the Rocky Mountains jagged jigsaw like teeth, cut and shaped the horizon where the clear blue sky met the mountains majesty. The calming silence being broken, only from time to time, by the chirping songs of a handful of nearby birds, it truly was a beautiful morning, a beautiful moment to be cherished and enjoyed.

After a ten minute interlude of quiet, I finally broke the silence and asked TP, "Did you happen to notice the incredible evening sunsets we've had every night since the Pope arrived?"

TP replied, "No, not really. I mean, the other night I was out on the balcony and did notice we had an incredible sunset with the clouds all red, orange and gold. But I didn't give it much thought. Is that what you mean?"

I replied, "Yah, I was out on the office steps the first night the Pope was in town, taking a break as sunset arrived, watching these beautiful cumulus clouds build up over the mountains. As a pilot, it's kind of second nature to keep an eye on the clouds, so when you're flying it becomes a habit. So you don't get yourself in a jam with the weather.

"Anyway, this huge bank of clouds built up over the mountains and then as the sun set there was an incredible display of color filling the western sky. I thought to myself, *God is just showing off for the Pope.* And I'm certain it had to impress the Pope, because it was truly a beautiful sight to see. I decided that night to make a point to check it out each evening, which I did and I was not disappointed. The same thing happened each night.

"The newspapers reported that every evening, starting about 4PM the Pope goes out into a garden at the inn for his evening prayers until 7PM. When I read that, it was like I understood. The Angels came every afternoon and prepared the evening sky for God to come, to listen to the Pope's prayers, and visit with this very special child of His. I think it's pretty incredible if you stop to think about it for a moment."

TP replied, "Sounds incredible, the way you explained it. I didn't realize it happened every night and I honestly never gave it any thought. But, if that's what the Angels were up to, it's pretty cool."

Quiet returned, and again you could hear the periodic chirping of the birds.

TP then spoke, saying, "You know what got to me? If it wasn't on the news every night and noted in the papers each day, I probably wouldn't have believed it, but did you notice there hasn't been any crime reported since the Pope arrived?"

Thinking for moment, I replied, "Well, now that you mention it, it does seem like there hasn't been any news about killings, robberies, shootings, and the standard fare of front page violence normally filling the first pages of the morning paper. You sure those news guys weren't so busy with the Pope they just overlooked reporting all the normal crime crap."

TP responded, "No, actually I was watching the news last night and one of the reporters commented on this abnormality; he was saying since the Pope arrived, calls to the police reporting crimes were almost nonexistent. It sounded like once the Pope arrived all the criminals left town and went on holiday. I thought the story was very interesting."

After a few moments, I replied, "Maybe it has something to do with all the FEDS moving into town a few months before the pope arrived. I don't know if you noticed, but it seemed to me like every fourth or fifth car on the streets, no matter where you went in town, were black sedans or SUVs with white government plates on them. They seemed to be everywhere. In fact I'd bet every government agency you can imagine has a huge task force deployed in Denver for this event. They probably have every phone in Denver tapped. And if you were ever convicted of a crime or arrested recently, you've probably had a government tail following you for the last month or so. You know the government, they want to know and control everything, but let's not start this conversation up or we'll be sitting under this tree for the rest of the day. Are you about ready to rock 'n roll? -- Then let's go!"

My gaze turned towards the command center, my thoughts running amok in my mind. I was trying to sort things out and create a new video in my mind of what I wanted to see happen in the coming hours, when suddenly, I saw a car I recognized meandering through all the police vehicles, trying to find a place to stop. It was my Lover Snugger, and my son Stephen. Seeing them arrive forced all the stress out of my body, I was so happy to see them. Stephen had jumped out of the car the moment it stopped, and as I walked briskly over towards them, he came running up to give me a hug. I grabbed him tightly and spun him around to let him know how happy I was to see him. I released him and went to the driver side of the car. As my snugger closed the car door, I wrapped my arms around her in a warm hug, and said, "Love you

Snugger! Thank God, the cavalry has arrived! You don't know how happy I am to see you."

Pushing me away, as she never appreciated public displays of affection, she said, "Stop it! I brought you boys something to eat."

Looking inside the car for the chow, I replied, "Oh Boy! Saved by the burger barn again! Thanks so much, sweetheart. Let's grab this stuff and take it over to the tables. Hey Steve, go find TP and tell him lunch is here."

Steve, reaching into the back of the car pulled out a cardboard box and said, "Okay dad, where is he?"

I replied, "I don't know, but check inside the bus. He's around here somewhere."

Audrey and I began removing the burgers and fries from the various bags onto the empty table to set up our picnic. Once all together, we sat down to eat. She was somewhat overwhelmed by the police command center and started the conversation off with a series of rapid fire questions as to what was really going on. TP and I explained all the happenings to both of them, getting an array of reactions from disbelief to outright amazement. Upon finally reaching the conclusion of our update, I turned to Steve and inquired, "What 'cha you got in the cardboard box, son?"

With a big smile covering his entire face, he went over to the end of the table where the mystery box had been sitting. Carrying it back, he returned to his seat, and as he opened the box, said, "I made some souvenir crosses for the marchers!" Reaching into the box, he pulled out half a dozen small wire crosses of various colors. He then added, "I want to give one to each person as they go by. So they'll remember us." Handing each of us a couple to examine more closely, it was evident he had crafted these small wire crosses with pride and love and wanted to share his love with the kids.

I was so impressed and proud of him I thought I felt the buttons on my shirt popping as I became speechless. It appeared he had gone into the garage and raided my reserve spools of electrical wire, white, yellow and red, and twisted, wrapped and tied off the wires in such a way as to form a cross. They were so simple, clever and well-crafted, I was amazed.

Based on the number of these crosses in the box, it was apparent he had not made them all in one evening, so I had to ask,  "Steve, these are beautiful, they're incredible! When did you make all these crosses?" He replied, "Tuesday night, at dinner, you explained about building the lemonade stand to take care of the marchers, and I decided they needed a souvenir. So I went out in the garage to figure out a way to make enough souvenirs and found a bunch of wire. I grabbed some wires and started twisting them around and they just came out this way. I've been making some every day and some each night. It was a lot of fun, dad! So anyway, I came over with mom to give them to the marchers when they come."

I was completely blown away. Here was my oldest son, from somewhere deep inside his heart, taking the time and effort to try and make things nice for the Pope's kids, all on his own initiative, with his own creativity, and in secret, not telling his mother or me what he was doing. I wanted to go somewhere and cry happily, as I had really just met and became acquainted with the incredible loving soul within my son. I suddenly realized I was always so busy and focused on work and my businesses, I had failed over the years to see and appreciate the incredible spirit within him. I was so proud and overwhelmed by his actions.

"That's such a cool plan, Stephen. You can also give them a cold soda with their cross if you want."

Inquisitively, he replied, "**Don't** they have to pay for the sodas dad?"

I sensed he didn't want to ask for any money when he was handing out his crosses, so I replied, "No son, when you're giving out a cross you can give them a soda for free. Okay!"

Relieved and happy, he replied, "Oh, that's great dad!"

Smiling, as we were both pleased with the outcome of the conversation, I said, "Son, after we finish eating, would you mind helping TP put some more ice in the trash cans? It's getting pretty warm and we want to try and keep them chilled." He nodded positively as he took another bite of his sandwich.

"So Snugger, what's your plan?" I asked as we finished eating. Before she could respond I added, "Why don't you let me show you around while we talk?" We both got up and started walking to the east, as I explained what she was seeing. She remained mesmerized by the fact we were smack dab in the middle of police command headquarters, *and still not in handcuffs.* As we passed them and waved, I noticed there were now more than two dozen people sitting on lawn chairs on the north side of the path to watch the marchers pass.

Having reached the east end of the lemonade stand area marked by two trash cans with plastic bags inside to receive the empty soda cans, we turned around and headed back west on the path. As we stood at the west end, in the shade of the tree, she finally said, "My plan is to leave Chris over at aunt Tanya's tonight. She'll bring him back tomorrow afternoon. Stephen and I are going to the Pope's mass tomorrow morning. Marilyn, my friend at the office, lives only a couple of blocks from the entrance to the park. We are going to spend the night at her house with some of my other friends from the office, so we don't have to fight the traffic and can get into the park early to get some good seats. Did you want to go?"

Answering, "No, I have no idea what time we'll get out of here tonight. We can't leave until the police are gone because of the license plate problem. We have no idea what time they're gonna break up and depart. Then we have to go back to King Soopers and settle up. So I have no idea when I'll be getting home. Its better you don't wait for me and screw up your plans, I'll be fine. I'll see if they are showing it live on TV tomorrow morning."

She responded, "Oh, I'm sure they will, it's been the only thing on the news all morning."

Smiling broadly, I asked, "So what do you want to do now? You want to stay and help sell sodas?"

Her retort was swift and immediate, "No!" Checking her emotions, by lowering her voice a notch, and to cleverly hide her true feelings about this undertaking, she continued, "It's getting so hot, it must be a hundred degrees and this is the only shade in the whole area. More importantly, I'm still not happy with your plan to try and make money off these kids. I know we could use the money, but it doesn't sit well with me. I'm not so sure it's such a good idea. And I don't even want to know how you're going to try to continue this right under the noses of the policemen."

I replied gently, "I know, but it seemed like such a good idea when I dreamed it up, and look at how it's fallen together. Everything will be okay. You'll see."

She turned, put her arms around me and resting her head on my shoulder, she whispered softly, "I know, I know, and I still love you. I'll go over and sit at the table for a little while or in the car and read the book I brought along, okay?"

I replied, before I kissed her, "That'll be fine, because I love you too!" We broke our kiss and headed back to the tables.

TP said, "Hey, let's take a walk a little ways down the path to see if we can see anything going on."

I replied, "Okay, let's go." As we arrived at the point in the path where the direction changed from almost due west to northwest, we stopped to gaze out over the horizon. To the west the mountains remained gorgeous, no smog. There wasn't a cloud in the sky. The temperature was warming up; it seemed to be about 90+°. The air was clear and crisp due to the lack of any humidity. I turned my gaze to the north and noticed between me and the city skyline, there seemed to be a small brown cloud, a kind of haze. At first I thought it must be smog, but on a Saturday smog would be very unusual and for some reason the cloud didn't have any height. I could still see the upper half of Denver's skyscrapers standing out against the clear blue sky. So I pointed this out to TP and asked, "What do you make of the haze?"

TP replied, "I don't know. It's kind of weird, probably some kind of dust in the air, reflecting the sunlight just right. Or maybe it's smoke from some strange chemical fire. It doesn't look like smog. If it was smog, I would think there would be more of it."

"Yah," I replied, "It seems really unusual. By the way, according to the TV weather report, it's supposed to be over 100° all day. Good soda selling temperatures, don't you think?"

With a quirky smile, he said, "Let's hope so, I could certainly use a little extra cash in my pocket right about now. You still think we can pull this off?"

Trying to interject some humor, I replied, "Yes, if we don't get arrested by the gestapo for violating a couple dozen municipal ordinances. And, more importantly, if the kids will all cooperate, and throw a measly couple of bucks our way as they pass by, we'll make sure they don't leave thirsty."

"You know," I said suddenly, "We need to quit calling them kids, they're actually young adults, I guess. We need to call them something else, you think?"

TP, gazing out at the horizon, responded, "Yah, sounds like a plan, I know a used car salesman that would call them 'mooches'. But, that don't sound too good, not classy. How about pilgrims? They are on a pilgrimage of sorts, even though it's been called a half a dozen different names like rally, conference, etc."

I replied, "I like the sound of that, let's call 'em pilgrims. That's a good one, from here on in, we'll call 'em *our pilgrims*.

"Well, I can't see any movement down the path. You ready to head back up to the lemonade stand?"

We put out our cigarettes and headed back to the tables, enjoying a truly beautiful late morning. As we were walking I voiced another concern going through my mind, and said, "I'm really afraid we're going to run out of Band-Aids in the first 10 minutes and I don't know what to do about it."

TP replied, "Me either!"

Upon our return, TP went back into the bus, as I meandered back over to the tree. Leaning up against the tree, looking down the path, I noted the time was about 9:15; reportedly the march was to start at 8AM. So I figured they had to be about 3 or 4 miles from the starting point.

I thought to myself, and then said out loud, *Hey there, John Paul, if you can hear me we're going to run out of band-aids and stuff real fast. We're really going to need some help here. I'm not so sure this was such a good idea; it may turn out to be a complete bust. But, if there's anything you can do, maybe put in a good word with the Good Lord for us, I'd sure appreciate it. Amen.*

My thoughts were suddenly interrupted as I felt someone tapping my arm. I turned and had to look down, and saw what appeared to be about a nine-year-old boy smiling up at me. I smiled back, and he said, "Hi Mister, can I help you guys? My mom said it would be okay!"

Smiling broadly, I replied, "What's your name young fella?"

"Bobby!" He replied proudly.

I countered, "Okay, maybe, but I gotta know, are you a hard worker?"

He replied, with enthusiasm, "Yes sir!"

Again smiling, I said, "Okay, you're hired! But first, we have to go over and double check with your mama, okay?"

He gave me a positive nod and off we went to check with his mom.

I actually had no idea what to do with him, but what the hell, any extra hand in a storm can always be a help.

CHAPTER 17

First-Aid

My Grandmother once said to me:

For the want of a nail, the shoe was lost,

For the want of a shoe, the horse was lost,

For the want of a horse, the soldier was lost,

For the want of a soldier, the war was lost!

Today I said:

TP,   For the want of a Band-Aid,

The First-Aid Station could be lost,

What are we to do?

As I walked up to where Bobby's mother was sitting, she saw me coming and rose as I said, "Hi my name is JD."

She shook my hand and replied, "Hi, I'm Tracy. I hope my son is not bothering you."

"Oh no, he only asked me if he could help us. It would be helpful if he could hand out sodas to the marchers as they come by. I wanted to check with you first - to make sure it would be okay."

She smiled down at Bobby. His face lit up with high hopes and expectations of a positive response from his mother. Then she said, "That's fine, as long as he doesn't get in your way. Is there anything else we can do to help you out?"

I said, "Well, since you asked, we have a problem and maybe you *can help*.

"We went over to pick up the first-aid supplies this morning and I don't think anyone at the office realized how early it was going be and have everything ready for us to bring out here. Consequently, we're really short on first-aid supplies. All we have is one little first aid kit. We are very concerned we may become overwhelmed and not have all the necessary supplies to handle the cuts, scratches and blisters we think the kids may have when they get to this point.

"I assume you live close by, across the creek, because I know you didn't drive in here with all the police equipment blocking the way. I thought maybe if you might have a box of Band-Aids, and maybe even some hydrogen peroxide it would sure help us out."

"Really!" She exclaimed excitedly, "I'm a nurse at St. Luke's and I've got some stuff at home I can bring over and in fact" . . . as she turned to the other ladies sitting nearby, now about a couple of dozen in number, and continued; "Hey everybody, is anyone else here a nurse?" Two other women got up and came over and the first said, "Yah, my name is Beth and I work at Denver General" (Hospital) and the other gal said, "Yes, my name is Karen and I work at Presbyterian Hospital." At that point Tracy interjects, "I'm Tracy, from Rose Hospital and well, this gentleman's got a first aid-station set up over there and he was unable to get all their supplies. Do you think we can maybe go back to our houses and put some stuff together to bring over to help them out?" As they each started nodding positively, other ladies having overheard the discussion jumped up and volunteered to join in.

I finally captured a break in the conversations taking place as they were getting organized and said, "Ladies, thank you so very much for your help. Bring all the stuff you're talking about over to the tables and we'll get everything set up properly. Again, thank you!

"Bobby, let's you and I go back over to the tables and start getting ready, while these ladies figure out what they can do to help us out." Bobby and I got back on the path and headed back to the tables. I looked back over my shoulder and I could see all those ladies heading over the bridge back to the housing development on the north side of the creek.

Bobby and I went over by the tree and I showed him where the sodas were, while explaining to him what we were going to need him to do. He asked if he could have a soda. I had to laugh, thinking about how many cans of soda there were in the bus, and said, "Certainly, Bobby. Today you can have all the sodas you can drink. You help yourself."

Twenty minutes later, here comes a parade of women carrying cardboard boxes, plastic bins and even some buckets, all filled with different kinds of first aid supplies. Everything from an extra-large bottle of hydrogen peroxide, to ace bandages, and boxes upon boxes of medical related supplies, hand soaps and lotions and even an array of medical instruments, including surgical scissors, different kinds of tweezers, a couple scalpels and almost everything you'd want to have for a full-blown first-aid station or full-blown emergency room. The supplies filled both tables and we all decided the eight large plastic bins used to carry most of the stuff in, could be used to bathe the feet or injury of the pilgrims once they arrived. If we were going to bathe their feet, it was obvious we would need some chairs for them to sit in and probably some rags for washing and drying. Once again, the ladies marched off across the bridge and about 15 minutes later there were two rows of four folding chairs facing each other with a bin to fill with water in front of each chair and a huge pile of clean rags between the chairs and the soda tables.

Then it happened. I remember, and I will forever remember. TP came sauntering up to me as I stood on the sidelines watching the ladies arrange all the supplies in just the right spot. After we lit up a cigarette, TP commented, "WOW!! These ladies are really something. These gals are a real God send!"

I blurted out, "God? He didn't have anything to do with them. They were sent by John Paul."

Then suddenly, I realized what I had said, and I most certainly didn't want to offend God.

So I quickly interjected, "Well, maybe I didn't state that quite correctly. I'm sure He - God, was involved somehow, maybe John Paul got the message and then maybe gave it the Holy Nod. And then God made it happen. I don't know! I have no clue how things like this work! I stood over there by the tree and asked John Paul for a little assistance. I never really thought to pray to God. I was having a thoughtful conversation, like I had John Paul on the phone or something, and asked him to intervene and help us out. And an hour later, we nearly have a full-blown emergency room in front of us. I mean, TP, I'm standing here in real-time, looking at real hard evidence of John Paul's answer to my prayer, my request. It's amazing!

"And yah, these gals are incredible. I mean personally, I was overwhelmed watching these ladies jump right in and help create a real first-aid station, and how this all came about. And it happened so shortly, if not instantly, after I said my prayer to John Paul. That's when the little kid, Bobby came up to talk to me, and I went over to get his mother's okay for him to help us out. Then all this just happened! I didn't have anything to do with it. I didn't lift a finger!"

Finally I stopped babbling, took a couple long drags on my cigarette, not looking up from the ground, afraid to hear TP's response.

Apparently after the appropriate pause length had transpired. TP finally said, "JD, every now and then, I really don't understand you. You're one of the brightest guys I've ever known, and then you tell me you're out here praying to a guy that's not even dead yet. I don't begin to understand your religious beliefs, but I can't imagine you're gonna pray for help from somebody still living. It makes no sense." I stood there, leaning up against the bus, trying to figure out if I wanted to even respond, and really get into this conversation, when suddenly TP saved me by saying, "Oh well, never mind!"

Promptly, I replied, "Thanks! Let's just watch the gals and try to enjoy the moment."

TP and I stood there in awe and utter amazement watching these ladies as they turned our well-planned lemonade stand into a first-class first-aid station. It was really something to see and participate in as it continued to develop. Finally, it seemed our three nurses had everything set up and arranged exactly the way they wanted it, as they headed over toward us.

Tracy smiled and said, "Well, guys, I think we've got you all set up to go," as she turned towards the tables and waved her hand as if she was making a formal presentation.

As she looked back towards me, I tried to come up with the biggest smile I possibly could, looked back and forth at each of the ladies and said, "You ladies are incredible, TP and I can't even believe what we've seen you gals do. It's really amazing, and from the bottom of our hearts, we want to thank you for helping us out. However, I have one last request. There are only the two of us, TP and me. Would you keep an eye on us, and if we get overwhelmed, would you three be willing to come over and help us out?"

They looked and nodded at each other and Tracy said, "Of course, we'd be delighted to help out if we can."

Thankfully, I said, "Ladies, we truly appreciate everything you've done to help us!" They turned, waving back, as they started walking back to their lawn chairs.

Flashing back to our last conversation, I couldn't resist and had to say, "There you go TP, real *Angels*, our very own real live *angels,* watching over us! What have you got to say about that? – No don't say anything - I was just being – well facetious, I guess."

"OK, whatever!" He replied, shaking his head as we walked over to the tables, to more closely examine the ladies' handiwork.

Without any question we were now truly ready for the onslaught to arrive. I caught Bobby running by and asked him over. I told TP I'd be right back as I was going to take Bobby down the path a little ways. As Bobby and I walked past the tree and down the path a bit, I finally stopped and squatted down, so we were eyeball to eyeball. Then I said, "Bobby, you see where the path curves down there?"

"Yes!" he replied.

After checking my watch, I said, "Okay, Bobby, here's the deal. It's 11:15 and the marchers should be arriving anytime. Now your job is to go down there at the curve and wait there. You keep watching down the path until you can see at least three people walking up the path towards you. As soon as you see them, you start running back to the bus, as fast as you can. When you get to the tree, you start hollering as loud as you can, 'The pilgrims are coming, the pilgrims are coming!' It's really important. Do you think you can do that for us?"

Nodding his head in a big up-and-down motion Bobby replied, "Yes sir, I can run real fast too!"

Smiling, I replied, "Bobby, you're a good man. If they don't get here in the next 20 minutes or so, I'll come down the path and check with you to see how you're doing, okay?"

"Okay!" He said, waving as he turned and began running down the path to the curve.

When I got back to the lemonade stand, I saw TP standing inside the bus and went over to visit with him. I stepped inside and said, "What's happening, man?"

Sitting in the driver seat now, smoking a cigarette, he looked over and said, "Well, the good news, of course, is we've got a hell of a first-aid station. The bad news, however, is while you've been off with the ladies, I've been here, trying to keep a low profile, and out of sight of the cops, and man we're getting killed. I'll bet they've consumed over two cases of soda so far, and not one dime, not one quarter, not even one penny, has been dropped in the coffee cans. They're ignoring the contribution request signs and I'm fearful the marchers are going to do the same."

After taking a moment to light up a cigarette, I finally inquired, "Do you think we're overpriced? Do you think we need to lower the price?"

He replied, "I really don't know. Maybe so, but my gut tells me we should wait and see how the pilgrims react to the price."

Thoughtfully, after a moment, preparing my thoughts, to reply gently, as I really didn't want to get into a mathematical pricing exercise with TP, in which he would correctly calculate and illustrate, a 50% price cut would equate to more than a 50% reduction in the profits we were supposed to make and split. So I said, "Well, I think your gut's right, but I think we should go ahead right now, before the circus starts, and make up a couple of replacement signs, one for each coffee can. Let's be ready to drop the price to, say, how about one dollar, if we have to, what do you think?"

As TP rose from the driver seat and reached across the bus to grab the remaining two marker pens, he replied, "Yah, I guess so. We need to be prepared, but man it is going to pulverize the profit potential. For all the effort and work we've done on this project, to anticipate such slim-pic'ens, it almost makes me physically ill just thinking about it."

It was evident my teammate was on a downer at the moment. Now it was my job to overcome my own depression which was beginning to set in, and try to re-light the fire in TP's belly. For, if you don't have a real fire in your belly, driving you to succeed, you'll never overcome all the obstacles which are always present on the path to success.

So, back out to the tables we went to make the backup signs for the coffee cans while trying our best to pump each other up during the ensuing conversation. The waiting, the anticipation and more importantly the overview of the whole situation as it related to the original concept of us both making a few grand on this adventure was really pulling us apart mentally and emotionally. I believe the biggest reason we didn't give up and abandon the project and head for the hills, at that moment, was because we were absolutely trapped by all of police vehicles surrounding the command center. We both agreed the only really bright star in the whole picture was our recently completed first-aid station, which now was so impressive we began to take great pride in what had been accomplished. This truly helped us overcome our momentary depression and rekindle the fires to get out there and do the very best we could.

We agreed finally, win, lose or draw we would put the monetary issues behind us and not worry about it until after we departed the lemonade stand. From this point forward, we would only concentrate on taking care of the Pope's kids and do the best we could for them. I don't know how we finally talked ourselves into this change in goals and mental thinking, but that's what we did, and in the end, we were both glad we did!

TP and I now sat at one of the tables somewhat bored, having another smoke break, comparing the time on our watches and mutually agreeing the correct time was 11:40 when we heard a faint cry.

CHAPTER 18

The Pilgrims Arrive!!

*More and more people followed suit, grabbing a soda and
stopping to take a break*

TP and I jumped up in concern, and ran to the path as we heard the cry again. It was getting louder! "The Pilgrims Are Coming!

The Pilgrims Are Coming!"

As we stopped on the path at the tree, we could see it was Bobby, running up the path as fast as he could, arms flailing wildly. Shouting over and over, "The Pilgrims Are Coming! The Pilgrims Are Coming!" Around the big tree trunk he came right up to us, out of breath but grinning from ear to ear, thrilled he could be the one to announce their arrival.

I bellowed, "Great job, Bobby, great job!" Then said, "Now keep going, run right past the policemen over to where your mother's sitting and keep hollering all the way! After you give your mom a big hug you can come back over here and we'll get ready to go to work, okay?" Off he went nodding happily and hollering all the way.

Steve was already standing over at the edge of the path with a handful of his crosses in one hand and an orange soda in the other. TP had moved over to the second table as I was pulling out an array of different flavored sodas, setting them on the table so they would be close at hand, with a coffee can for contributions nearby. It was about high noon as the first pilgrim passed the tree. I walked up to him as he approached, and asked, "Cold soda?"

He shook his head negatively, and said, "No, thanks, I have my own water." He grabbed a string hanging off his back pack, with a thermos dangling from the end of the string to show me, as he continued on without missing a step.

He was the first pilgrim, leading the pack. We waited. It was a few minutes before a small group walked into the shade of the tree. I headed towards them and said:

Cold soda? You guys want a cold soda? Anybody for a cold soda?

Pilgrim #2:   No thanks!

Pilgrim #5:   No, thank you.

Pilgrim #7:   No thanks!

I hollered out again:

"Sodas, ice cold sodas, anybody need an ice cold soda?" I continued to query, standing right on the edge of the path, holding out a soda in each hand, smiling and looking each one squarely in the eye as my voice rang out while they kept marching by. Many simply nodded negatively as they continued on. So I tried to get a little more aggressive, and put a little more emotion into my pitch:

Pilgrim #22:   No thanks!

Pilgrim #27:   No, but thanks for offering!

Pilgrim #35   Yah, thanks.   Boy!   Just what I needed!

As I reached out and handed him a soda.

Pilgrim #49:   No thanks, the last pilgrim in the group said, as he went on by.

There was a break in the parade of pilgrims; the path was once again empty. Steve was over grabbing another handful of crosses to hand out, and as I approached him, I said, "Steve, how's it going?"

Excitedly, he replied, "I gave out a bunch of crosses, dad. They really liked 'em, and were really happy."

I inquired, "How about sodas, did you give away any sodas?"

He replied, "No," as he continued to gather more crosses, and I turned to look for TP.

Bobby appeared in front of me happy and smiling, and said, "I gave out 2 sodas and one man gave me a dollar and I put it in the can!"

I responded, "Good job, Bobby! You can take a break for a minute before the next group arrives, okay!" He nodded and ran off. I saw TP heading towards the bus and went over to talk to him.

I asked, "TP, how did it go?"

He replied, "Not good, I couldn't give away a single can of soda."

So I gave him my results, including Bobby's and Stephen's reports. As I tried to analyze what was going on, TP finally stated, "This is a frikin' disaster. We can't even give away the sodas for free!!" His voice filled with disgust and disappointment.

His words began filling me with chagrin; I had to nip this in the bud. I began, "TP, did you notice, it seemed like the more athletic individuals were leading the march? They had good physiques and their leg muscles were well toned. Most of them were carrying water. Maybe all we're seeing so far are the kids in really good shape. I'll bet as the march goes on the condition of the marchers will deteriorate. I think the less prepared and weaker marchers will be the ones who need to rest and rehydrate. I believe it's a bit early to let what happened get us down, or give up and throw in the towel at this point."

TP shrugged his shoulders, lifted his cap off his head and wiped his brow with his forearm, and remarked, "It sure has gotten hot hasn't it?"

Recognizing TP was really saying, *yeah, okay, I hear you, but I don't wanna talk about it*, I acknowledged his comment with an 'Ok,' as we headed back to the tables.

After another smoke break, the peace and quiet at the lemonade stand for the last 20 minutes was suddenly broken by the sound of singing. Curious, we got up and went over by the tree, and saw a large line of heads breaking the horizon on the path, while the singing was getting noticeably louder. The path at the point the pilgrims had reached was much wider, probably 15 feet across. The pilgrims were now visible from the waist up. It was evident there were about a dozen people in a line across the path, marching together. As they continued forward, we could see the size of this crowd continue to grow.

We raced back to the tables. When we checked the path again as they were coming up to the tree it looked like there were at least 300 or 400 people in this group. They were pretty tightly packed together, and as they reached the tree they were forced to shrink the width of the lines across the path from 12 or so people, to 6 or 8 across, which slowed the pace of their march. They were singing along, happy as larks. The first half a dozen lines to pass seemed to want to keep the pace going uninterrupted, so none stopped to take a refreshment.

But, as the necessary compression slowed the pace more and more, people started to stop and get out of line for a soda. We noticed Bobby directing marchers over to the trash cans to select a soda. More and more people followed suit, grabbing a soda and stopping to take a break, while talking to their fellow pilgrims. Many even grabbed a second soda as they restarted their march to the park. TP and I were giving out sodas pretty fast. It was exciting to finally see people taking advantage of the lemonade stand. Then suddenly it was quiet again; the group had come and gone. I grabbed Bobby and TP. We proceeded to check everything out to evaluate how we'd done.

After inspecting the contents of each trash can it was obvious we needed to add more sodas and ice. TP and I began making trip after trip, back and forth, carrying two cases of soda each to the trash cans. We had long since given up trying to keep only one flavor of soda in each of the cans. We continued to pour case after case into each trash can, until the trash cans were over two thirds full. After finally filling the last trash can, TP mentioned, "Well I guess we need to ice 'em down now, huh?" I nodded affirmatively and we took the last of the empty cardboard boxes back to the bus, breaking them down so they would lay flat.

TP stepped into the bus and pulled my empty boxes into the bus behind him. I leaned up against the side of the bus and lit up a smoke. As Bobby approached I said, "Bobby, would you run over where we set up the chairs and grab two of those plastic pails sitting over there?"

He replied, "Okay!"

TP stepped out of the bus with a hammer in one hand and a crowbar in the other. Extending the hammer to me, said, "Here you go - you'll need this!"

Inquisitively, I replied, "What in the hell is this for?"

He chuckled, and said, "Wait until you get down underneath the bus and try and get some of the ice out of there, you'll see."

Grinning from ear to ear, Bobby returned carrying the two empty pails and TP said, "Bobby, JD and I are going to crawl under the bus and spread these plastic bags out. Then we'll start breaking off ice and pushing it out to you. You put the ice in the pails, and once they're full, you run over and pour them over the soda cans. I need you to do that until the water and ice is about this far from the top," indicating with his hands, a height of about 6 inches. Then come back and do it again, got it? Bobby nodded affirmatively as TP and I began to crawl underneath the bus.

It was close quarters; there wasn't much room. Examining our stash of ice I instantly understood why TP had provided me with the hammer. Apparently, as the pile of crushed ice began to melt over the four big blocks of ice underneath, the cold from beneath then froze the melting ice as the water trickled downward, leaving a giant block of ice lying before us. After my first half dozen swings of the hammer, I finally broke off about a 1 pound chunk, about 5 x 6 x 8 inches. Wow! It sure took a lot of effort to break off one piece. Closer examination revealed that below the outer 2 inch shell there remained evidence of individual ice cubes frozen together.

TP had been correct in his assessment early this morning, when he elaborated on his idea to turn the berm and the frame of the bus into an ice chest to preserve the ice. I found it really interesting how it turned out. The broken ice chunks slid easily across the plastic bags as the ice continued sliding out from under the bus. I could see Bobby's small hands grab the chunks and heard it land in the bottom of the plastic pail. The plan was good. I began hammering away in front of the axle while at the same time, TP was using his crowbar to hammer and pry at the other end of the enormous ice cube we had created, sliding his successes, one after another, out from under the bus to Bobby.

After a while I was actually getting quite chilled. I called out to Bobby, "How we doin' Bobby, are all the trash cans full yet?" In a loud voice, he answered, "No, there's one more to fill!" TP nodded in acknowledgment and we both returned to hammering away at the ice. About 10 minutes later, we both had enough ice harvesting for a while. We rolled and crawled out from under the bus. The warm air felt good as I was actually quite chilled by this point. We helped Bobby fill the two pails with the last of the ice we had shoved out, and sent him on his way.

TP returned the tools to the bus. I picked up a pail in each hand and headed over to the trash cans, searching, unsuccessfully, for the remaining trash can in need of the ice I had carried over. Bobby had done a really first-class job. I ended up spreading half of one pail of the ice over the top of all the trash cans which were now all topped off. I then carried the pails over to where we had lined up the lawn chairs with plastic bins in front of them and poured out the remainder of the ice, some into each of the bins.

Then I leaned over to set the empty pails back out of the way, and when I stood up and began to turn around, there stood a police officer. I smiled and greeted him, "Hi there, Officer, how are yah?"

He replied, "Fine, thank you. My boss asked me to come over and ask you if you guys would mind going over to the east end of the path and round up all those empty pop cans over there." Turning as he spoke, and pointing to the east, he continued, "There's quite a pile of them over there." He turned back to face me as I looked in the direction he had pointed to, unable to see the pop cans he spoke of on the far side of the command center.

TP walked up and nodded to the policemen, while the officer continued, "It's a safety thing. We want to make sure our pathway is clear, in case there is an emergency and we have to mobilize some of our vehicles onto the path. Would you guys mind taking care of it?"

Nodding my head and smiling, I replied, "Of course officer, no problem. Consider it done. In the meantime, would you like to take some cold sodas over to your crew?"

He answered, "Well, your offer, it's very nice, but only if you're sure you have enough..."

Enough, I thought, *what's he talking about - you can see through the windows how full the bus is -- there must be around 7000 cans of soda in there, maybe it's his attempt at humor.*

"... The heat has really been tough on us over there, with no shade or cold refreshments; it would be real nice - thank you." While he was talking I had turned around and grabbed the two ice pails and was extending them to him as he finished speaking.

I then said, "Here, take these and fill'em up to carry 'em. Please, take as many as you need. When you're done, if you would, please bring the pails back over here." As I pointed to the now official storage spot for the pails, he smiled and nodded as he thanked us again and headed over to the loaded trash cans.

I lit up a smoke. TP followed suit, as we waited for him to get out of earshot. Finally, TP whispered, "What are you doing? What did he want?"

I looked up at TP and smiled. For some reason I felt good, but I thought I would have a little fun with TP, so I whispered, "Keep it down, I just bribed the whole police force!"

I was having great difficulty holding my laughter back as I watched TP's face contorting into an expression of complete bewilderment as he said, "Oh shit, that's just what we need, you're going to get us into trouble with the cops for sure." His expression was priceless and I couldn't hold it in any longer. I broke into complete laughter at TP's expense. It was too funny! I finally regained my composure and explained the true nature of the policeman's visit and admitted my graciousness was nothing more than a simple act of attempted kindness being extended to the policemen. I told him it was just good PR. TP then expressed his displeasure and a lack of appreciation of my humor, as we walked back over to the bus to get more trash bags and head over to clean up the east end of the lemonade stand.

Empty soda cans were strewn everywhere. The two trash cans were so full they looked like ice cream cones with pointy tops. This was going to be a job. I started picking up empty cans, throwing 'em into a trash bag as I tried to get closer to the trash cans. We were both picking up the outliers as we moved towards the trash cans. I finally tired of bending over for a single can and then started kicking 'em towards the trash cans. Then it dawned on me, we ought to try squashing them first, as I woke up to the fact they might not all fit back inside the bus when we leave. So I said to TP, "Hey, you think we ought to crush some of these cans before we pick them up, to try and reduce the volume a bit?"

TP, stopping for a moment, said; "Yep, that's a good idea, let's do it." We then both began, almost like a dance, stomping on the cans, as we pushed them towards the trash cans with our feet. When a group of cans came together, the dance would begin again, watching each other as we did our dance.

We really looked silly, and began laughing as we watched each other stomping cans, intermittently stopping to pick up the debris we were creating. It looked like we had each crushed a small mountain of cans and soon only the full trash cans remained. I had TP hold open his bag against the lip of the first trash can and started pushing the cans precariously perched above the lip into the bag. Then we did the same thing to the other trash can. We could now lift the full plastic bags and tie them off as we removed them from the trash cans. After inserting new empty plastic bags into the trash cans, we noticed a few more empty cans in the tall weeds nearby, and tossed them into the ready to go trash cans. We picked up the first load of our booty, about six bags each, and trudged towards the bus and stuffed them in, returning a few more times to snag them all..

Walking around, I undertook a visual inspection of the readiness of the entire lemonade stand area. Upon the conclusion of my inspection I felt pleased. Yet something was bothering me, something wasn't quite right. I continued looking around, but couldn't figure out what seemed to be wrong.

TP came up to where I was standing, literally smack dab in the middle of the lemonade stand area, and said, "How about a smoke break?"

I turned to face him, and said, "Sounds good!" While lighting up it came to me! I uttered, "AHH-Hah! TP, check it out," I exclaimed suddenly, "The sky over the path, it's not blue anymore, it's brownish. It's like the haze we saw earlier." I began turning, 360°, looking at the sky, which had been bright blue and cloudless except for the area north of the path earlier. I said, "You know this is really weird TP! We can't see the mountains anymore. In fact, our visibility has been reduced to about 300 yards. And don't say it's smog. It doesn't have any odor, it's not like LA or New York City smog which smells so bad you swear you can taste it. This stuff is odorless.

As TP turned and scanned the sky, somewhat amazed, he muttered, "Yep, I see what you mean, it is kind-a-weird!"

At that moment, the cry rang out again, "The Pilgrims Are Coming!" Bobby was back on the job. Running over to one of the trash cans, he grabbed a couple of sodas and headed over to the north side of the path. Steve was standing east of him.

TP and I got a soda in each hand and returned to the edge of the path, waiting for the pilgrims to arrive. After a few minutes the second wave arrived and we repeated our efforts as before.

This time however, I disposed of the first two cans instantly and returned to the trash can for more sodas, placing four in the crook of my left arm. The cold against the side of my body felt so good, as I walked back to the path a few feet away. Quickly, two cans were grabbed up. Then as three pilgrims walking together approached me, one of them asked, "Can we have a soda?" I was so delighted to respond, "Absolutely!" I grabbed a soda off my arm and handed it to the speaker, the other two reached over and each grabbed a can. As they were opening them, I inquired, "Would you guys like to make a contribution?" As I reached down and grabbed the coffee can by my foot with the 'contribution' sign facing them, one of them replied, "Well, we don't have any money." Surprised they would say that, I acquiesced and replied, "Okay, don't worry about it, you guys keep marching on. You're over halfway there, but it's a bit of a trek up the hill. So take it easy and don't wear yourselves out!"

The pilgrims continued to come. I continued to solicit a contribution for the sodas I was handing out, without any success whatsoever at all. In desperation, I changed my pitch and began hollering, "Cold sodas, only two dollars," over and over without a single taker.

So very frustrated, I changed my pitch again and began hollering, "Cold sodas, only a dollar!" Again, over and over, I made the call. I walked past the tree down the path, head-on into the oncoming marchers, with an arm full of cold sodas. I was hoping all the while, TP and the kids were faring better than I and were filling the other coffee can with money. After passing through the tree's shade and back into the sunlight, I decided I didn't want to carry the sodas back with me so I started holding them out as the marchers came by. They were quickly taken from my outstretched hand. I couldn't see any sense in carrying them all away back to the tables, anyway.

I was completely crushed. I couldn't believe, despite my best efforts I couldn't sell a single stinking can of soda. Always having believed myself to be a master salesman with unbelievable closing skills, here I stood looking into a trashcan full of ice and sodas realizing once again, I was a complete failure. I was feeling really sorry for myself. Then something clicked in my mind as my thinking continued to spiral downward.

We needed to train the pilgrims! Somehow, we had to demonstrate and put on a show to get the pilgrims off the path, and over to the tables and trash cans, to start taking the sodas, and leaving a contribution. I ran over to where TP was standing and explained my idea.

He finally said, "Well, why not, whatever we're doing now ain't working. So what do you think we should do?"

I responded, "I don't know, yet, but go get Steve and Bobby and bring them over to the tables and I'll figure it out, okay!"

At the tables, I began running previous video tapes in my mind. I noticed in the filmstrip, as a few people started drinking sodas around the tables, the percentage of the people around the tables drinking sodas increased. Now I had to figure out how to turn this image in my mind into a reality.

As TP and the kids came up, I said, "We've got to get a bunch of these kids drinking sodas, so we're going give them away for a while. We have to start building a crowd around the tables. Steve, you and TP go over by the second table and start trying to direct some of the marchers into the table area. Tell them the sodas are free. Bobby, you and I'll do the same right over there and see if we can't build up a crowd." Off we went.

At first, we had to drag some of the pilgrims kicking and screaming over to the table. But soon, with a lot of effort and some salesmanship, a small crowd had begun to form. As it grew we had to go over to the trash cans and start handing out sodas, and help people find their selection, to keep the momentum going. More and more started coming over to the tables, grabbing a soda and pausing to chat among themselves. Finally, it seemed we had achieved success.

I stepped back away from the tables to observe the growing crowd. My gaze meandered around the area, stopping to focus on the lawn chair rest area. All the original chairs were filled with resting pilgrims, as were a number of additional chairs which had been placed nearby. Apparently some of the neighborhood observers had been kind enough to bring their chairs over and donate them to the cause. I decided to go over and take a closer look. The seated pilgrims were removing their shoes and socks and rubbing their feet. Those with bins of water in front of them were soaking their feet. The nurses, like little honeybees, were busily going from pilgrim to pilgrim, each carrying a box of Band-Aids, applying Band-Aids here and there. As one pilgrim finished redressing his feet and walked off another sat down in the empty chair to repeat the process. I walked up to Tracy and asked, "How's it going, Tracy?"

Smiling, she replied, "Good, really good! We've been so busy. And we need fresh water. The water in the bins is getting so dirty," pointing, as she and I started to walk down between the rows of bins.

I stopped and said, "They are getting pretty nasty, I'll take care of it."

I walked over and grabbed two pails and headed over to the trash cans. I immersed them both into one of the trash cans filling them with ice cold water. Returning to the bins I had the pilgrim sitting in front of each bin pour out the dirty water and then refilled it, while exchanging pleasantries with them. I repeated this process until there was fresh water in all the bins.

I stood in the center and in a raised voice asked, "How's everybody doing?"

Everyone started to respond positively with one pilgrim pointing out the cold water was reducing the swelling in his feet. Several others then concurred, and expressed their gratitude for the relief being provided. I was really overwhelmed by the warm feeling I felt inside, recognizing the appreciation of our efforts being conveyed to me by the pilgrims. It made everything feel so worthwhile.

Back at the tables, the plan was working, almost! The number of people standing around drinking cold sodas had substantially increased. Sodas were being handed out to everyone. But still, no one had made a contribution. But seeing the relief and gratitude expressed by the pilgrims overshadowed the lack of contributions.

We continued to hand out sodas like mad and my concerns and stress seemed to kind of fade away. I finally said to TP, "Can you make up new signs saying 'Contributions', with no price, and put them on each of the coffee cans. Put one on each table, and we'll wait and see what happens. We'll put our trust in the Good Lord!" I thought to myself, *OK, Lord, it's all up to You and John Paul now, amen.* TP did as I asked as the second wave of pilgrims was finally departing the area. We didn't know how long it might be before this respite would be over.

Once again, TP and I stood by the tree, looking down the path while we took a smoke break and chatted. I said, "How come you and I are not covered in sweat anymore? Your shirt and mine, they're both dry. Does it seem cooler to you?"

TP replied, "Interesting point. I hadn't noticed or paid any attention, but now since you mentioned it, yah, I think it is cooler. I think it feels like it's in the mid-80s."

I replied, "I think you're right. I noticed, also, no matter where you're standing, you still can't see any blue sky. It's like the sky turned to this brownish tinge. I can even look up at the sun without squinting or blocking my eyes, and see a high overhead shining sun. It's really weird. It's like the Good Lord created this canopy-like effect to reduce the temperature without creating darkness, which complete shade would result in. I mean, I'm no longer sweating like a pig and I am actually quite comfortable. Really weird isn't it?"

TP rejoined, "Yep, it is weird. Hey Look! Here comes the next wave!"

Back at the tables, we began making preparations for the arrival of the next wave of pilgrims. Steve came up to me and said, "I only have eight crosses left. After I give them all out, Mom and I are going to leave." After giving him a big hug, I squatted down, and with my left hand on his shoulder, I said to him, "Steve, I am so very proud of you and I want to thank you for helping us out. And, I want you to know how much I love you!"

He smiled, and replied, "I love you too, dad. I hope you make a bunch of money!" He turned and ran off to his chosen spot on the path to await the arrival of the third wave. TP and Bobby had been out policing empty soda cans and returned with bags of empties filled to capacity, which they threw in the bus. We decided we needed another trashcan for empty soda cans near the tables.

We proceeded to move all the cold sodas from one trash can to another nearby. We were getting ready to dump the cold water and remaining ice on top of the sodas, when we stopped in mid-effort. We looked at each other and suddenly it came to us, let's go pour this ice and water into the foot washing bins in front of the chairs. Together we grabbed and lifted the heavy trash can, less than half full of sloshing ice and water, and carried it over to where the chairs were lined up in front of the bins. Then we began moving from bin to bin filling each with fresh ice and water for our next round of arriving pilgrims. We were once again ready to go, thinking it would be more of the same - happy pilgrims, slowing down as they approached the lemonade stand, and in most cases stopping for a moment to catch their breath.

The third wave sputtered out fairly quickly. Maybe a couple of thousand pilgrims had marched by, with only about 1/3 stopping for refreshments and/or rest. Again, it seemed like we were seeing more well-conditioned male athletic types going by with a few females mixed in. Steve came by to tell me he had given out his last cross and was headed home with his mother. And once more the lemonade stand turned quiet.

I stopped for a moment and watched Steve and his mother driving out through the trees, when suddenly it dawned on me, I'd forgotten to get some money from her. I was furious with myself. I couldn't believe I completely forgot I had no money. I guess I thought subconsciously, there would be a bundle of money from the contributions at the end of the day. *Ain't that some stinkin' thinkin'*, I thought, as I continued to regret my failure to ask her for some money before she left.

Across the path all the observers returned to their chairs and began chatting amongst themselves. The police command center continued to be relentlessly active with officers and police vehicles coming and going. TP and I settled into a couple of the folding lawn chairs to rest and chat while we waited for the onslaught we knew was yet to come. TP confirmed my estimate of about 4,000 pilgrims passing by so far. For some unknown reason I was no longer concerned or worried about the financial aspects of our adventure.

I was also no longer concerned about running out of ice, sodas and medical supplies, a concern which had been gnawing away at the back of my mind as I noted the number of bags full of medical trash and empty pop cans being stuffed into the bus. We still had about 60 to 70% of the sodas left and there was still a mountain of ice under the bus, which in and of itself amazed me. So I was, in fact, calmed by my belief the Good Lord and John Paul were helping take care of business.

I was actually beginning to enjoy myself and felt good about helping so many people at one time who were unquestionably, totally focused and committed to their mission to reach the park, to see and hear their beloved Pope John Paul II. To a certain extent, I envied them, as I could not understand their motivation and extreme efforts just to see and hear this individual, John Paul. I wondered if I had actually missed out on something, something I did not know or understand, like they did, which seemed to fill them with such joy and happiness. I couldn't make sense of it or figure it all out.

CHAPTER 19

The Fourth Wave

It suddenly hit me like a ton of bricks, this is why we were REALLY here,
and this was what it was all about.

TP and I sat underneath the big tree resting in its shade, chatting aimlessly as we continued to wait for the next wave of pilgrims. It seemed like they were way past-due. They should've been here already.

Yet they still had not arrived. We were ready for them. All the small bins had been filled with fresh water. All the trash cans were filled to the top with sodas and ice. And thanks to the neighbors, the first-aid tables were re-supplied and abundantly overflowing with supplies.

Our chatter stopped suddenly, as we both focused our gaze on the changing sight before us. I couldn't believe what we were seeing. TP said, "JD, man, look at that!"

I replied, in complete disbelief of what I was seeing, "Yah, unbelievable!" What we were seeing, coming around the curve and up the incline, was a multitude of people plodding, literally plodding along, packed so tightly together it looked like they were a solid dark mass, oozing along in unison. Behind the first half dozen rows of marchers, individuals weren't even recognizable as they blended together. It looked like in front of the crowd were the walking wounded. People with their arms on the shoulders of the persons on either side of them, moving slowly and gingerly.

Overcoming our bewilderment, we jumped up and started running towards the crowd. The injured were being assisted by their companions and it was as if the thousands of people behind them did not want to pass them by, maybe out of sympathy, but more than likely, out of respect. There were so many! It suddenly hit me like a ton of bricks, this is why we were REALLY here, and this was what it was all about.

A young girl, about 20 years old, with long black hair was at the front of the pack. She had one arm over the shoulder of the young fellow on her left, while the one on her right was supporting her elbow with his forearm, their hands locked together. She was trying to walk like a ballerina, on her tip toes. Her tennis shoes had been oozing blood, some of which had become hardened and caked on.

As we pulled up in front of her we didn't even stop. We started walking backwards, so as not to stop the forward progress. I looked at the two guys assisting her and said, "Could you guys use a break?" As they began to nod gratefully, I said to the young girl, "Are you okay sweetheart, you're almost there. We have a first-aid station right around the corner." I raised my voice a little so the other two guys could hear me and said, "Okay, here's what we're going to do. In a moment, TP and I, as I nodded in his direction and looked at him and then back to her, we are going to turn around and you're gonna walk up behind us and then we're going to lock our arms behind you. Then we're gonna get our arms right behind your legs and lift you up. It's an old military maneuver so don't worry. Once we're alongside of you I want you to put your arms over our shoulders, so you can hold on as we keep moving. Do you understand what we're going to do?" She nodded affirmatively as we continued walking backwards.

TP and I nodded to each other and did an about-face. As the three of them came up behind us, TP and I reached behind her legs and we grabbed each other's elbows. We then started to lift her up as her helpers moved to either side of us and she put her arms over our shoulders. TP had to scrunch down a bit to adjust for our disparity in height. TP started calling out, "Your left, your left, your left your right, your left!" That did it! We were in lockstep together, which allowed us to pick up the pace.

Moving quickly now, we reached the tree and one of the nurses grabbed a lawn chair out from in front of the water bin, so we could walk right up to it. I said, "Sweetheart, what we're going to do is take you right over to the water bin. Then we're going to lower your feet down into the water. When you feel the bottom, I need you to try and stand up for a moment, so we can get the lawn chair right behind you, so you can sit down. Now hold onto TP and me and we'll help you, and try to keep most of your weight off your feet, okay?" As she gave us a positive nod, TP and I began to lower her feet into the bin. She let out a pretty good scream as her feet hit the ice cold water. The lawn chair appeared instantly behind her and I said, "I know it hurts, it's the cold water. Go ahead and sit down now. The chair is right behind you."

Seated now, she began to cry. I wasn't sure if it was from relief or pain. I assumed the latter. As TP and I knelt down in front of the water bin, with as much assurance as I could muster in my voice, I said, "Sweetheart, don't cry. You're safe now. We're gonna take care of you. You're gonna be just fine," trying to add some tenderness near the end of my little speech.

Through her tears, with tremendous emotion, she immediately replied, "Thank you, but I have to get to the Mass. I have to, and I can't walk anymore!" With empathy, I replied, "Look, you don't worry about that right now. You let me worry! I'm sure I can figure out a way to make sure you get there, so don't cry. I'll figure out a way." Instantly regretting what I said, I wanted to bang my head against the pavement or something, because I had no clue how I was going to resolve her problem. But more important was the task at hand. TP, the nurse, and I had to figure out a way to get her shoes and socks off without hurting her, so we could see what was wrong with her feet.

Her feet were soaking in the bin and she was probably feeling some relief from the reduction in swelling. Our nurse had gone over to help the guy a couple chairs down who also seemed to be in pretty bad shape. All the chairs were being vacated for the more serious medical issues arriving. I said to TP, "Let's go over by the path and talk for a minute."

As we rose Tracy came over to survey the situation. I asked her to join TP and me in the discussion. I then said to Tracy and TP, "I personally experienced a situation like this during the battle of KheSon in Vietnam. My boots filled up with blood, and hours later, when we tried to remove them, it was like my skin was being torn off my body. It was so excruciatingly painful. It took two wonderful nurses, to painstakingly cut my boots off with scissors and a lot of water. I remember as they were trying to remove my socks, I thought they were taking the soles of my feet off as well. So my recommendation is - we cut the shoelaces, and if we can, pull out the tongues and cut them off, then begin cutting the rest of the shoes off her feet. What do you think Tracy?"

She replied, "I think that's a good idea, but you'll have to go slowly, especially when you get near the open wounds causing the bleeding. Do you guys want to start and then holler for me when you need me, so I can continue to help some of the others?" TP and I looked at each other and nodded our positive responses.

Kneeling in front of our wounded pilgrim again with TP, I said, "What's your name Sweetheart?"
"Kathy," she answered.
I then said, "Kathy, what a cool name for such a pretty girl. We're going to go ahead and fix you up now. While TP goes over and gets some supplies, I'll explain to you what we're going to be doing here." TP left to get what we would need from the first-aid table and I explained to Kathy what we were going to do, step by step.

Upon his return we hunkered down and began the process. Since the water in the bin had turned bright red we could no longer readily see the details of her tennis shoes. We had to gently lift each foot out of the water as we worked on it. Painstakingly, we proceeded, cutting away a small piece of tennis shoe at a time and then returned her foot to the water to soak some more. Fortunately, TP found two pair of curved surgical scissors with really sharp blades, and a rounded tip on one blade, making the cutting process a whole lot easier than it could've been. As the process continued, TP and I took turns chatting back and forth with Kathy. Although it was mostly idle chatter, it seemed to put her at ease, and she became much more relaxed. From her conversation it was easy to realize her tears and sadness were directly attributable to her fear she might miss the Pope's mass and sermon.

Once we had removed both shoes and large portions of her socks, we decided we should try some of the liquid hand soap and see if we could wash some of the remainder of the socks off her feet. So we knelt there washing her feet with the soap, over and over again to release the remainder of her socks which had adhered to her skin like glue. Cutting off pieces of sock, as it was released, we had reached the point where the remainder of the sock on each foot was definitely covering open wounds. I went to get Tracy. TP took the bin into the weeds on the north side of the path to dump the water and refilled it with clean water. I brought Tracy back and she examined Kathy's feet. She then complemented us on a job well done, and said she would take it from here. Kathy thanked us both a couple of times, and I told her to continue resting, as I would stop back later to check on her.

Suffering pilgrims continued streaming in, now sitting on the ground trying to help themselves as they waited for assistance. Time was no longer being measured or kept as TP, the nurses, and now others, and myself continued hopping and running from one wounded pilgrim to another, trying to aid and assist each one. Band-Aids and bandages were flying off the supply table. Bucket after bucket of ice water was being passed around, and small amounts were poured over open wounds. Sodas were being consumed so fast the trash cans were nearly empty again.

More observers came over and helped refill the trash cans with sodas and ice. Two ladies showed up with a cardboard box full of additional medical supplies. It was a sight to see. So many people coming together, working to aid their fellow human beings, while contributing as much as they possibly could to the common goal without asking or expecting anything in return!

Sometime later, as the rush finally subsided, it was definitely time for a smoke break, which we took as we walked over to the tables. I was really hot and tired. My body temperature began dropping as I swirled my hand around in one of the trash cans full of ice water, searching for a black cherry soda. I was in awe at what I was seeing. Hundreds of people filled the lemonade stand. They were everywhere, either sitting on the ground cross-legged with their shoes off rubbing their feet, or lying down with their heads resting on their backpacks. The empty soda can trash bins had long since filled to capacity, resulting in empty soda cans lying scattered everywhere. All around the tables and the eight main lawn chairs, medical supply trash was reaching a depth of inches and more. There was a constant shift of people as those feeling rested got up and headed on down the path. New arrivals came over, and found their spot.

Getting a chance to catch my breath, watching what seemed to be complete chaos was making me feel really good inside. I suddenly realized if you watch pure random chaos in motion intently, long enough, patterns develop, and in this case those patterns were beautiful. And combine with it the wonderment and the sense of satisfaction in actually doing something proving to be so worthwhile. Then I think you get as close to heaven as possible, while standing alive on this planet. I stood there completely immersed in the fascination of the action, and overwhelming enjoyment of the moment, wishing I could capture it, share it with everyone, and keep it with me forever.

TP's arrival in front of my face broke the magic of the moment, as he said, "Man, we got a lot of work to do! We gotta refill the sodas and ice them down. We gotta get this medical trash picked up before a breeze comes up and blows it everywhere, and for certain, we have to get all these empty soda cans picked up! You ready to get back to work?"

I replied, "Yep, but let's first go over to where the observers are standing and see if we can recruit some help. What da-ya think?"

He exclaimed in reply, "Now that's a great idea!"

Standing in front of an array of observers, some sitting, others standing, I blurted out, "Hey everyone, can I have your attention for a moment.   Apparently the other folks who were supposed to come help us couldn't get past the police barricades. There's only the two of us and we really need some help!   We need help getting more sodas out of the bus over there, and ice 'em up.   And we really need a number of people to help us pick up all the empty soda cans, so they don't become a safety hazard.   Can, or would, any of you folks be willing to come over and help us out for a few minutes?"   Amazingly, hands were going up in the crowd standing behind the rows of lawn chairs, as a dozen people sitting in the chairs also stood up.   I responded instantly by saying, "Oh, thank you all!   Please, follow us over to the table area and we can start there!"

TP took a bunch of the volunteers over to the bus to start bringing out sodas and more ice.   Working quickly, I assigned three people to use empty pails to take the water out of the trash cans to refill the wash bins the pilgrims were soaking their feet in. The remainder were broken into two groups.   One to go around collecting trash and the other to pick up empty soda cans. Moments later I asked the group remaining to take some trash bags over to the east end of the lemonade stand area and police the soda cans over there.

Volunteers took cold sodas out of the trash cans and replaced them with warm sodas, adding more ice after every few cases, then topped each trash can off with some of the already cold sodas removed earlier.   Soon there wasn't an empty soda can in sight, nor was there any more trash lying around.   Over by the bus, there remained three people helping TP try to stuff a couple of dozen trash bags, full of empty cans, into the bus.   All the while, the pilgrims kept on marching by.   Incredible!   What would've taken TP and me hours to handle was done in 20 to 30 minutes.   I went around thanking all our volunteers.

"How full is the bus now?"   I inquired of TP as we headed back to the path.

He replied, "I started at the back of the bus and have been jamming those bags in as tight as I can from floor to ceiling.   We are about half-full! There are three kids under the bus breaking up ice. They're doing a great job, and think its real fun – go figure. Just between you and me, I think we have more empties than we've put out, but how can that be – we're the only game in town. I have not seen one empty can which didn't belong to us – it seems strange. Maybe it's just my imagination."

Replying I said, "How much soda do we have left?"

He responded, "Only about 35% of what we started with. We might run out before this is over."

Continuing my inquiry, I asked, "How about the ice?"

"Ice, now that we have plenty of. Seems the more we chip off the more it grows. It's really astounding how well it's holding up! You pull a soda out of any of the trash cans, and it's ice cold. The water in the trash can is icy cold, go figure!"

Coming back up to the path we noticed a flurry of activity in our lawn chair area. We walked over and determined our three nurses were overwhelmed. We each knelt down in front of a pilgrim and began to chat with them as we helped remove their shoes and wash their feet. For the next hour or so we never moved from our spot kneeling in front of a lawn chair, washing the feet of the pilgrims.

We knelt there, chatting happily with one pilgrim after another as they came and went. Helping them to remove their shoes and socks, then washing, rinsing and even drying their feet. Applying hydrogen peroxide and Band-Aids to minor open wounds and burst blisters, we placed gauze pads on tender calluses and bunions and taped them securely in place. From time to time, as we encountered swollen and tender blisters we would holler for one of the nurses, who would come over with their scalpel-like knives, and swiftly lance the blister, providing the pilgrim with much-needed relief. Then we would take a piece of rag and try to press the fluids out of the wound, discard the rag in the pile beneath the chair, re-clean the wound and bandage it up. In most cases we would turn their socks inside out by rolling them down to the toe. Then after washing the socks out, gently place the sock over their toes, and roll it back up over their ankle so the outside of the sock was now the inside.

Somewhere along the way as TP and I chatted intermittently, he said something I still cherish in the back of my mind, "Hey, JD, wasn't there something in the Bible about Jesus washing somebody's feet?"

I replied, "As I recall, I do believe there were a couple stories about feet washing in the New Testament. I'm trying to remember. I think you're right. I think Jesus washed somebody's foot, feet, I mean, but I don't remember the specifics. What I do remember was the story about the prostitute, Mary Magdalene. Now she was something special. I forget how it came about, but she ended up washing the feet of Jesus, but she didn't have a towel, so she used her long hair to wash and dry His feet as she proclaimed her love for Him.

"He apparently was so touched by this event he told her she was forgiven - for all her sins, and something to the effect of - she didn't have to worry about the street bullies and other assholes calling her a sinner. I thought it was a pretty cool story when I first heard it, in second or third grade.

"Then, when I was probably in fifth grade, I got my mother to explain to me what a prostitute was, and I finally understood the significance of the story and could absorb better, why Jesus was so touched by this lady of the night and her actions, and conveyed His endearing Love to her. I still think it's a great story. Why did you ask?"

Starting to grin, he looked over at me and said, "Well, after all that, it doesn't matter. It just came to mind, you know -- 2000 years ago?"

After a pregnant pause, trying to anticipate his next comment, I said, "What about 2000 years ago?"

He replied thoughtfully, "I don't know, I can't figure this all out. You know - you and me of all people, sitting here, spending a Saturday afternoon washing strangers' feet? This is so bizarre! So I was thinking, and then remembered the Bible, but I couldn't recall the story and I was just trying to tie everything together. You know what I mean?"

Looking his way, trying to formulate a response, being just as confused as he was now, smiling broadly, I finally said, "Well, if you're thinking, maybe we might get our sins forgiven, then you better make sure you get your pilgrims' feet really clean!"

Starting to chuckle, he instantly retorted, "So what, you want me to scrub harder, 'cause you know, there ain't enough feet here today, to get **all my sins** forgiven." Our pilgrims started laughing with us. All four of us were now laughing heartily.

For me it was a precious moment. I was still bewildered by the enormity of the situation in its entirety, all of the activity surrounding me. More amazingly, my own participation in what seemed like pure bedlam. It was the spontaneity and knee-jerk reaction to each event as it happened, resulting somehow in the proper response, to allow all the different activities going on simultaneously to continue to flow uninterrupted and unfettered with no plan, no organization and no leadership. Complete strangers pitched in to make things happen and cause every obstacle that appeared to be overcome, and every crisis to instantly fade away.

I hadn't observed such a thing since Vietnam, when I ended up being flown out to a hospital ship during the three-day battle of Khe Son. I ended up helping unload a never ending stream of airships as they hovered over the landing pad, bringing in the wounded around the clock. Due to the civilian casualties mixed in with the soldiers, all injured, some maimed and so many dying, this devastating experience is an ever recurring nightmare in my mind. Now here I kneel, washing the stranger's foot in my hand, awash in the mayhem of the moment. But this time, it is great joy, not overwhelming sadness that fills my heart with this experience.

As TP and I finished tying the shoelaces for our pilgrims and heard their expressions of thanks, we heard a voice cry out, "**Help!** Can someone **help us,** please?" We rose, said goodbye to our pilgrims and ran over to the path where a group of 4 or 5 pilgrims were doing their best to carry a young girl, about 16 years old.

CHAPTER 20

Emergency . . .

*... it was time to give God an **Emergency call***
with high hopes He would help...

We could see the bone protruding through her skin above her ankle. It was evident she had a compound fracture of her right tibia and needed emergency care.

TP and I jumped in to help get her over to a lawn chair. TP went to find Tracy while I helped her try to find a comfortable way to rest her leg. Looking at a scarf which had been tied slightly above the wound as a tourniquet, I asked the folks who were with her how long it had been on. Everyone shrugged and then our victim chimed in, "Someone put it on right after I broke my leg." I immediately loosened it to allow blood to flow to her foot for a little while. I threw out the water in the two bins closest to me and ran to get fresh water. By the time I returned, all three nurses were busy attending to our newest wounded pilgrim. I refilled the water bins and backed off, so as to not be in the way.

Turning to TP, I said, "Looks like our nurses have it under control. When I went to get the water I noticed we're really low on sodas again. We need to go refill the soda bins."

TP nodded and off we went. Having found out how easy it was to recruit some help, we got a couple helpers and began, once again, parading back and forth carrying case after case of sodas over to the tables. It was getting harder and harder to get the ice broken off of our ice cube underneath the bus. The outer shell kept getting thicker and thicker requiring more and more effort to break off chunks. But we hung in there banging away on our small mountain of ice until all the soda bins were filled with ice. Our helpers had emptied the overflowing trash cans over on the east end of the lemonade stand. We did the same around the tables, under the tree, and then jammed a mountain of trash bags into the bus. Now everything was once again ready to go.

Although the pilgrims continued marching by, the breadth of the parade seemed to have shrunk, from six or eight abreast to three or four, but the never-ending stream continued on steadily. The lemonade stand remained near capacity as people continued to come and go. So many had passed I could no longer guess how many pilgrims had passed by, it was so many.

We walked up to the nurses to ask about our wounded warrior. They told us they had stabilized the leg and stopped the bleeding and got her leg all bandaged up, but she needed to get to the hospital. Tracy was over talking to the police to make arrangements. I knelt down on one knee next to our patient and said, "How are you doing sweetie?" Smiling weakly, she replied, "Much better! I was walking along and my foot, I lost my footing on the edge of the path and my leg broke. I don't know how it could have happened, I was just walking along."

I smiled and chimed in, "Not to worry, you're in good hands, and we'll make sure you're taken care of, so your leg will heal perfectly. What's your name?"

She replied, "Vicky." In response, I said, "Well Vicky, my name is JD and this is TP - if you need anything at all, just ask one of the nurses to come get us, and we'll take care of you. Would you like a cold soda?"

Nodding her head, happily, she said, "Oh yes, please!"
I queried, "We have lemonade, orange, black cherry …"
She interrupted, "Orange, orange, please!"

TP immediately took off to retrieve the soda as I replied, "TP will be back with your soda in a moment." Almost as quickly as I completed the sentence, TP was handing her a cold orange soda. She smiled broadly and thanked us.

As I stood up, TP said, "Well, shall we go back to washing feet?" I nodded and we returned to our former positions, kneeling in front of our pilgrims.

Once again we were busily washing the feet of the pilgrims before us, chatting aimlessly. And like a giant high speed buzz saw, irony was cutting through my mind and reducing it to a pile of sawdust. Here I knelt washing the feet of strangers, policing empty soda cans time after time, trying to not think of how I was **not** going to be arrested for the theft of seven pallets of sodas, and/or be able to make the next mortgage payment. I had squandered my entire net worth on what turned out to be a terrible idea, to produce a concert. And a little over a year ago or so, I was the #2 guy heading up a Denver government agency office - only one tick from an executive officer contract, with delegations of authority over 1.2 billion dollars of disposable assets, and three hundred employees working for me. I pissed off one of the largest newswire services in the world and most importantly, put my family in financial jeopardy. Just how in the hell did I get myself into this mess, how many really bad decisions had I made, and how would I ever recover, I thought over and over and over. Until suddenly, my thoughts were interrupted, thank God.

Feeling a tap on my shoulder, I turned my head and looked up to see the uniform of a police officer standing behind me. I started to rise, my mind racing again, thinking, oh, what now, what's wrong, what kind of trouble are we in now? Fully erect, I could now see all the 'scrambled eggs' (the gold leafs embroidered on the bill of his cap) on his hat, denoting a command officer.

He said, "Excuse me, I'm sorry to interrupt you. I'm the Division Commander for this station and we have a problem. The nurse, Tracy, said she thought the station wagon behind the bus might be yours. Is that your vehicle?"

TP was now standing next to me as I replied, "Yes, that's my car. Is there a problem?" He replied, "No, there's no problem with your car. I wanted to ask if you might help us out."
I responded, "Sure! How can we help?"

He then explained, "Tracy told us we have to get the girl with the broken leg to the hospital right away. We don't have any patrol cars nearby; all we have is our big equipment trucks. We've been trying to get a car in here for the last 20 minutes, unsuccessfully. The traffic between here and the park is terrible. So I wanted to ask you if you would transport her to the hospital for us. Your station wagon would be perfect for her to be able to lie down during transport."

Without hesitation and with great relief, thinking at least he wasn't going to arrest us, I responded, "Of course! I'd be glad to help!" Looking at TP, I said, "Can you take care of everything while I'm gone?"

TP replied, "Well, how are you gonna get back?"

"Good question!" I replied. Turning to the police officer, I said to him, "Commander, he's right. I bet you have a lot of the streets around here blocked off for local traffic only, right?"

He answered, "Affirmative, we have traffic control barricades at every intersection."

Thinking for a moment, I said, "Commander, can you write me a note I can take with me, giving me the authorization to get back in here?"

He responded, "Yah, I can take care of that."

I replied, "Okay! Let's do it. However, I have a favor to ask."

He queried, "What's that?"

Turning, I pointed over towards our first wounded warrior, still sitting patiently under the tree, now next to a young man, with his left foot completely bandaged up, and said, "See those two pilgrims sitting underneath the tree over there? The skin on the bottoms of their feet was broken open so bad, we destroyed the girl's shoes getting them off and we couldn't get the guy's shoe back on. They simply can't walk any further. They have family and friends at the park waiting for their arrival who will be able to provide further care for them. Will you make arrangements with the next patrol car coming in here, to have them taken out to the park?"

Nodding affirmatively, he said, "Certainly, I'll make the arrangements. In the meantime, I'll have a couple of my officers go over and carry the girl over by the police trucks and make sure you have room to get out."

Replying I said, "Okay, I'll go over and move the car nearby, and thanks for taking care of the kids under the tree."

As he turned, he said, "And thanks for helping us out!"

TP and I started walking towards the car. We were both a bit jittery from the encounter. TP said, "Well, at least we weren't in trouble. When you get ready to move the car, I've got to figure out some way to hide the missing license plate."

"Ya, I know, but we got bigger problems. I forgot to ask mama for some money when she brought our lunch earlier. I'm hoping I have enough gas to get to the hospital. I know there's not enough to make the round-trip. So we need to make a plan in case I don't make it back. I'll call Audrey when I get to the hospital, if I make it. If I don't, I'm sure I can flag somebody down to help me make sure Vicky gets to the hospital as quickly as possible. If I get to the hospital and Audrey doesn't answer my call, I'll head back and hope for the best. "So here's the plan. If I'm not back by the time the command center has moved out of here, you need to head out and follow the route I'm going to give you and look for me on the side of the road. I'll wait for you, so I can come back and help you clean up and pack up to return all the remaining sodas to the store."

TP replied, "Well you don't have to worry too much about returning sodas. Judging by how many trash bags full of empties we've stuffed into the bus, there won't be much to return. In fact, I'll be surprised if we have any left at all."

His offhand comment, taking the wind out of my sails, caused me to say, "Oh, thanks for that! Now I have to worry about that again! By the way, while I move the car, you want to check the contribution cans? I haven't looked in them all day. See if there's any money in there I can use for gas." As TP turned, I added, "Hey, while you're over there, stop by and tell our wounded warriors we took care of their problem, and they'll be taken out to the park."

TP, smiling, said, "Yah, that'll lift their spirits." And he took off.

About two dozen trash bags filled with empty soda cans were lying alongside the bus waiting to be stuffed inside. I decided to move them to the back of the bus and piled them in front of the empty license plate holder.

As I got into the car, TP came up holding his outstretched hand in my direction, "Here you go, there was $2.43 total in the two cans." As he handed me the money, he added, "I'm sorry. I feel really bad, I just don't have any money to add to it."

Resigned to the circumstances and somewhat depressed, I softly replied, "It's okay TP, you hold the fort down while I'm gone, and I'll pray John Paul and the Good Lord will take care of the rest and get me back here."

As I backed the car up to where the police officers had brought the girl, I rolled the window down and said, "TP, help me get her loaded up, will you?" TP lowered the tailgate as I got out from behind the wheel. I folded the back seats down and climbed in. As the police officers sat her down on the tailgate, TP cradled her head and shoulders as she started to lie back down. We spoke with Vicky and directed her, as we gently lifted her into the back of the station wagon. She was short enough, she fit perfectly.

As TP closed the tailgate, the police commander and Tracy walked over. He handed me a hand written note instructing all police officers to allow me to pass. I shook his hand as I thanked him. Tracy then handed me a note and said, "JD, give this to the doctor in the emergency room when you arrive. It explains everything we did for Vicky."

I replied, "Okay," as I climbed in the car and fired up the engine to leave.

I followed the police truck, as it backed out of the way, and as I broke through the trees, I was blown away by the size of the crowd being held back by the police barricades. Trying to figure out why they were all here, I looked into the rearview mirror and was surprised to realize, between the trees and the police trucks, you could see the pilgrims marching by on the path. The number of people watching the parade of pilgrims was astounding. Even though there were a few chairs scattered about, the majority were all standing, filling the roadway and the lawns up to the edge of the houses, packed closely together. I was only about 5 feet past the police barricades when I had to stop. I simply couldn't move any further because of the crowd of people. I noticed two police officers walking up behind the car in my rearview mirror. They walked out in front of the car and started to move the crowd out of the way so I could proceed. I finally reached the intersection to make a right turn, enabling us to slowly begin the journey.

Cars were parked back to back, up both sides of the street, with people milling about in the center of the street as we progressed to exit the housing development. As I continued, meandering down each street very slowly to avoid running over any pedestrians, I took the opportunity to chat with Vicky. I learned she would turn 17 years old later this month and she was from New Zealand. As we continued plodding along, she told me she was extremely happy and excited about coming to the United States to see the Pope. She had really fallen in love with the Rocky Mountains. She thought they were incredible.

After clearing the police barricades at each intersection, we finally made it to Yosemite Street. Vicky explained how much she was enjoying the trip so far and how much fun she was having, getting the opportunity to see and experience so many of the wonders Denver provided.

I made the left turn and was finally able to pick up speed to 40 mph, and proceeded to the interstate. As I waited for traffic to clear to make a left turn onto the I-225 northbound entrance ramp, I said, "Vicky, I'm going to be picking up speed now, in order to get you to the hospital as fast as I can. I'll try to make it a really smooth ride for you, so don't be afraid if it seems like were going pretty fast, okay?"

She replied, with a smile in her voice, "OK, I'm not afraid, I trust you, and God's with us!"

I entered the highway at 90+, with my hazard lights on and flashing the headlight switch on and off. Traffic was light and I tried to stay in the right-hand lane as much as possible, in total fear of running out of gas at any moment, as the gas gauge no longer had any elevation whatsoever. I wanted to be fully prepared for when the engine died, to be able to pull over to the side of the highway safely. I remained amazed as we continued down the 8 mile stretch of highway, as fast as I thought was reasonably safe, and the engine continued running.

As we progressed down a long stretch of empty highway, I detected a note of concern in Vicky's voice when she inquired, "Is the hospital very far away?" So I thought I should include in my response something soothing and amusing to calm her anxiety, and said, "No, it's not far. And it's the same hospital where I gave birth to my second son."

After a short pause, she finally inquired, "Pardon me, I don't think I understand what you mean."

Chuckling heartily, I replied, "Well, let me tell you. One night about 3:30 AM in mid-July 1988, my wife woke me up, saying, 'Wake up, wake up, my water broke, it's time to go to the hospital.' Before we left the house, as I waited for my wife to finish dressing, I called my sister and told her to bring my older son Stephen and meet us at the hospital. We had this plan all arranged earlier. Once we got to the hospital we went to the maternity floor.

"Stephen and my sister, Tanya, waited with me patiently as I held my wife's hand during her contractions. About every 10 or 15 minutes the nurse would come back in and tell us they were still trying to contact my wife's doctor, with no success. After what seemed like hours my wife told me the baby was coming and she couldn't wait any longer. So I went up the hall to speak with the nurse, and explained the situation to her. Then she tells me - not only had the doctor not returned his pages or calls, she also admitted she wasn't actually a nurse, she was just a nurse's aide and couldn't really do anything.

"Becoming concerned, I dispatched her to the emergency room to find the on-duty doctor. I had Stephen hold his mother's hand and asked Tanya to check the bathroom for towels, and if there was more than one to wet half of them down with warm water, and see if she could find some scissors, and string or suture material, in any of the drawers and cabinets along the wall. I went over and washed my hands and put on a hospital gown, grabbed this little stool on wheels over in the corner, and rolled it up to the center of the action.

My wife let out with a scream, 'He's coming!' I replied, 'Okay, I'm ready! Push!' And with the next contraction, she pushed and my son's head appeared. I held his head with my left hand and turned his right shoulder, and then hollered "push" on her next contraction.

"Seconds later, I had my new son in my hands. I cleared his mouth and heard him cry out as he took his first breath. Tanya wrapped a towel around him as I lowered him into a horizontal position. I instructed Stephen to grab the suture string and scissors and to tie off the umbilical cord in two places and then his big brother cut the cord. I then placed the newest member of our family in his mother's arms, and at that very moment, you'll never guess who finally shows up? A doctor, the only doctor in the whole hospital apparently, saying, as he came in the door, 'Hi everyone, I'm Doctor Jones and we can get started now, sorry it took so long.' It sounded so funny. We all started laughing - even my wife.

And that's how I gave birth! So Vicky, now you can remember, along with your other memories of this trip, you actually met a man who gave birth to not one, but both of his sons. I learned how to do the second delivery from the doctor of my firstborn, who allowed me to deliver my first son. Which is how, I knew exactly what to do! I haven't told this story to anyone for a very long time. I wanted to share it with you, because those two events were the most memorable, fantastic, and incredible moments in my life. And they took place right inside the hospital we are pulling into right now!"

Turning into the emergency room driveway, I heard her soft reply, "That was such a nice story, thank you for sharing."

I began honking, as we rolled up to the doors and stopped the car. I turned around in my seat and put my hand on Vicky's shoulder, and said, "We're here! You lie still while I go in to get some help to get you out of here."

She replied, "Okay, I'm fine!" As I got out of the car I thought, boy, this girl has some grit! The outside bank of automatic sliding doors opened as I approached running head on into three guys pushing a gurney through the interior doors. I explained the situation to them while I opened the tailgate and they locked the brakes on the gurney. Two of them jumped up inside the car and began to lift her, as the other attendant and I lifted her legs and moved her onto the gurney. They headed into the hospital while I grabbed her backpack. Mission accomplished - I made it. Vicky was safe and sound at the hospital. *Thank you Lord!* I thought as I took her backpack and Tracy's note inside.

A lady from admissions was already filling out forms as I walked up to the gurney in time to help Vicky get her passport out of her backpack. A doctor and a nurse appeared and began to talk to her about her injury. I handed the doctor Tracy's note, while the nurse began to cut away the bandage on her leg. Finally, the doctor said, "Well, Vicky, the folks who helped you out on the path did everything correctly, and your leg looks real good. So we're going to take you down to x-ray to get a picture to make sure everything's ok and then we'll get you into a cast."

Directing my only concern to both the doctor and the admissions lady, I said, "I want to make sure there isn't any problem with her being admitted, since she's from New Zealand?" They both responded with assurances directed to both me and Vicky, that yes, she would be admitted and treated. It was no problem for them to take care of her. Vicky smiled with relief and again thanked me. I smiled and wished her the best during the remainder of her stay and her trip home. I then went to the front counter to use the phone to call Audrey. For a good 10 minutes, I tried repeatedly, hoping she would answer, to no avail.

Outside I closed the tailgate and climbed into the car, hesitating and thinking about turning the key to start the engine. Man, this situation really sucks! The more I thought about it the worse it got. Finally, I decided to turn the key to the on position to see if there was any movement whatsoever, on the gas gauge, hoping my fears would abate by the sight of some movement. After three attempts, hope took a hike. The gauge didn't move at all.

Boy this is a real sticky wicket, I thought. I remembered those words being expressed to me by a British sailor I had made friends with, just before we got our asses kicked in a bar fight, while I was on R&R in Hong Kong a hundred years ago. I felt like I was about to get my ass kicked again when I ran out a gas on the way back to the lemonade stand. I concluded the nearest gas station was going to be too far away for my $3.43 to get me there and then back. I might just as well see how far I get. At least then I'd be on the route I had given to TP so he could pick me up.

In desperation, I decided it was time to give God an *Emergency call,* with high hopes He would help me out and keep this boat afloat, and said out loud, *Lord, the only way I'm going to make it back is if you keep the engine running. Thanks for your blessing no matter how it turns out. Amen!"*

CHAPTER 21

Pope John Paul II's Mass

"I came that they might have life, and have it abundantly. "
(Jn 10: 10).
(The Event Tag Line.)

I thought, it's so dark, why is there no light?? Oh yah, you have to open your eyes! So why is it so hard to do that? Let's try opening just one eye. Ahh, finally, let there be light, the red numerals 12:38, what the hell is that, it don't matter, let's just go back to sleep.

Let's try again, the red numerals 1:55, oh, man, it's the damn clock, it's almost 2 o'clock, and from the light coming in around the drapes, it's gotta be afternoon. I gotta get up and get some coffee.

The freshly brewed coffee smelled so good, as I took my first sip and lit up a cigarette. Thinking, oh yah, Stephen and Snugger are at the Pope's Mass and Chris is over at Tanya's. After nearly 12 hours of uninterrupted sleep, I still felt a bit groggy. Then I heard the door open as Chris came running up the stairs with his aunt close behind. After a few hugs, Chris announced he was going over to a friend's house. Tanya and I sat down at the kitchen table to chat for a while. An hour or so later, Stephen and Audrey arrived and joined us at the kitchen table.

Tanya, turning to Stephen asked, "So what was it like?" He replied, "It was really cool, but man, it was so hot. And there was a lot of walking!" I interjected, "Did you get to see the Pope?" He answered, "No, we were too far back, but we did get to see his all white helicopter fly in and land. I'm gonna go over to Anthony's house, see you guys later," as he rose to leave.

I stopped him, saying, "Steve, before you leave would you do something for me?" Anticipating some dreadful task was about to fall upon him, he retorted, "Okay, what?" I replied, "Relax, it ain't a big deal, I need the station wagon moved into the garage. Can you take care of that for me?" Knowing full well he loved to get behind the wheel of the car at any opportunity, without any response, he turned and headed for the door.

Shaking my head, I said, "Watch this, let's give him a minute." We heard the station wagon engine turning over and over with no success. Finally after a number of tries, we heard the car door slam.

Moments later, he stood at the kitchen table and said, "It won't start!"

I replied with a touch of sarcasm, "Well, you took off before I could even finish what I was going to say. Last night when I got home, about 1:30 in the morning, as I rolled over the curb and up into the driveway the car died. It was out of gas. It had been out of gas for the last 20 or 30 miles I drove it, but that's another story."

Very sarcastically, he retorted, "Ya, sure, dad, so what am I supposed to do?"

Smiling, I replied, "Grab the 5 gallon gas can in the garage we use for the lawnmower, and put it in the station wagon, be sure and leave a couple of inches in the bottom of the can to help you get it started again. We'll have to pour some gas directly into the carburetor to get it fired up. You go ahead and get the gas in it, and then take the air filter off the engine. I'll grab a glass and come out and join you in a minute."

Steve headed out the door and Tanya inquired, "What did you mean when you told him you drove while it was out of gas for 20 or 30 miles?"

I answered, "Nothing ever gets by you does it, Tanya?" As I got up to get a glass out of the cupboard to pour fuel directly into the carburetor,

I continued, "The short story, yesterday when I got to the lemonade stand, the fuel gauge was on E. After I turned the car off, I only turned the ignition on to check the gauge, and it did not move. I was out of gas.

"Later in the afternoon, I was asked to rush a girl to the hospital and made it back to the lemonade stand. Then, last night I drove from the lemonade stand to King Soopers, and then home. It was weird. The car just kept running and running until I pulled into the driveway where it died. I've run out of gas couple times in the past and the gauge was not bottomed out, either time. Hell, that big V-8 takes a half a gallon of gas just to get out of the driveway in the morning. Go figure! Will you gals give me a minute to go out and help Steve get the car started before we continue this conversation. I really want to hear Audrey's version of the Pope's Mass."

Walking up to the car door with an empty glass in my hand, I asked Steve, who was behind the wheel, "What'cha doin'? I see you got the air filter off. Did you put in the gas?"

He responded, "I'm checking the gas gauge dad. I wanted to see if it was broken. I turned on the ignition before I put the gas in and it didn't move. So, I thought I would check it after I put the gas in. The gauge seems to be working fine. I put 3 or 4 gallons in the tank and the gas gauge shows we have almost ⅛ of a tank now."

I responded, "Well, that was good thinking! Go ahead and try to start it now. Be sure to pump the gas pedal like mad!"

After a couple of good tries, I said, "Never mind! We're going to have to put some gas directly in the carburetor. Do you know how to do that?"

He nodded negatively. I continued, "Okay, grab the gas can and let's pour about a half an inch into this glass. Then we can pour it into the engine easily." After we opened the latches on the two carburetor float covers we saw there was no gas in the carburetor. After filling both floats, Stephen tried to fire the car up again, without success. The engine sputtered a couple of times and then backfired ending our first attempt. I knew the fuel lines and the pump were both empty so we'd have to try again. Steve refilled the floats and on his second attempt the engine finally fired up. I had Steve put the car back together and park it in the garage as I went inside to hear the rest of the story.

I sat back down at the table and Snugger said, "Sounds like you got the wagon running again."

I replied, "Yep, it was completely bone dry. Even the gas pump itself was apparently empty. So it took a little extra effort to get it going."

Tanya then queried, "Well, mom, Steve gave us a sweet - but awfully short story. Think you might expand on your son's story and tell me and your old man the whole thing!"

Chuckling softly, she replied, "Yes, I can. It all started late yesterday after dinner when Steve and I went over to Mike and Marilyn's house because it's only a couple blocks from the entrance to the park. My friend Karen came over too. We watched TV for a while and then sat around and talked. I told them about how you guys were out at the march site and had found yourselves smack dab in the middle of the police command center trying to sell sodas to the marchers while you were pretending to be a first-aid station. Needless to say, everyone laughed and cracked up, as I told them the story. They thought it would make a great TV comedy. We went to bed early so we could get up at the crack of dawn.

"We departed about 5 AM in Mike's car and headed for the dam. We drove in as far as we could and then had to walk the rest of the way. It seemed like about a 2 miles to the actual area for the Pope's Mass. By then it was about 8 AM. The area cordoned off was huge. It was at least 300 yards wide and probably more than a quarter-mile long. They had roped it off in blocks about 30 foot across and 15 foot deep, creating narrow aisles running from the stage to the end of the area with wider aisles running from left to right.

"The marchers had come in the night before and many were still in their sleeping bags. It appeared the area set aside for the marchers was about 300 yards between the stage and the visitor section. We found a spot about 30 feet behind the marchers area where we spread our blankets and claimed our turf for the remainder of the day.

"We mingled with some of our neighbors on their blankets next to us, chatted and just walked around as the park filled up. Suddenly, the entire crowd focused on the arrival of the Pope's helicopter increasing everyone's anticipation. The heat of the day was really beginning to climb as we continued to wait for the Pope to begin mass.   Medical personnel were roaming around throughout the crowd carrying IVs and trying to attend to people who were beginning to suffer from the heat. It was a very long walk to the port-a-potties, and some people were trying to minimize their water intake, in a strange battle between having to go pee, and passing out from the heat. It became somewhat bizarre as the day wore on. A few attendees were carried off on stretchers as they succumbed to the heat. Fortunately, no one in our group required medical assistance.

"Finally the Pope began mass and it seemed everyone was thrilled the event had begun. It felt like there was a sense of well-being consuming the entire crowd and everyone individually. Unlike a normal Catholic Church service where there are points during the mass when a person kneels or stands, everyone remained stationary, unmoving, seated, in the chairs they brought or on blankets. I think it was to reduce the likelihood more people would be overcome by the heat.

"I couldn't see the Pope because he was so far away. But I could hear the mass clearly on the loudspeakers. I was so thrilled to have this experience. During his sermon it was like the sound of his voice captured you and filled you with this feeling of sweetness. His words could fill your mind with understanding, like when he started, he said, 'Jesus speaks these words in the parable of the Good Shepherd. The Good Shepherd: what a beautiful image of God! It transmits something deep and personal about the way God cares for all that He has made.'

"I felt it was so important these days for everyone to hear him say, 'The Spirit has led you to Denver to fill you with new life

to give you a stronger faith and hope and love. Everything in you
– your mind and heart, will and freedom, gifts and talents –
everything is being taken up by the Holy Spirit in order to make
you 'living stones' of the 'spiritual house' which is the Church.

'This Church is inseparable from Jesus; He loves her as the
Bridegroom loves the Bride. This Church today, in the United
States and in all the other countries from which you come, needs
the affection and cooperation of her young people, the hope of her
future. In the Church each one has a role to play, and all together
we build up the one Body of Christ, the one People of God.'

"And the best part, near the end of his sermon was when he
said, 'Jesus himself provides the answer – and the answer is a
supreme declaration of Divine Love, a high–point of the Gospel
revelation concerning God the Father's love for all of creation.
The answer is already present in the parable of the Good Shepherd.
Christ says: 'The good shepherd lays down his life for the sheep'.
Christ the Good Shepherd is present among us, among the peoples,
nations, generations and races, as the One who 'lays down his life
for the sheep'. What is this but the greatest love?'

"During the sermon and actually during the entire mass the
activity and movement of people continued relentlessly. There
were medics and parishioners and pilgrims coming and going back
and forth throughout the entire service. So it was bit difficult to
focus completely on the Pope's sermon, but what I did hear, I truly
enjoyed, and was glad I went to the event. It seemed like there
must have been at least a couple of hundred people passing out
communion. In each section, Catholics rose and went down the
aisle to receive the host blessed by the Pope. Shortly after
communion, the mass concluded with the Pope's blessing.

"Afterwards, people rose and began to peacefully and
quietly stroll back towards the parking lot or the port-a-potties to
exit the park. In a way it was sad the event was over, but on the
other hand, it was so good to be up moving and headed out of the
hot sun. Despite having been cooked well-done and a nasty
sunburn, I feel really good about having attended the Pope's
Mass."

[A Special Note: The preceding text, quoting the words spoken by the Pope, as recalled by my wife, were 'copy and pasted', from a copy of John Paul II's sermon, verbatim, from the Vatican's website, to ensure accuracy over recall.   And to this day, she still cherishes her memories of her day with Pope John Paul II.]

Looking at me with that special look of hers, my Lover Snugger then asked, "So how did it go out at the lemonade stand? Were there a lot of pilgrims - and were you able to sell enough sodas to pay for them?"

One thing I'd learned over the years about my loving wife was that whenever she was concerned she always got directly to the point, and expected a direct and succinct answer.   In this case, and under the circumstances, there was no simple answer.

Feeling extreme consternation, I finally answered, "Yep, after you left the pilgrims continued to come.   They came, and came, sometimes in large groups or waves, but always with a pretty continuous stream of people marching on.   It really was something to see.   As for paying for the sodas, you can relax, we didn't have to pay anything at the store, and I don't owe the store any money, but we also didn't make any money.   I'll explain everything - it's kind of a weird story.   I'll start with when I returned from a trip to the hospital to finish the day.   So sit back and relax, and give me a moment to get a fresh cup of coffee."

Having explained the hospital trip, I sat down at the table and continued, "Here's the rest of the story, my love.   I'll call it;"

     # The Cleanup Detail

I pulled in behind the bus and parked the car back at the lemonade stand, thinking as I got out and shut the door, how incredible it was to have made it back while the gas gauge remained stubbornly locked in place, below the E.   I looked around for TP as my gaze traveled across the landscape.   I couldn't believe what a total disaster area the lemonaid stand had once again become. Seeing TP headed my way from over by the path, I met him near where the lawn chairs had been lined up. We watched an older woman fold up the last two lawn chairs and begin her trek towards the bridge. The observers had finally given up the ghost and departed, so much for recruiting help to clean the place up.

TP broke through my thoughts when he said, "Where the hell you been? We got killed! Just killed! Wave after wave came through here a little while after you left, and we were completely covered up! I couldn't keep up with it. There's only about a dozen sodas left in the bottom of one of the trash bins. The others are out of both sodas and water. I couldn't find time to get over and get more ice. We used nearly all the ice water from the trash cans washing the pilgrims' feet."

Looking around, I replied, "You know TP, I've seen real, actual battlefields that didn't look this bad. This is a king size mess. It'll take forever to clean it up.

"I see we're out of first-aid supplies."

Nodding, TP responded, "Yah, and that ain't all. As best as I can tell, underneath all the trash bags in the bus, there's only a couple dozen cases of soda left, maybe. The only thing we have left is a supply of ice. I don't understand it, but there's still a mountain of ice under the bus, go figure. By the way, **where were you?**" Then, with a measure of frustration for emphasis, he added, in rapid-fire succession, "You were gone a good two hours, to go what, 20 miles, maybe? You stopped for gas and a beer? If you didn't, how did you get back here? I sure could have used some help here, you know!"

"Sorry about that," I replied. "It took forever just to get to Yosemite Street. I put the pedal to the metal all the rest of the way and reached the hospital pretty quick. It took about 15 minutes to get her tucked in. And no, I didn't stop for gas and you know I don't drink, not even beer." Reaching in my pocket and pulling out the $3.43 to display, I added, "See, I still have our gross receipts in my pocket! And I have no clue how I got back here, the gas gauge still refuses to move!"

Smiling, I then continued, "Stop bitchin' for a minute, take a look out on the western horizon and tell me what you see."

He turned his head for a moment and then looked back at me and said, "The mountains, so what?"

I answered, "I gotta tell you something, and you need to stop and listen for a minute. In case you don't remember, when I left, I couldn't see; we couldn't see the mountains because of the haze. I'd gotten so used to it I didn't even pay any attention to it on the way to the hospital. But on my way back, as I came around the curve on I-225 past Parker Road, I could see the bank of haze clearly, sitting over on top of the dam and filling the lower valley to the north and west as far as I could see. And from my vantage point, I could tell it extended upwards 800 to 1000 feet, the same altitude as the downwind leg of a landing pattern at the airport. Once I reentered the haze, I could no longer see the blue sky until I reached the crest of the hill on the Yosemite Street exit ramp. Once again I had an un-obscured view of the sky, and the mountains to the west, and a check in my rearview mirrors reflected the haze covering my view to the east. "Now, would you be kind enough to explain to me what I observed, what we both observed all day?"

TP looked down at the ground, removed his hat and wiped his brow, then said softly, "I have no idea, I can't explain it. I've seen it, I saw it and now it's gone. You got me on this one. Strangest thing - it is noticeably hotter standing here in the sun. In fact, let's go over to the shade. Maybe we can give away the last of the cold sodas." And with that we walked over, grabbed a couple of sodas, and began to offer them to the scattered few pilgrims continuing to come by, sporadically, mostly in single file.

An extended period of time passed without the passage of a pilgrim so we decided to begin policing the area. We grabbed a couple of empty trash bags from one of the tables and began picking up discarded soda cans lying around everywhere. I was on the back side of the tree with a half-full bag of empty soda cans when I noticed two figures coming up the path. I set my trash bag down and went over and got two cold sodas, an orange and lemonade, and went back to the tree to meet our pilgrims. They were noticeably different from the pilgrims who preceded them. It wasn't necessarily the red ribbons tied to their left arms, their well pressed clothing, or their extra-large backpacks which definitely looked like military issue, but there was something different about them for sure. I walked up and offered them a cold soda. They both graciously declined as TP walked up beside me.

Then one of them, directing his inquiry to me said, "Who are you gentlemen with?"

Feeling a little trepidation, there was just too much authoritarian tenor in his voice, I thought a lighthearted or even a somewhat humorous reply was appropriate, and said, "Each other, why do you ask?"

When they looked at each other, I thought I might have got 'em to almost smile, but with a bit more authority in his voice he queried back, "What are you doing here?"

Taking a deep breath, throwing my shoulders back and standing as a erect as possible, in full military posture, I took a step towards him, as if to defend the lemonaid stand, and said, "If it's any of your business, we set up this lemonade stand this morning to provide some cold refreshments for the pilgrims, and ended up turning it into a first-aid station, and all day long we've been tending to the injured kids with bleeding and torn up feet. We even took one of the youngsters to the hospital. Now, just who are you guys?"

"I'm sorry, I didn't mean to offend you. We're with the Vatican. We're the cleanup detail, and our job is to make sure that no one got lost, injured, or left behind. We are the end of the march. "There is no one behind us."

Relaxing my posture and stepping back, I said, "It's OK! We actually had a good time today helping out."

Before I could continue, while his sidekick was pulling pad and pen out of his pants pocket, he said, "Can you give me the name of the party you took to the hospital, and which hospital you took them to, so we can follow up?"

I provided them with the information they were asking for about Vicky, and then added to my answers, "She was doing fine when I left her."

He replied, "Thank you. We appreciate what you did and the information, and I want to thank you both for what you have done here today. We have to continue on now."

I responded, "You're welcome and if you don't mind, would you guys mind stopping by the police command center over there, and tell the Commander - he's the one with all the scrambled eggs on his hat - *the march is officially over*, so we can all get out of here."

Smiling, he answered, "Yes, of course, thanks for mentioning it."

They waved as they strolled over to the command center, which I prayed would be the commander's cue to button up his operation and get out of Dodge. So TP and I could leave as well. It had been a very, very long day.

TP and I went back to our policing duties. The knowledge that this would be the last time we had to do this was fuel enough to ignite our afterburners, and provide the energy necessary to complete our task. Suddenly TP hollered from over by the tables, "Hey, JD, get over here, you gotta see this."

Dropping my trash bags, I ran over to see what he was hollering about, and said, "What'cha got buddy?"

His face beaming with wonderment, as he said excitedly, "Look at this," as he extended his right hand, palm up, out to me. "Look what I found in one of the contribution cans!"

"Wow!" Astonished, I gazed upon a golden coin, shining brightly in the reflecting sunlight, lying in the palm of his hand. "What is that?" I asked eagerly.

Still in awe, TP, now holding the coin between his thumb and finger, so we could examine it more closely, and see both sides, said, "I don't know. I was picking up the cans to throw them away and this was in the bottom of one of the cans. It's like a commemorative coin with the Pope's face engraved on it. See it says, 1993, and looks like Latin words. You got any idea what it says?"

Taking the coin from TP to examine it closer, I answered, "Well, my last Latin class was in eighth grade, but let me see it close up."

Turning it around in my hand, I said, "Looks like highly polished bronze, and on this, the front side, apparently there's no Latin translation for the word Denver and the next two words mean the 'Month of August', followed by the date of 1993. On the backside, I think the two individuals are Saints Peter and Paul, facing each other, underneath some kind of holy hat.   The inscription on the outside edge is bit tougher, I don't recognize the word *mondialis,* but based on the other two words, which mean youth and day we could assume *mondialis,* means world, with VIII meaning 8. So I think it says, *world youth day 8.* But, I wouldn't bet on it!"

Papal Coin Picture from VaticanCoins.com

Handing the coin back to TP, I commented, "That is just so cool! I wonder who left it for us -- was there only one?"

"Yah," TP replied, "So what do you want to do with it?"

Thinking for a moment, I responded, "I don't think it has a lot of value -- except maybe to us, and maybe someday it'll have some value. I wish they would've left two of them, so we could each have one. But, since there's only one, I want you to have it! You worked so hard on this project, and all day today, without stopping, and it's the only thing of value we have to show for it. So you take it! May it always remind you that God is by your side!"

"Thanks, my friend, it will!" He replied, with an appreciative smile, as he slipped it into his pocket.

Later, having completed our policing duties, dusk arrived as the last police truck backed out and drove away. We began unloading the bus to make room for the tables, chairs and trash cans. Despite our best efforts we didn't see a way to get it all back in the bus. So we put the tables and chairs in the station wagon and refilled the bus with the trash bags and cans.

It was evident, if we tried to put the last dozen trash bags in the bus, TP would be unable to get to the driver seat. So we decided TP would get into the driver seat, and then I'd stuff the last few bags in around him.

First we took a smoke break and formulated a plan for our departure. As night settled in fully, we lit up our cigarettes and sat down, leaning up against the rear tires of the bus, and in the darkness, our planning discussion, our second board meeting, began:

TP: When we pull out of here why don't you follow me, so I don't get stopped for no license plates, in case the cops still have their barricades up.

JD: I don't think there's much chance of that happening in the dark. I didn't see any streetlight poles, and I'm sure the police are out of here by now anyway. I'm more concerned about my gas situation. I'm not even sure the car will start, and even if it does, I'm not certain how far I'm gonna' get. So how about you follow me in case I need some help getting the car off the road when it dies.

TP: (starting to chuckle) Yah, that is a better idea, but then you'll have to run the rest of the way behind the bus, because there's no room for you in the bus anyway. (Now laughing heartily together - much to my chagrin)

JD: Very funny, aren't you the comedian! The car has no gas, got it! I don't think I'm gonna get anywhere near the store before I run outta' gas. So we need a plan. I don't wanna' drive around while we try to figure out what we're doin' once we get there. If we get there, I don't wanna' have to drive one more foot than is absolutely necessary.

TP: Okay, right. But how are we going to get the sodas out of the back of the bus? This is going to be a real bitch. I won't be able to open the side door to exit the bus without a bunch of trash bags falling out. Then, if I stop the bus 4 or 5 feet short of the dock to open the back door, a bunch of those trash bags are going to come pouring out on me. Then we'll have to move them out of the way, so I can back all the way up to the dock. I don't know how else we can do it.

JD: You're right. That's the only way we're going to get it done. But I'll be there to help and maybe someone from the store can help us as well. If I make it to the store, I'll park in the first available space. I'll then go through the front doors, find James and get him or someone else to open the dock door. You continue around to the back of the store and wait for me. I'll be out there as soon as I can. First we'll take some trash bags out of the front so you can get in and out. Then we'll go to the back of the bus and open the door and move whatever falls out of the way. Then I'll guide you until you're up tight against the dock. How does that sound?

TP: Sounds like a plan to me. So, have you figured out how you're gonna explain the shortage in our soda inventory?

JD: No, haven't got a clue. I'll just wing it, once we determine how bad it's gonna' be.

TP: Oh, not to worry, it's gonna be bad. I mean, just look at the bus! I can't even believe the number of soda cans we've bagged up, its thousands, not hundreds. And you know what's bothering me? I know, I flat out know, I picked up more of our empty soda cans than we put out - more than what we had to start with and I can't come to terms with the facts!

JD: TP, I don't want to go there right now! What do you think the scrap value is going to come in at?

TP: Well over $100, maybe even $200, I think.

JD: Think it'll cover my bail if the store has me hauled off to the slammer? I mean, if they do, I assume you'll figure out a way to get my raggedy ass out of the hoosegow!

TP: Of course, buddy. I'll even bring you a new toothbrush in case there's a problem getten' you out!

JD: Oh, thank you so very, very much. With friends like you who needs any enemies. One last thing, with the way we're parked, once you get the bus started up, I'll back up sharply to the north, you then back straight out and let me pass in front of you, so you can follow me, okay?

TP: Fine by me! You about ready to go? What time is it anyway?

JD: Its 2030, time to rock 'n roll. Let's make like a couple of birds and get the flock outta here and write The Last Chapter to this story!

CHAPTER 22

TLC

...if you believe in God,

let's just consider it some kind of small miracle...

Well, after the bus had warmed up for a couple of minutes, I finally garnered the courage to turn the key in the ignition, and to my surprise the car fired up.

Thank you, John Paul, take me home, please, I prayed silently, as I put the car in reverse and moved out of the way.

In the quiet of the night with my window down, I could hear TP rev up the engine of the bus, but it wouldn't move. Then as he increased the acceleration, more and more dirt and pebbles started to fly, as the tires spun vigorously, while the bus failed to move at all. I could see from the directions of the spray of the dirt, he was trying to move, both forward and backwards, with no success. I turned the car off and went over and pounded on the door. He turned off the engine, and we moved some of the trash bags out of the way, so he could climb out and determine the problem.

After a walk around the bus to check for any obstacles, TP finally said, "JD, pull your car over so we can shine headlights underneath the bus to see what's the problem here." I pulled the car over as requested while TP began to crawl underneath the bus. I turned off the car, but left the headlights on and went over to see if I could help out.

He rolled out from underneath the bus as I walked up, and said, "You will not believe this. Part of the undercarriage and both sides of the rear axles are completely encased in our ice mountain. I don't know where this ice is coming from, but I swear there's more ice than we put under there. It's got us completely locked in place. We're gonna have to get under there and chip the ice away until we can break free."

In complete disbelief, I exclaimed, "AWW Shit! What the Frake! What the Frake else is going to go wrong?!" I was so pissed off! I couldn't believe it.

When TP said, "What are you so upset for? We just gotta chip away the ice, and we'll be good to go."

Approaching complete rage, I howled, "And where are the tools? Remember, yours are under a couple hundred bags of trash and my tire iron is underneath all the tables and chairs and only the Good Lord knows how long we'll have light before my battery dies."

I screamed out loud into the sky, "Good grief, Lord, how long are You going to keep us here?" Having got that off my chest, I kicked the dirt with my foot as I walked over to the bus to help TP began to unload the bus. Again!

There was no doubt both TP and I had long since passed the point of exhaustion. After half an hour of beating the crap out of the iceberg holding our bus hostage, reloading the station wagon and bus with all the trash, I stood there, listening to the screeching sound of the bus. Scraping against the ice, the bus moved about eight feet backwards when once again, the rear tires began spinning. This time TP pulled forward as far as the bus would go before it hung up again. He then put it in reverse, and gunned it.

We could hear the bus breaking up the ice. But again, the bus got hung up before clearing the iceberg.

TP pulled the bus forward and repeated the process. He had more running room this time. He floored it in reverse, and the front of the bus rose up with the front tires 6 or 8 inches off the ground. The rear tires dragged the bus over the top of the iceberg until, in a small cloud of dust, the front wheels of the bus hit the ground with a thud upon clearing the iceberg. For the first time, we could see the entire iceberg in the headlights of the bus.

I was utterly amazed at its size - it was huge! I walked over to take a closer look at it. It was a big solid block of ice, sitting there on dry dirt with no pooled water anywhere around it. I tried to understand how a couple of dozen bags of cubed ice could have transformed itself into a much larger block of ice in the middle of August, after sitting out for over 12 hours in temperatures of 100° since midday. I could not formulate a logical explanation or understand what I was seeing and touching. I stood up, wiped my wet hands on my jeans, waved to TP, and headed over to my car.

I drove through the trees for the last time with TP close behind me. As we meandered out of the housing development, I drove with a constant eye on where I could pull over when the engine died, silently praying all the while, *'Take me home John Paul, please!'* We turned left off Yosemite onto Hampden Avenue and continued through the curve where Hampden turned into Havana. Upon reaching King Soopers, I elected to continue on to Mississippi so I had a light for the left turn. I pulled into the first parking place I could find. As I turned off the engine and removed the key, I said another silent prayer, *Thanks for the ride John Paul, thanks for getting me here. I can walk home from here, if necessary!*

TP continued on around to the back of the store, as I walked through the front doors looking for James. He walked up after having been paged and greeted me with a big smile, saying, "JD, it's good to see you. Did you have a successful event?"

Returning his smile, I replied, "You bet! Wow, it was a tremendous success but totally exhausting! Sorry we're running a little late."

"No problem. Let me get the paperwork so we can settle up." He replied.

I answered quickly, "Good, TP's on his way around to the dock door so we can unload the returns."

After a shuffle through some papers, James grabbed his clipboard and came out from behind the counter. We began walking to the rear of the store when he said, "So do you have a lot of returns?"

Trying to think fast - was this the opportunity to try and explain everything, or no - wait and see how much the total bill is first, I replied, "Actually, I don't really know. After we got set up, TP recruited some helpers. They kept the sodas flowing throughout the day, so I didn't get much chance to see how the inventory was holding out this afternoon. And throughout the day, we were filling black plastic trash bags with empty cans and throwing them into the bus. The bus is completely full, so I can't tell how many cases may be on the bottom. TP thought there might be two maybe three dozen cases left. But we won't know for sure until we can unload the bus."

James responded, "Ok, so what happened? How did it go? Were there many marchers?"

"Well," I replied, "Where to start. It really went well, and we truly enjoyed the experience. There were so many marchers - I would have to guess a minimum of 20,000, maybe as many as 30,000. And once they started arriving about noon, they just kept coming, wave after wave. It truly was a sight to see. I'm guessing their march was about 20 miles and we were at about mile post 14.

"Despite being tired, thirsty and hot they were happy and excited, laughing and smiling, and so polite. There was a kind of spirit, a spirit of joy and happiness, which surrounded and accompanied them, as they marched on. I've never experienced that kind of feeling in a large crowd of people before. You know, like at a ballgame or concert how the people around you seem so self-consumed, and focused on either getting to their seats or getting out of the venue. You know what I mean?"

James replied, thoughtfully, "I think so. I mean, I've never felt joy and happiness at a football game, just the excitement. But I would agree, getting into the stadium, and leaving the stadium, always feels like such a grind. There's no feeling good about it, you just can't wait to get to your car and get out of the traffic.

"Hey, Tony, get Greg and help these guys out. They're gonna be returning some cases of soda on the dock. Go ahead and open the door, then set up some pallets, and stack each different flavor on a different pallet. I have to go back up to the front of the store. Page me when you guys are ready to take the final tally."

"Thanks James!" I responded.

Once Tony opened the dock door, I jumped down from the dock onto the pavement, and went over to the bus, as TP opened the side door. We started to unload bags out the front door to an area about 10 feet away on the tarmac. I told TP I would guide him backwards to the dock and tell him when to stop.

To insure we would have room to open the back door before coming up against the back of the dock, I went to the back of the bus and stretched my arms across the back door, so I would know about how much room we needed, and then signaled TP to begin moving backwards. Once in place, he killed the engine and came to the back of the bus to assist in the unloading.

We decided one of us would hold the door partially open while the other pulled bags out to prevent a cascading effect. Our fear was, if the bags on top fell out and hit the pavement and broke open, we'd have another mess to clean up. Tony and Greg couldn't help but notice how fatigued we were and how slow this process was going. They jumped down and pitched in to help us out. Now we're cooking! TP decided we'd removed enough bags, giving him enough room to dig through the remaining bags, and move them around as the pop was unloaded. We now backed the bus against the dock. I climbed up the ladder to the dock and looked in the back of the bus. The sight made my stomach queasy;

I didn't see two or three dozen. What I saw was only a half dozen.
I thought, *this is going to get ugly.*

We all agreed TP would hand the sodas up to me on the
dock, I would hand them to Tony and Greg, who would stack them
on the pallets. And the process began, two cases lifted up each
time.

Twenty minutes later, I said softly, so Tony wouldn't hear
me, "TP, what's going on? You keep on handing up more sodas?"

TP motioning for me to bend down, whispered, "JD, I
don't know what's going on. I move a couple of bags and there's
two more cases of soda, so I pick them up and hand them to you.
When I turn back around, the space on the floor is empty. So I
grab a couple of trash bags nearby, and put them in the empty
space, and find two or four more cases, and hand them up. Then I
move the trash bags I just put down, in the empty space, and
there's more soda. I can't explain it! Shush! Tony's coming up
behind you."

Tony inquires, "Are we done?"
I reply, "Almost Tony, looks like we have a few more."
He answered, "Okay, no problem, keep 'em comin'," as I
handed him two more cases of pop. Turning to take two more
cases from TP's outstretched arms, I heard Greg tell Tony he was
going to go get some more pallets lined up.

Two by two, the sodas continued to come out of the back
of the bus. It was baffling! There was no additional working room
being created in the back of the bus from the removal of the sodas.
The 2 by 2 foot of floor space TP had been working in was not
increasing in size. The bags surrounding him, stacked to the
ceiling, remained in position, unmoving. But, every time TP
moved a couple of the trash bags close to his feet, more cases of
sodas appeared, as if they had been there the whole time. I looked
back into the store at seven pallets lined up, side-by-side with
various heights of sodas stacked upon each of them, in total
disbelief.

"Where are they coming from?" I thought.

We continued on! Finally, I heard Tony say, "Okay, we're done! All seven pallets are full!"

TP was about to hand me two more cases. I turned to TP and said, "Quick put those back, we're done!"

After he set them down, and covered them with trash bags, he turned and extended his hand to me saying, "Gimme a hand, I gotta see this!"

Standing on the dock next to him, I whispered, "**Don't say a thing!**" We walked over to the pallets. I felt compelled to raise my hand and arm over the top of the first pallet, and let it brush across each pallet, in amazement of what I was seeing, as we walked around both sides of all seven pallets. I was checking to see if they had, in fact, stacked the same flavor of soda on each individual pallet, as we continued our unofficial inspection.

To say I was totally blown away is a complete understatement of my astonishment and bewilderment at what I was seeing. I simply could not believe my eyes, or my touch, feeling the products stacked before me. The sensations traveling throughout my entire being were indescribable. I wanted to say something, anything, but I remained shocked and speechless! Continually asking myself, *"What is happening here?"*

Unknown to me, Tony had already gone to get James, and as we were coming back around to the dock side of the pallets, I heard James say, "All done?"

Looking at James, I was still so dumb struck I couldn't think of what to say.

Finally, I stammered, "Yah, but I feel really bad. After all your efforts and help James, it looks like we are returning everything. Your guys did all the stacking on the pallets. TP and I pulled them out of the bus and handed them off to Tony and Greg to stack them properly, by flavor, onto the pallets. So do you want to go through and count each pallet?"

James was walking around the array of pallets inspecting each one, when he replied, "No, I can tell from the way they are stacked on the pallet, they're all here. Because they're all the same height and width, I only have to count the number of rows on one pallet. I'm checking now, to see if each flavor is accounted for, and the last one here, the lemonade, makes the inventory complete. So, I guess there's no charge and nothing for you to pay for, everything has been returned.

"Based on what you were saying earlier about the number of marchers going by, and looking at all those trash bags on the ground out there, and in the bus, I would've thought you used them all up. I don't understand how all these pallets are standing here and your bus is still full of trash bags."

I didn't want to leave James with a bad taste in his mouth, so as he continued, using one of the pallets of soda as a tabletop, to finish the paperwork on his clipboard. I walked over and placed my hand on his left forearm. "James, I can't thank you enough for everything you did to help us out. I can't explain. I have no explanation, to answer your question. And, I don't know how to say this, but what you did, and everything you did - was tremendously beneficial. Those kids marching by were hot tired and thirsty, **and because of what you did**, they had a chance to stop, take a break and get a cold drink before they continued on."

James had stopped writing on his clipboard and was looking intensely into my eyes as I continued, "**We were able to help those kids because of your help**. Somehow, we ended up with a bus full of empty soda cans, and you ended up with your entire inventory returned. I can't explain this, but if you believe in God, let's just consider it some kind of small miracle and forget about it, with my thanks, prayers, and eternal gratitude for your help."

He replied, "I don't understand what's happening here. And I'm not sure I understand exactly what you're trying to say, but I guess if we helped you out somehow, I'm glad we could be of service. And I still want to thank you for choosing King Soopers." We smiled and shook hands. James grabbed his clipboard and disappeared through the swinging doors into the store. TP and I walked outside onto the dock, as the door was being lowered down into a closed position, and we began stuffing the trash bags back into the bus.

After several attempts, we got most of the trash bags back into the bus. The remainder kept falling out, as fast as we put them in. So we decided to close the back door and drag the remainder in through the front door. We began by pushing and stuffing bags to the rear of the bus to make some room forward. There was so little room. We worked in complete silence, neither of us saying a word. It was almost robotic, dragging, pushing, and stuffing the bags back into the bus.

I threw the last bag in as I climbed in and sat down on the top step. We had gained just enough room so we didn't have to stuff bags in around TP now. Saying, "TP, do me a favor. See the streetlight over by the tree on the edge of the parking lot? Drive over there and park the bus for a few minutes, would you please. I need a moment - to think quietly. Thanks!"

TP hadn't closed the door, so as I sat on the steps at the door, and looked out to the west, I could see the moon, some stars, and parts of the mountains reflecting the moonlight. It was approaching midnight as I sat there in the dark, oblivious to TP's presence, trying to wrap my brain around what had just happened. It seemed like the more I thought about it, the more my mind became completely befuddled. Nothing, absolutely nothing I could think of, helped me to make any sense out of what I had just participated in. The more I thought about it the more my head pounded.

TP finally chimed in, almost reverently, "JD, what just happened?"

Unable to formulate a response, the silence continued on for another 10 or 15 minutes. I then spoke, "TP, I have no idea what happened. I can't seem to wrap my brain around the last couple of hours. If you're not in a rush to leave, I'd like to sit here for a little bit longer, in the quiet, and think about it."

After a while, TP responded, "Yah, okay, I think I know how you feel."

About twenty minutes later TP mumbled, "I can't understand what happened, I can't believe what I saw! I keep looking in the rearview mirror, just to make sure the trash bags are still there! Can you tell me - is this what you'd call a miracle?"

It took a while for me to conceive a response. Minutes later, I replied, "TP, I honestly do not know! On the one hand, it seems so spooky, and on the other hand, there should be a logical explanation. Yet, instead of feeling trepidation from a spooky event, I keep getting this warm fuzzy feeling, until my brain bogs down trying to understand everything. There have been a couple of times in my life, especially in Vietnam, where I'm sure what took place was a miracle. But, at the time, I shrugged it off as extreme good luck, or coincidence. It wasn't until years later that I could accept those events as miraculous."

The silence returned. A while later, TP responded, "Yep, I think I know what you mean. I've been thinking about some strange events when I was *in country* as well. But, this night, there was no extreme danger, no bullets flying, or life-and-death events to deal with. Do you think it was a miracle? I mean, how else can you explain what happened?

..."Wasn't there a story in the Bible about Jesus feeding the multitudes with baskets of fish or something?"

I snapped back, "Let's not even go there. That's a biblical story, and Jesus was the main character, and the multitudes witnessed it, in real time. Right before their eyes, they got to see the fish multiply, and then they got to eat 'em.

" I don't even want to think about a couple of beat-up old war horses like us, being the main characters in a miracle, which really took place, for the benefit of the Pope and his kids. Every pilgrim that wanted a cold soda got one, as many as they wanted, and they don't even know how it happened."

TP responded, "Are you saying the miracle was for our benefit?"

I replied, "**I don't know whose benefit this miracle was for.** I prefer to think it was just God's way of ensuring we didn't get stuck with the tab.

"The really big question is - why didn't He just let us find a bag full of money out there in the parking lot, to pay for the sodas. Instead of having case after case of aluminum cans, filled with soda, perfectly wrapped in a printed cardboard container, appear repeatedly. It seems like that must have been a lot more effort. I don't get it."

After a while I added, "Maybe God was pointing out, **money isn't the answer to everything**. Just maybe, He wanted to demonstrate that the correct answer to everything is just **Trust in God**.

"Anyway, we have to get past this conundrum, and make a decision to accept what happened, miracle or not, and figure out how we're going to deal with this."

Answering me instantly, "What do you mean?   What's there to deal with?"

I responded intensely, "Do you really think we can tell anybody else, except my wife and kids, about what happened here tonight?"

With a bit of light laughter, the first of the night, TP retorted, "Got it! If we told someone else they would think we had completely lost our minds, were drunker than skunks, or were out to create some kind of scam trying to make a buck. Right?"

I responded, "Exactly - absolutely nobody is going to believe us! I don't even know how we could tell the story, - our story, -- the Pope's story, -- the pilgrims' story, - of what happened anyway. I have no idea of whose story it is to tell!! Think about it! If the story ends here, where does it begin? How can you condense everything into a 10 minute story?

"Hell, James would probably lose his job if the store got a call every five minutes from someone checking to see if what happened was really true. Eventually, you and I'd have our mugs on the front page of newspapers and tabloids everywhere! I've been there, done that once, it's a horrible experience. No thank you! We're gonna have to agree to keep this our secret! - You think?"

Once more, silence filled the air and time. A dozen minutes later, TP replied, "You're right! I certainly don't need the notoriety either. Let's make a pact, right here, right now, we tell no one about what happened here tonight, agreed?"

As I reached over to grasp his extended hand in agreement, I added, "Except for my wife and the kids, right?"
While shaking my hand, he agreed, "Right! We'll only break this pact - if we are both in complete agreement, okay?"
Nodding, I answered, "Done deal! Agreed!"

Suddenly, I felt better. Trying to figure out a logical or scientific explanation of the night's events -- all of the day's events. It was overwhelming. Then suddenly it no longer seemed important, or worthy of further contemplation, or thought. It was like, because it was now a completely sealed secret, and no one else had to know, a huge weight rose up off my shoulders and faded into the night sky.

Ten or maybe fifteen minutes later, the silence was broken when TP asked, "You ready to go?"
Much happier now, I replied, "You bet! Take me to my ride, 'James,' and we'll head to the barn!"

Feeling really good, as I stepped out of the bus by my car, I heard TP holler, "I'll follow you home!" Raising my right thumb over the roof of the car in acknowledgement, I climbed in and thought, *'Hey there, John Paul, and You too my Lord, of course, thanks for an incredible day and it's okay if the car don't start, Amen!'* The key turned in my hand, and lo and behold, old Bessie fired right up, amazing!

Less than ten minutes later, I took my foot off the accelerator a couple of feet from the driveway entrance, and let the car coast up over the curb and onto the driveway, rolling up clear of the sidewalk. At that exact moment, I pressed on the brake pedal, and the engine died! I looked in the side mirror to ensure I was clear of the sidewalk and threw the car into park. I jumped out into the middle of the front lawn, with my feet wide apart, my arms spread as far as they would reach, and screamed out at the top of my lungs "**Thank You Lord! And you too John Paul**! You guys got me all the way home! Thank you, thank you, Amen!"

TP jumped out of the bus, saying in a muffled shout, "What are you doing? It's 2 o'clock in the morning, the neighbors are gonna call the cops."

In a softer voice I replied, "It's okay, I'm done, just a little prayer of thanks. Not to worry, the neighbors will be fine. And I'm fine. My prayers were answered. I'm home again, and the day is finally done, so a prayer of thanks was in order.

"Can you believe it? As I rolled up into the driveway and put my foot on the brake, **the car died**, finally out of gas, **for certain this time**. Unreal, HUH?"

Shaking his head, TP replied, "Yah, pretty amazing, how about I give you a hand unloading the wagon."

"Thanks, buddy, let's do it," I said, opening the garage door, which automatically turned on the lights, so we could see what we were doing.

Finished up, TP climbed back into the bus and plopped down onto the driver's seat while I sat back down on the floor of the bus, at the edge of the top step, to hear TP say, "How yah' feeling at the moment?"

"Physically, I'm totally exhausted. But, inside, I feel really good. Mentally, I'm stoked. The last 24 hours have really been an incredible experience, and I'm really glad to have shared it with you. I really enjoyed it."

After a moment or two, TP responded, "Thanks for that, I had a good time too. It was a kick in the ass, wasn't it? I mean, in my wildest dreams I would've never thought I would spend a hot August afternoon in the sun, on my knees next to you, washing strangers' feet as they passed by.

"On the one hand, I have to laugh at myself, and then this warm fuzzy feeling kinda' takes over, and then it feels like this is something really cool, to do, or to have done. You know what I mean?"

Thoughtfully, I answered, "Well, yah, sorta, I mean, there were so many different things. When I start to think about it, I go into some kind of overwhelm. It really helps to have someone to talk to about it. If I'd been by myself, right about now the neighbors would be calling for the guys with the straitjackets to come get me."

Laughing, TP replied, "So what are you gonna do now?"

Seriously, I answered, "That's the scary part, I have no clue! I really don't know, TP, how about you?"

After a thoughtful moment, resting his forearms on the steering wheel and leaning forward, looking straight ahead through the windshield, he calmly answered, "I think I'm gonna go rustle me some cattle. Wanna come along? It's really hard work, but we could make some really good money. What do you think?

"Wow! Now that sounds really cool." I added, "Do you have an extra horse, and maybe some tack? I only rode bareback once and damn near got killed." Stifling my laughter, I added, "A couple of things though. Please tell me, cows don't drink sodas, do they? And we won't have to wash them, will we?"

Then I lost it, I couldn't keep a straight face. I burst out laughing.

Laughing heartily with me, he retorted, "Yah - I got a really old mare you can ride. She's a bit lame, but you probably won't even notice. And all you'll have to do is hold the cow down on the ground, while I put a red-hot branding iron on her rump. Sounds like fun, Huh?"

"Sign me up, partner! Sounds like a great adventure," I replied.

After laughing with gusto at ourselves, probably from pure exhaustion, we shook hands, and said good night.

I stepped out of the bus and turned to wave, when TP said, "Oh, hey JD, I almost forgot, we've still got four cases of soda left over, up front here, besides the other two cases by the back door. Two lemonades, and two black cherries, what do you want to do with them?"

With an inquisitive look, I replied, "You have got to be kidding me! Now you're gonna tell me, not only did we return all the sodas to the store with two to spare, but now, you're telling me we have four more cases! You can't be serious!"

TP got out of the driver's seat, moved some trash bags around, and as he stood up and stepped out of the bus, in his hands were two cases of black cherry soda. The night, I mean the morning, just turned from weird to really, really weird. I stood there looking at the two cases of soda in TP's hands and was overwhelmed with astonishment. How could there be even more sodas?

TP interrupted my bewilderment, when he said, "Here, you want 'em?"

I finally cleared the fog in my mind enough to say, "Yah, we're partners right. You keep the lemonade, and the orange, and whatever else you find in there, okay!"

Grinning from ear to ear, he replied, "Works for me, I never liked black cherry anyway!"

Still befuddled, I finally answered, "Don't call me tomorrow and tell you me you found more sodas, okay!"

TP fired up the bus and pulled away from the curb, homeward bound at last. I was tiring of standing on the sidewalk, looking at the two cases of black cherry soda in my hands, which were starting to get heavy. Gingerly, carrying these two special cases of sodas, I crossed the lawn, brought them into the house, and set them down carefully on the dining room table, and sat down, -- (looking over into the living room, I nodded and pointed) – see they're still sittin' there.

Finally, I couldn't sit there any longer, staring at those two cases of sodas, so I got up and went to bed.

Pausing for a moment, I realized I'd reached the end of the story. But, my audience remained spell bound with an inquisitive look on their faces. I suddenly realized they were waiting for an explanation. Having none, I took a deep breath and continued.

So there you have it, my Love. A true story, the story, my story, the whole story . . . and I'm stickin' to it, 'til the day I die!!

Now, my Love, I know what you're looking for! And last night, I searched every nook and cranny of my conscious mind, and then as I dozed off, I searched the vast expanse of my subconscious mind. And then I traveled through millions of galaxies looking and searching, and finally, in some remote corner of the universe, I surveyed its entirety, all without success. I just couldn't find it, to present it to you, - that which you desire most at this very moment - **an explanation!** I couldn't find it. I don't have it. And **I can't give it to you.** However, I did find that my love for you stretched all the way out - to the edge of the universe.

So now, notwithstanding my failures, what I need - and want, more than anything else . . . is a hug.

Softly she replied, "What do you mean failures, the lemonade stand was such a success, and you did it!" She pushed her chair back from the kitchen table, rose up, and came to where I was leaning against the counter. And with a smile, and a sparkle in her beautiful blue eyes, she reached up, put her arms around my neck, and gently pulled me close, brushing my lips with a kiss so tender and loving, it made my toes tingle, . . . and with that kiss, I recalled TP's question that haunted me last night, and suddenly I understood, …

It's God's Story ... His Miracles

Demonstrating His love for us,
for the benefit of everyone.

And we lived happily ever after!!!

Always keep your heart full of Love and Forgiveness,
for we never know who
The Good Lord will select next -
to serve – *to help*

Make Miracles Happen!

It could be You!

The End

Thank you my Lord!

EPILOGUE:

•

Approximately a week after the Pope left Denver, headlines announced that Michael Jackson was arrested on charges of child molestation. We were relieved we had not succeeded in our efforts to complete the concert project and caused the personal introduction of Michael Jackson to the Pope. Today I believe that if Michael Jackson knew of the pending charges, he probably had hoped the issues would be resolved prior to the concert.

•

One Thursday afternoon in mid-1994, the GAO delivered their completed *Archibald* report to the Chairman of the FDIC and informed him that it would be delivered to Congress on Monday. The next day the Chairman resigned. Archibald's job had finally concluded, successfully.

•

TP and I saw no reason to tell the story during the Pope's life. After his passing many discussions concluded with the decision to maintain the secrecy of the story. The real reason motivating me to come forward at this time, was the nagging recollection of TP's angel's words, and the repetitive news stories of the church's inability to convey Sainthood on John Paul II due to a lack of miracles as required in that process.

•

Without a doubt, John Paul had a very special relationship with God, His Son Jesus Christ and the Holy Spirit, as evidenced by the unexplained events which occurred in the unfolding of the Pope's plan, to meet and speak with his young followers. Although the success was in part the work and efforts of hundreds if not thousands of individuals contributing in some fashion to the progress and completion of World Youth Day 8, 1993 it was, without a doubt, sanctioned and orchestrated by the presence of the Spirit of God.

•

A couple of years after the story, Paula Westerfield fell ill and passed away suddenly during final negotiations of a performance contract as a featured headliner, at a major Vegas strip hotel.

The Impact After 20 Years

•

I began to see John Paul's commitment to his mission of sharing his knowledge of God's love for all mankind with the world. He understood its value and importance, and formulated a plan to share it, to preach it, and to explain it. And that's exactly what he did, with extraordinary success! What an incredible and visionary man!

•

In retrospect, what impresses me the most about Pope John Paul II was his leadership and commitment to his missions - one to the church itself and the other to his congregation.   Once he recognized his mission to lead and guide a changing church — to enact, correct and nurture the reforms of Vatican II, he developed a plan to achieve and executed it.

•

John Paul IIs true love though seemed to be his other mission for his congregation - creatively conceiving the concept of world youth day event rallies as his means and method, to share his love and his message, with everyone, everywhere. His focus was on the young, soon to be adults, whom he cherished while never allowing the bureaucracy of the Church or the Vatican itself to interfere with his commitment to his missions.   He always just kept on truckin'.

•

Enjoy and take from the story, not just the fact that Blessed Pope John Paul II was an extraordinary person, who through his daily activities manifested God's love, but that God's love manifests itself in each of our individual lives when we open our hearts to Him, as exemplified by God's actions during World Youth Day 1993, and now written and recorded within the pages of this story.

  May God Bless You Always!

Drafted To Serve
www.DraftedToServe.com

His Prayer Garden 1993 - Allenspark, Colorado

Saint John Paul II
Making Miracles Happen

A True Story as told by **JD**

---

*"I started reading this morning and then I couldn't put it down.
I finished this afternoon ... let's make it a movie..."*
Mike O. - Executive Producer, Las Vegas, NV

*"The content does indeed capture the reader. I was doing the happy
dance, singing, 'This is why I became an editor!' and my own dog
looked up at me like, 'lady, what are you doing?' I was certainly
pulled into the story, and couldn't wait to read more."*
Lee Ann R. - Book Editor, New York City, NY

Great American Press.